JavaFX™ Special Effects

Taking Java™ RIA to the Extreme with Animation, Multimedia, and Game Elements

Lucas L. Jordan

Apress®

JavaFX™ Special Effects: Taking Java™ RIA to the Extreme with Animation, Multimedia, and Game Elements

ISBN-13 (pbk): 978-1-4302-2623-9

ISBN-13 (electronic): 978-1-4302-2624-6

President and Publisher: Paul Manning
Lead Editor: Tom Welsh
Technical Reviewer: Sten Anderson
Editorial Board: Clay Andres, Steve Anglin, Mark Beckner, Ewan Buckingham, Gary Cornell, Jonathan Gennick, Jonathan Hassell, Michelle Lowman, Matthew Moodie, Duncan Parkes, Jeffrey Pepper, Frank Pohlmann, Douglas Pundick, Ben Renow-Clarke, Dominic Shakeshaft, Matt Wade, Tom Welsh
Coordinating Editor: Debra Kelly
Copy Editors: Sharon Terdeman and Vanessa Porter
Compositor: LaurelTech
Indexer: BIM Indexing & Proofreading Services
Artist: April Milne
Cover Designer: Kurt Krames

Distributed to the book trade worldwide by Springer-Verlag New York, Inc., 233 Spring Street, 6th Floor, New York, NY 10013. Phone 1-800-SPRINGER, fax 201-348-4505, e-mail orders-ny@springer-sbm.com, or visit http://www.springeronline.com.

For information on translations, please e-mail info@apress.com, or visit http://www.apress.com.

Apress and friends of ED books may be purchased in bulk for academic, corporate, or promotional use. eBook versions and licenses are also available for most titles. For more information, reference our Special Bulk Sales–eBook Licensing web page at http://www.apress.com/info/bulksales.

The source code for this book is available to readers at http://www.apress.com.

Dedicated to my wife, Debra. I love you, and I love our future together.

Contents at a Glance

▓ **Chapter 1: JavaFX Design Considerations**..1

▓ **Chapter 2: Effect: Particle Systems**..23

▓ **Chapter 3: Effect: Visual Transitions** 49

▓ **Chapter 4: Effect: Animated Lighting**...71

▓ **Chapter 5: Effect: Advanced Interpolators** 87

▓ **Chapter 6: Effect: Physics** 113

▓ **Chapter 7: Effect: Animated Image Sequences** 137

▓ **Chapter 8: Effect: Animated Gradients** 153

▓ **Chapter 9: Effect: Audio Visualizer** 177

▓ **Chapter 10: Effects: Physics and Particles** 201

▓ **Chapter 11: Pulling It All Together: Clown Cannon** 215

▓ **Index**..241

Contents

Contents at a Glance..v

Contents vi

Foreword xii

About the Author xiii

About the Technical Reviewer xiv

Acknowledgments xv

Introduction xvi

■ Chapter 1: JavaFX Design Considerations...1

   Graphics and Animations in Applications 1

      Controls and Layout 1

      Graphics 5

      Animations 8

   Designers and Developers 9

      Workflow 9

      Showing off the Platform 12

      Setting Realistic Expectations...12

   JavaFX 13

      Scene Graph..13

Designer Tools 14

Deployment 18

NetBeans 18

Open Source Tools 20

GIMP 20

ImageMagick 21

Blender 21

Inkscape 21

Audacity 21

Summary 21

Chapter 2: Effect: Particle Systems 23

Basic Principles 23

Visual Density 25

Particle Appearance and Behavior 25

Animation Implementation 25

Example 1: Core Classes 25

Example 2: Adding Some Controls 29

Example 3: Transparency 35

Example 4: Blend Mode 38

Example 5: Nonuniform Nodes 40

Example 6: Direction 44

Example 7: Nonlinear Paths 46

Further Considerations 47

Summary 48

Chapter 3: Effect: Visual Transitions 49

Getting Started 49

Example 1: Fade Replace...53

Example 2: Slide Replace 56

Example 3: Flip Replace...58

Example 4: Wipe Replace 63

Example 5: Burn Replace...66

Further Considerations 69

Summary 69

■ **Chapter 4: Effect: Animated Lighting**..**71**

Lighting Basics 71

Animating Light..73

Distant Light Example 75

Point Light Example 77

Spot Light Example 80

Light and Shadow Example...83

Further Considerations...86

Summary 86

■ **Chapter 5: Effect: Advanced Interpolators** **87**

The Basics 87

Visualizing Interpolators...88

Built-In Interpolators 91

Custom Interpolators 94

Extending Interpolator..95

Quadratic Interpolator..96

Cubic Interpolator..97

Polynomial Interpolator 99

Windup-Overshoot Interpolator...101

Step Interpolator 103

Transition Example 108

Fade Transition 110

Slide Transition 110

Flip Transition 111

Further Considerations 111

Summary 112

■ **Chapter 6: Effect: Physics** **113**

Simulation...113

Third-Party Implementation 114

Simple Example 115

Pendulum Example 122

Teeter Totter Example 126

Transition Example 128

Further Considerations 135

Summary 135

■ **Chapter 7: Effect: Animated Image Sequences** **137**

Creating Images..137

Implementation...143

Further Considerations 151

Summary 152

■ **Chapter 8: Effect: Animated Gradients** **153**

The Basics 153

Paint Types 153

Proportional...155

Animations..159

ix

Simple Color Example 159

Simple Linear Gradient...160

Simple Radial 163

Multi-Colored Linear 165

Animated Stops..166

Animate Opacity and Stops 169

Progress Bar 172

Summary 175

Chapter 9: Effect: Audio Visualizer...**177**

What Is an Audio Visualizer?...177

Audio and the JVM...179

Audio and JavaFX..179

Java Sound 180

JavaFX and Java 186

Audio Visualizations..188

Controlling the Audio...190

Bars..192

Disco 194

Wave 198

Summary 200

Chapter 10: Effects: Physics and Particles **201**

Particles as Bodies 201

Emitters as Bodies 209

Summary 214

Chapter 11: Pulling It All Together: Clown Cannon **215**

Design Phase 215

Game Design..215

Graphic Design...217

Implementation...222

Game Life Cycle 223

Round Life Cycle 230

Summary 240

■ **Index**..**241**

Foreword

JavaFX. Oh boy, another new technology purporting to be the long-lost missing link between your math-fueled, unshaven, back-end developers, and latte-sipping, *Mac*-using, front-end *designers*.

We've heard all this before: Flash, Flex, Silverlight, AJAX, and heck, even GWT have all surfaced in the past few years—all attempting to solve the problems of delivering rich interfaces across devices as diverse as television set-top boxes and mobile phones. But none of these has captured the broad audience that Java serves. Much as Java functioned as the stepping-stone toward computer operating system agnosticism, JavaFX may well be the springboard for device agnosticism. The idea that applications no longer must be coupled to a particular device is, frankly, transformative, and worthy of serious consideration.

This book, written by my friend, colleague, and neighbor, Lucas Jordan, provides an outstanding run-through of most of the compelling reasons to consider JavaFX.

By focusing on rich graphical tools that assist in the creation of deeply immersive application experiences, Lucas taps into the essence of what makes JavaFX an attractive technology. Whether the subject is JavaFX's outstanding designer-developer workflow, unique declarative syntax, first-class support of Java technologies, rich graphics API, or innovative effects tools, Lucas shows you everything you need in a manner that is straightforward and compelling.

If you are considering using JavaFX in the near future, read this book. It will provide you with everything you wanted to know about JavaFX's ability to produce rich, immersive interfaces.

If you haven't yet thought about using JavaFX, read this book—it just may change your mind.

Ryan Donahue
Manager of Information Systems
George Eastman House, International Museum of Photography and Film

About the Author

 **Lucas L. Jordan** started his love of computers with a Commodore 64 and BASIC in the 1980s. This love survived the DOS and Pascal years to blossom into a successful career as a Java developer. He is currently working on back-end systems for EffectiveUI, and he hopes one day to make it as an independent game developer. Keep your eye on claywaregames.com.

Lucas also enjoys organic food and swimming whenever the western New York weather permits.

About the Technical Reviewer

 **Sten Anderson** has been working with Java since the late '90s and is currently a Senior Consultant for the software consultancy Citytech in Chicago. Sten blogs about Java, JavaFX, Groovy, and any number of other things at http://blogs.citytechinc.com/sanderson/.

Acknowledgments

First, I would like to acknowledge the people who encouraged me to work with computers: Harold Shermer (grandfather), Yvonne Jordan (mother), Len Wilcox, Matthew Godleski, David Eck, and Bill Simons.

Second, I would like to acknowledge EffectiveUI, my current employer, for providing me with the opportunity to meet the Java community face to face at JavaONE 2009.

Third, I would like to thank Apress and all the hard work everyone put in to get me through my first book.

Lastly, I would like to thank all of the people who are still my friend after me telling them, "Sorry I can't, I have to finish my book."

Oh, and Jim Weaver for putting me in touch with Apress in the first place.

Introduction

Goal of This Book

This book is intended to show off some interesting visual effects that can be implemented in JavaFX. The chapters explore particle effects, realistic animations driven by physics, and a number of other techniques. The first set of chapters look at each effect in isolation, and then the last chapters look at some of these effects in combination. The book concludes by presenting an entire sample application.

The book's goal is to provide a developer with a number of new tools that can be used to spruce up an old application or used in a new application. Given the newness of JavaFX at the time this book was written, I suspect that most developers are in the evaluation phase, exploring whether JavaFX is a worthwhile technology for some new project. I hope some of the effects in this book will convince you that JavaFX has a lot of promise.

While always keeping the needs of developers in mind, I will also spend some time looking at why applications require graphics at all, and how leveraging experts in visual design and user experience will greatly improve the end result.

This book was written by first messing around with JavaFX code to produce something interesting, then writing a little about it, and finally cleaning up the source code with the help of my technical reviewer. I bring this up to point out that the accompanying source code is really the heart of this book; it drove the content of these chapters. For the book to achieve its goal, I believe it is best consumed with the code handy. Go fire up NetBeans and run the example code as you get to each chapter, I think it will add a lot. Besides, this book is in black and white, while many of the examples are rich in color.

Who This Book Is For

This book is not an introduction to JavaFX. I assume you have played around with JavaFX already and hopefully have written an application or two. JavaFX is different enough from Java and other common languages that I urge anyone interested in this book to spend some time with JavaFX first. Just becoming familiar with the numerous curly and square brackets that get littered throughout JavaFX source code is a good start. This will help you to understand the concepts being presented, instead of fighting with syntax. JavaFX code can be surprisingly short and powerful, but some of that brevity comes with a cost in clarity or obviousness.

Additionally I expect you, the reader, to have some experience with computer graphics, such as coordinate systems, polygons, transformations, colors and gradients, and trigonometry. If you feel that brushing up on any of these topics is worth your while, I would like to recommend the online course "Computer Sc-Computer Graphics" from the Indian Institute of Technology Madras (IIT Madras) by

professor Dr. Sukhendu Das. The class is presented on YouTube at the following URL:
`http://www.youtube.com/view_play_list?p=338D19C4OD6D1732`

If you are a JavaFX expert already and just want to get to the effects, jump to Chapter 2 – but come back and read the section Designers and Developers in Chapter 1 sometime.

Who This book Is By

I think it is worth giving a little bit of background on my development history. My hope is that by sharing where I come from as a developer, you will be able to better understand my opinions and my interest in JavaFX.

Like so many of us, I started playing with computers at a young age. My early, pre-career computer programming was mostly in BASIC and Pascal. Using these tools, I tried in vain to reproduce a number of video games I was very fond of. I had neither the time nor the experience to create anything of any real value, but I learned a lot about 2D graphics in the process.

In college I was introduced to Java and fell in love with the language and with Swing. When I graduated I got a number of contract jobs writing Swing applications. This was a great experience, since I had to learn the hard way about things such as testing code and the truth about cross-platform deployment, and, most important, it taught me about how users use applications.

I remember presenting a new feature to a client; I think it was a tool that laid out printed labels. My client sat down at my app and starting clicking randomly; he had no idea how to use the "clever" interface I had devised. I tried to explain how some combination of mouse gestures and key presses produced the desired results. He didn't get it and I rewrote it. This showed me the value of using standard things such as buttons, sliders, and wizards to meet the expectation of the user. This is not to say there is no place for innovation, of course there is; computer interfaces have been evolving since they were invented, but the changes come in small steps.

Later, a small company that specializes in Rich Internet Applications (RIAs) hired me. This was my first experience working with user experience designers who have made it their career to understand how people use applications, and to create interfaces that meet those expectations. Most of these designers don't know how to code; they create PDF documents explaining the interface and a developer implements it. There is an example of one of these wire frame documents in Chapter 2 in the section Designers and Developers, where I explain how they are used.

Working at a company that put design first showed me the importance of having these specialists involved in a project. Many developers and graphical designers use the term "developer ugly" to refer to the quick and dirty graphics that developers create while in the process of getting the app to work. Developer ugly can also apply to user experience decisions as well. I don't intend to say that all developers lack the skills or the design sense to create nice-looking images or elegant UIs. I am pointing out that when you have your head down in the code, worrying about thread synchronization or something, it is not the best time to create an icon for a button. Just as graphic designers have all day to iterate over their creations, a user experience designer has all day to contemplate the UI. So I say, let specialists do their job. And of course, great projects take shape when all of the specialists work together.

So now my day job is implementing designs by other people, and at night I continue to try and create simple but fun video games. It is this endless tinkering that led me to JavaFX and to write this book. So while I try to address design issues as they come up in this book, my primary concern is getting it to work. I hope that the techniques in this book will enable a developer presented with a design challenge to say, "We can do that."

Chapter Overview

The following is a brief description of each chapter. Most of the chapters present a stand-alone effect and show how it is implemented. Feel free to read the chapters out of order, except for the last two, Chapters 10 and 11. Those two chapters rely on the foundation presented in the earlier chapters.

Chapter 1 briefly investigates why user interfaces work the way that they do by looking at them in a historical context. It further explains the roles of designers and developers and offers some suggestions on how they can work together. The chapter finishes by showing how this collaboration works when using JavaFX.

Chapter 2 shows how to implement a particle effect in JavaFX. We look at how particles are animated and how they can be blended together to create some surprisingly nice results. The sample code that accompanies this chapter is a playground for testing different combinations of properties of a particle effect.

Chapter 3 introduces how JavaFX can create animations, which are handy for transitioning the user from one panel to another. These transitions are common in RIAs and cell phones, and JavaFX is very capable of reproducing these effects.

Chapter 4 reviews lighting in JavaFX and how the different types of lighting affect the appearance of a node. The chapter also explores how lights can be animated to create a number of compelling visuals.

Chapter 5 looks at the Interpolator API in Java FX and shows how it can be extended to create new interpolators. The source for this chapter is an application for testing the effects of using different interpolators and is fully explained. The last part of the chapter shows how interpolators can be used in conjunction with the transitions from chapter 3.

Chapter 6 shows how to include an open source physics engine call Phys2d in your application. This chapter uses a number of examples to show how the physics engine is used and how JavaFX can be used as a presentation layer for the simulation.

Chapter 7 presents a technique where animations created with other tools can be used in a JavaFX application. The code provides a pattern for efficiently loading a large number of images and animating them.

Chapter 8 looks at gradients in JavaFX and how they can be animated. The animation of gradients in JavaFX is a little different than other animations in JavaFX and explains how they work. A final example shows why you might want to use animated graphics in your application.

Chapter 9 combines Java Sound and JavaFX to create visualizations of audio in a JavaFX scene. This chapter covers the basics of using Java Sound as well as how to expose the audio stream in a JavaFX-friendly way.

Chapter 10 combines the techniques from Chapter 2 on particles and Chapter 6 on physics to show how the two can be used together to create some interesting animations.

Chapter 11 presents an entire JavaFX application called Clown Cannon reviewing the design process for the application and how the techniques from the previous chapters are combined. How the application manages its state is also explored.

CHAPTER 1

■ ■ ■

JavaFX Design Considerations

This book was written to demonstrate how JavaFX can be used to create visually rich applications. It does so by presenting a number of techniques and explaining how they work in JavaFX. Before we explore the code, it is worth our time to look at the design of applications. Design is the process of planning what the application will do, how it will look, and how it will be implemented. This chapter starts with some thoughts on creating the content of applications in general, and ends with specifics related to working with JavaFX.

When exploring the creation of content, we will look at both the details of the workflow as well as why the content is created the way that it is. We will also look at design from a usability perspective, exploring how the workflow of the application you create is as important as the rest of the design. Lastly, we will look how JavaFX can be used to turn a design into an application.

Graphics and Animations in Applications

Graphical user interfaces (GUIs) are so common now, it is sometime hard to explain to people that it was not always this way. A screen, keyboard, and mouse are how most people interact with computers. But graphics in general are used in several different ways. The most basic way is to simply show the user something on the screen. This might be as simple as displaying an image or drawing a chart.

But GUIs are more than just displays; they also allow the user to interact with the content on the screen. In order to enable the user to accomplish a task, controls must be presented that they understand. Each control must be drawn on the screen, and how these controls are drawn can have a surprising effect on the user. Attention must be given to the quality of the rendering, consistency, and the look of the applications as whole.

The term *look and feel* is often used to describe the GUI as a whole. The set of controls used and how they are drawn comprise the *look* of the application. Once the user starts actually using the application, the *feel* becomes important.

The following sections explore the controls used in an application, how they are drawn, and how animations combine to create the complete *look and feel*.

Controls and Layout

As time marches forward, the set of controls that are common on the desktop changes. Exploring the default components that come with a particular UI technology shows us what users expected when that technology was current. For example, below are the components that come with AWT, Sun's UI technology from the 1990s.

```
java.awt.Button
java.awt.Checkbox
java.awt.Choice
java.awt.Dialog
java.awt.Image
java.awt.Label
java.awt.List
java.awt.Scrollbar
java.awt.TextArea
java.awt.TestField
java.awt.Window
```

As you can see, there were really very few choices. If you compare the list above with the one below, which shows the Swing UI controls, you can see the new paradigms that were introduced in the last 10 years.

```
javax.swing.JButton
javax.swing.JCheckBox
javax.swing.JCheckBoxMenuItem
javax.swing.JColorChooser
javax.swing.JComboBox
javax.swing.JDesktopPane
javax.swing.JDialog
javax.swing.JEditorPane
javax.swing.JFileChooser
javax.swing.JFormattedTextField
javax.swing.JFrame
javax.swing.JInternalFrame
javax.swing.JLabel
javax.swing.JList
javax.swing.JMenu
javax.swing.JMenuBar
javax.swing.JPasswordField
javax.swing.JPopupMenu
javax.swing.JProgressBar
javax.swing.JRadioButton
javax.swing.JScrollPane
javax.swing.JSeperator
javax.swing.JSlider
javax.swing.JSpinner
javax.swing.JTabbedPane
javax.swing.JTable
javax.swing.JTextArea
javax.swing.JTextField
javax.swing.JToggleButton
javax.swing.JToolBar
javax.swing.JTree
```

The bold items represent controls not available in AWT. At some point, the engineers at Sun must have decided that these new items were standard and useful enough to include in the default set of controls. While it is true that AWT represented the intersection of controls from all the platforms supported by Java in those days, and thus was limited by cross-platform constraints, it is still interesting to see AWT lacked a radio button. There are some other interesting additions, such as the toolbars and trees. These components are so common now—it's hard to imagine life without them.

The list of Swing components also shows a paradigm that is now almost extinct, the JDesktopPane. This component, in conjunction with JInternalFrame, allowed the application developer to create a windowed environment inside a host window of the OS. This paradigm was very popular at one point, but today, it is considered bad form. The argument for not using windows within windows is something like, "The OS already has windows, why make the user manage another set of windows that might work slightly differently?" I think this is a valid perspective, but of course there are always exceptions and plenty of applications out there work this way today.

Regardless of the exact set of controls available, there are still numerous decisions on how those components are laid out. Consider the humble login dialog found in many applications, composed of a few labels, two text fields and a button or two. Figures 1-1 and 1-2 show two different login dialogs.

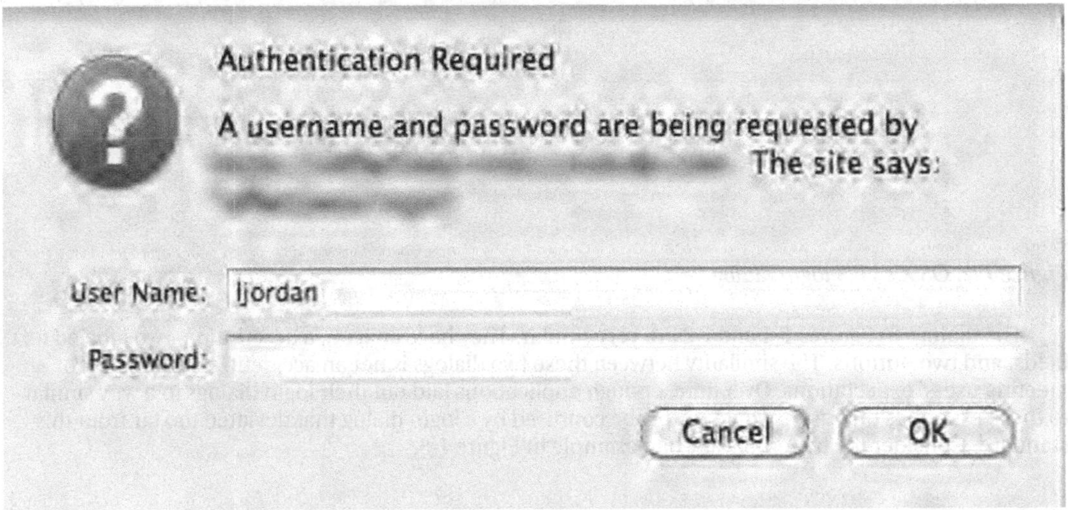

Figure 1-1. Firefox login dialog

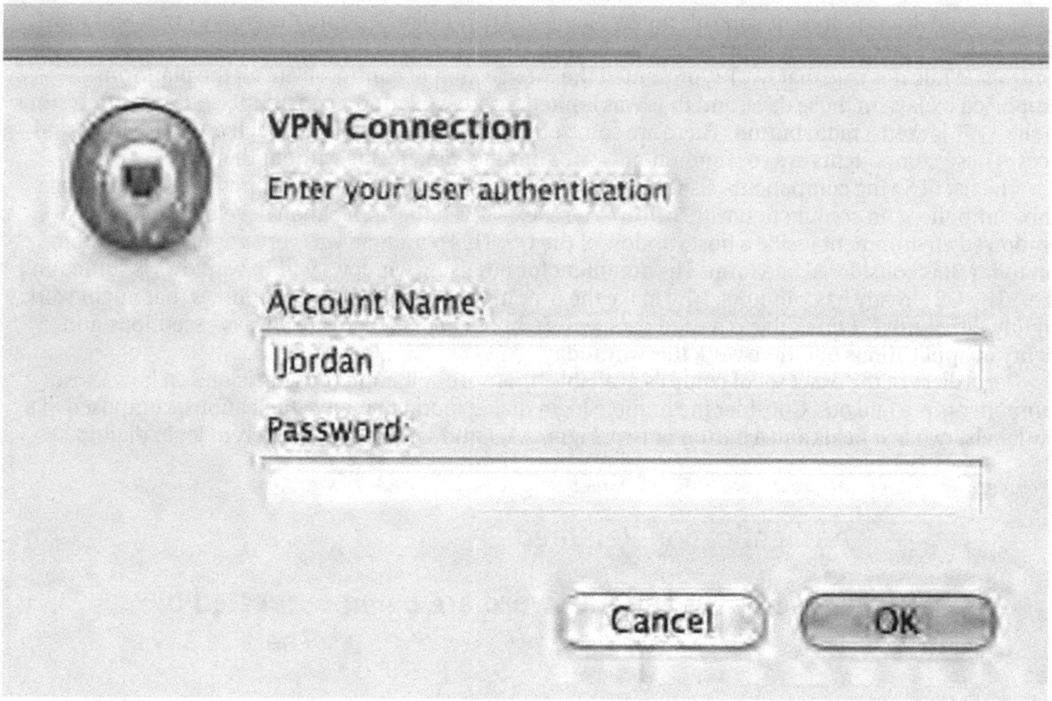

Figure 1-2. *OS X's VPN login dialog*

The dialogs in Figures 1-1 and 1-2 are very similar. They have an icon, a description, two labeled text fields, and two buttons. The similarity between these two dialogs is not an accident—it is a matter of meeting users' expectations. Over time, enough applications laid out their login dialogs in a way similar to these examples that users would simply be confused by a login dialog that deviated too far from this standard. Consider the hyperbolically bad example in Figure 1-3.

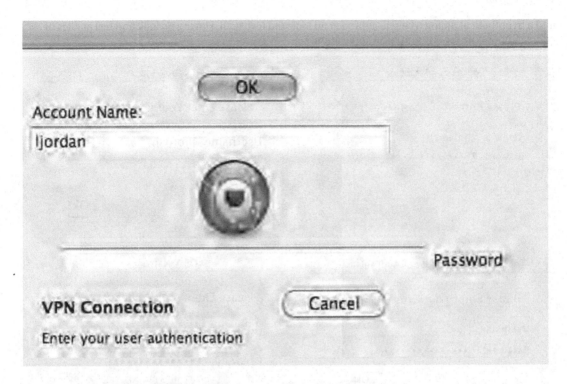

Figure 1-3. Hyperbolically bad login dialog

Figure 1-3 has exactly the same components as the dialog in Figure 1-2. The only difference is the layout, but the layout is so poor that no one would ever actually create a dialog like this. I presented an example this hyperbolically bad so there could be no arguments about its merits. The dialog in Figure 1-3 might even be perfectly functional in the sense that if you filled out the right information you would be authenticated. But the number of users who would be stopped in their tracks is very high.

Of course, most applications are considerably more complex than a single dialog, but I think the point holds about fulfilling user expectations when possible.

Graphics

Given a set of controls, there are numerous ways to lay them out on a panel. There are also numerous ways to draw each component. Every modern GUI toolkit allows the developer to customize the look of each component. For example HTML has CSS to control the layout and look of the components on a web page. Java's Swing has the concept of a LookAndFeel class. As any Swing veteran knows, Java comes with a number of look and feels built right in. Generally, the look and feels fall into one of the following categories; legacy, cross-platform, native, or customizable.

By examining the Java look and feels, you can get a sense of how the look of components has changed over the years. Just like the set of components has changed over time, the look of those components has evolved as well. Figure 1-4 shows several Swing look and feels, the default JavaFX look, and a hypothetical dialog trying to approach no look and feel at all. Having no look and feel at all is of course impossible for any graphical application.

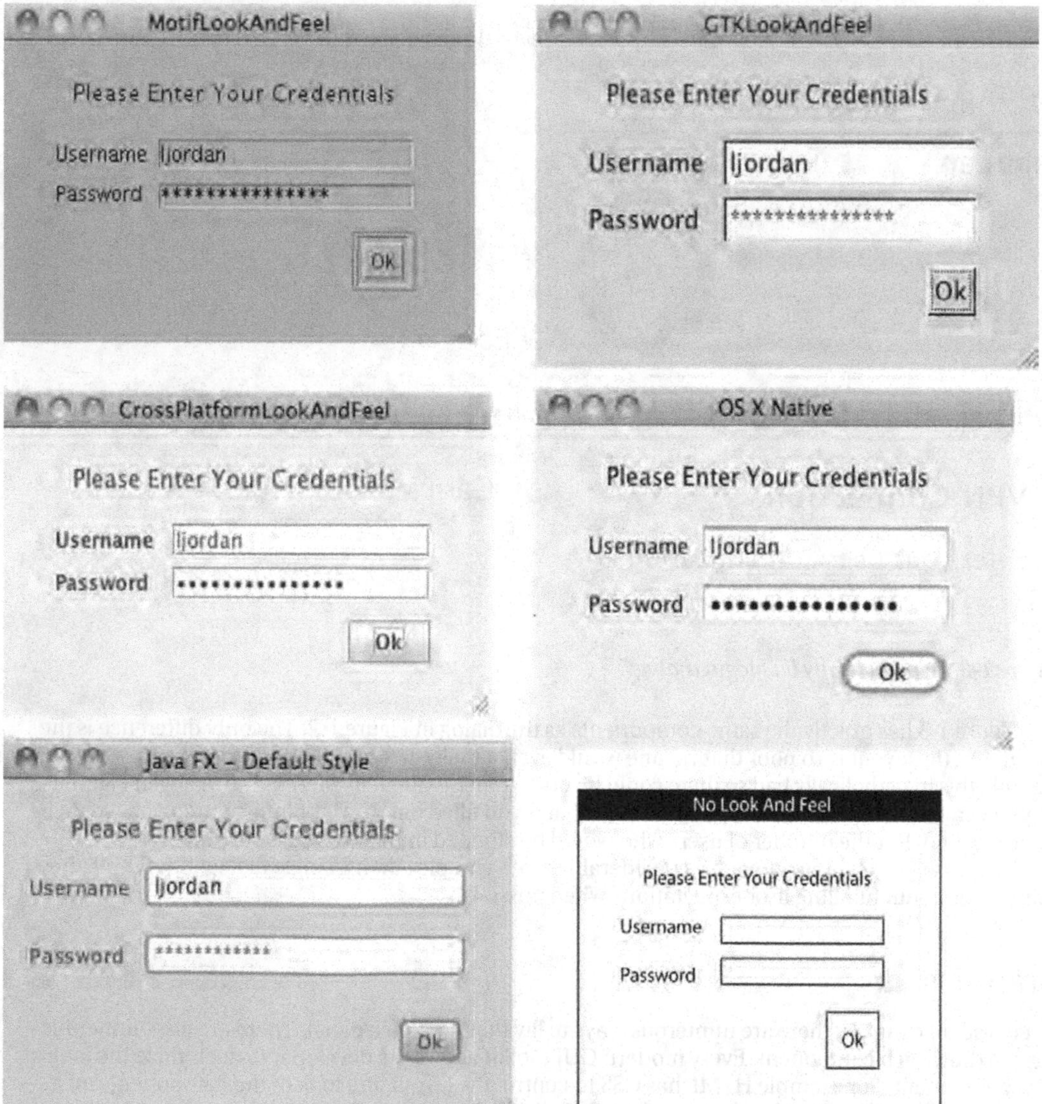

Figure 1-4. *Look and feels*

The six dialog boxes in Figure 1-4 have an identical set of components and identical functionality. The differences between them are strictly in the style used to draw each component. The top two dialogs, Motif and GTK, speak to an older aesthetic; they both use very simple bevels around each component. The simplicity of the bevels is partly a function of the computation horsepower at the time, but not completely. Presumably people thought they looked good, too. The GTK one is still OK by my standards, but I am sure my graphical designer colleagues would disagree.

The cross-platform look and feel and OS X's native look and feel represent a more modern look. The bevels are subtler, and gradients are used on the button. The JavaFX look is also modern in the same way with regard to gradients. It drops the sense of depth in the text fields and instead gives them a rounded corner.

The point of exploring the differences between these looks is to highlight the numerous design decisions that went into them. Each of those decisions becomes part of an application and influences how the user perceives the application. For example, the native look tries to blend in with the rest of the OS, effectively passing the decision-making on to the OS makers. If the application looks native, the user is more likely to trust the app and have confidence in it. As any knowledgeable designer will tell you, confidence is part of the *experience* and is as important as the flow or layout of an application.

Consider the difference in confidence that might be evoked if the user was presented with the cross-platform look rather than the Motif look. I suspect most users would be suspicious of the Motif version, while not even noticing the cross-platform one. This is because the Motif version looks older. So by making this simple decision, you improve the experience of the user by preventing unnecessary worry.

I tried to create a dialog with no look and feel in Adobe Illustrator, as shown in the bottom right dialog in Figure 1-4. The fact is that even this minimalist look still involved design decisions. Should I give the dialog a black border? Maybe I should use gray instead of black, perhaps that is more neutral? In fact, I could not create a neutral dialog. No look and feel is still a look and feel.

The examples in Figure 1-4 show default looks, without any customization. All graphics packages allow some customization. Java and JavaFX both provide powerful tools to make an application look any way you can imagine. Figure 1-5 shows a login panel with a completely unique look.

Figure 1-5. Custom look

In Figure 1-5 you can see a graphical style unlike those presented before. The components on the panel appear to float due to the drop shadows. There is a background graphic whose function is strictly aesthetic. The layout and set of components of this dialog are well within user expectations, but the colors and shapes used to decorate it may be completely new to them. This might be bad if the dialog does not look like the rest of the application. Conversely, this graphical design might be a good thing if the set of colors and shapes indicate a familiar and trusted brand.

Animations

Let's consider all changes on a screen an animation, including simple actions like replacing one panel with another or highlighting a button when the mouse moves over it, as well as the more blatant animations found in computer games. Each change happens for a reason, and understanding why these changes are important will guide us in creating compelling applications.

Let's start with the simple example of a wizard for setting up an e-mail account. The first panel might contain a few text fields asking the user for her e-mail address and password. The second panel might contain a few checkboxes that allow her to customize how the application behaves; perhaps it lets her select if e-mail should be stored locally or on a remote server. Each panel of the wizard will have a number of buttons along the bottom, most likely a Cancel button, a Done button, and a Next button.

When the user encounters the first panel, only the Cancel button is enabled. As soon as the username and password are filled in, both the Done button and the Next button would become enabled. This simple animation of enabling the buttons informs the user of a few things. First, enabling the Done button tells the user he has filled in the required information. Second, enabling the Next button tells the user there are more options if he is interested.

There are other subtle animations involved as well, like when the mouse moves over a text field, the cursor should change to a vertical line, indicating that text can be typed into the field. The mouse cursor might also change when it moves over an enabled button, or the button itself might change. These little cues help users perform their tasks and would be missed if absent.

In most applications that contain wizards, clicking on the Next button causes one panel to be instantly replaced by the next one. It's easy to imagine that this transition from panel to panel could be much livelier. Perhaps one panel slides out of the way while the next panel slides into view. Would this animation add anything to the user's experience? It is a question that can only be answered if you know more about the application. For example, if the application is for setting up a bank account, such frills might distract users or, worse, make them think the app is silly or child-like. These are not attributes a bank wants associated with its applications. However, if the application is a video game, these sorts of flourishes are almost expected.

Apple's iPhone provides an interesting study on how animated transitions promote a sense of simplicity. Almost every time the screen on the phone changes content, there is some sort of transition. This is due to two factors. First, Apple made it extremely simple for developers to include these effects in its applications. Second, Apple uses those transitions to great effect in its own applications.

Another obvious example that uses animations in an application is the progress bar. This invaluable component gives the developer a chance to explain to the user that things are going to take a little time.

Each of the animations mentioned above is used in applications because of a conscious decision, just like the choice of controls and the layout and rendering of the application. These elements combined are the design of the application. The next section will discuss in some detail the advantages of working with professional designers and how best to collaborate with them.

Designers and Developers

Developers are the people who understand the technology; it is their job to take an idea and implement it in code. In some ways, this is the most complicated part, involving the herding of billions of bits of data through the most complex machine. On the other hand, it is the simplest. When writing software, developers have the luxury of knowing when they are done. Does the app work or not? Does it match the design? These simple tests make software development akin to engineering, while design is not.

Design in this context refers to both graphical design and user experience design. Though many people correctly distinguish between the two, I want to talk about the design as a whole. Design is the process of planning, which is the foundation for all endeavors. When creating an application, it is the design that takes an identified problem and presents a solution. Theoretically, we write software to solve some problem. A clear vision of the problem and its solution is often what separates a successful project from an unsuccessful one.

It is true that we can measure the success of a design by how well the problem is solved, and this is why design can never be engineering, since we so often lack the ability to measure how well a design solves a problem. For example, if you are designing a game, there are probably two problems you are trying to solve—lack of money and boredom. Or, to put it positively, there are two goals you wish to achieve—to make money and to entertain people. These goals are probably not isolated; it seems reasonable to assume that the retail success of a game is a function of how well it entertains. However, measuring how well people are entertained is much harder.

Consider that the entertainment value of the game or the ease of use of an application is the sum of all of the design decisions. Now consider that the set of decisions is humongous and composed mostly of answering questions like "Should the background of this screen be Blue(r=42,g=57,b=144) or Blue(r=42,g=27,b= 222)?" or "Should the field for a social security number come before the field for birth date or after it?" While it is true that user testing can provide excellent insight into the success of a design, it would be impossible to measure every combination of possible answers. At some point, the designer simply has to use her instinct to come to a decision.

Workflow

I am a strong believer in iterative process. I find, as a developer, it is much easier to make many small changes than create an entire application out of whole cloth. I think a lot of designers find it easier to improve something that exists than to create a completely new design. Basically, it is easier to fix mistakes you already made then fix mistakes you have not yet made. That's what the iterative process is all about, setting up development so each new feature is a small change.

With that in mind, let's consider the creation of a simple application. This sample application will be a single panel used to graphically show the size of files in a directory. The first step is for an experienced designer to draw the application, like the diagram in Figure 1-6.

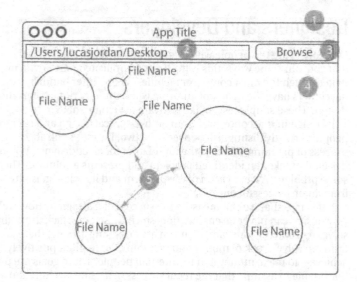

Spacial File Browser

This application presents the files in a directory as circles which are proportional in size to the size of the file.

1. The window chrome.

2. Text path showing the current display directory.

3. Button allows the user to select a dir from a file dialog.

4. Display field for the files.

5. A circle presenting a file, the name is either displayed within it or next to it depending on the file size and the length of the file name.

Figure 1-6. *Initial design document*

Figure 1-6 shows a sketch of this new application on the right, decorated with numbered points. On the left, each point is described. Little details are added as the designer thinks of them; for example, it occurs to our imaginary designer that the file names will not necessarily fit within every circle. So she comes up with two strategies for displaying the names. She is also familiar with the practice of having both a text field and a button for selecting directories, so she includes that in the design.

While it would be possible to simply go and create this application, why not give our designer some feedback from the developer's perspective? This will give her a chance to iterate over her design and make improvements. I would bring up the following points.

- What happens if the user types a bad path into the text field?

- How exactly are those circles laid out, are they just random? Can they overlap?

- What if the file name is really long? Should we abbreviate?

- Does the application remember which directory it was looking at between runs?

If the team agrees that regardless of the issues brought up, the basic design is solid enough to move forward, then a graphical designer can start doing his work while the developer gets started on evaluating technologies and creating the first version in code. Figure 1-7 shows the first mock-up by our graphical designer.

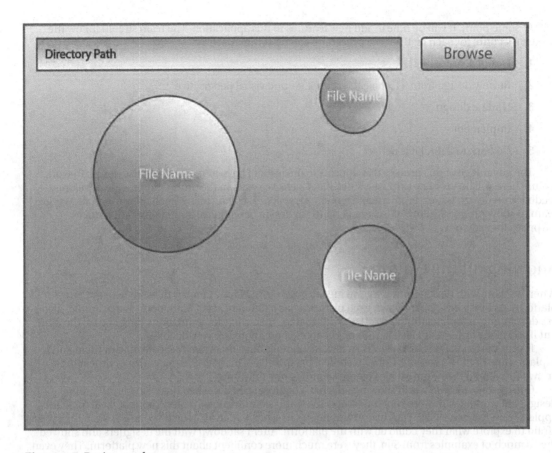

Figure 1-7. Design mock-up

Figure 1-7 shows the design from the experienced designer realized with color. The graphical designer was directed to make the application friendly, so he opted for thick lines and pastel colors. From a developer's perspective, I would ask these questions of the graphical designer.

- What is the proportion used on the gradients?

- Is the direction of the gradient random or driven by something else?

- Are these all of the colors we should use or are they just examples?

- The path field is overlapping one of the files, is that what we really want?

While there is a still a lot of work to be done on this application, the basic framework is in place. Most importantly, questions about how the app works and looks were asked early. Of course, development issues do arise: maybe we can't get the layout of the circles just right. In this case, hopefully the issue was identified early in the development process, allowing the design team to rethink the feature.

At some point, it will be time to add new features to this application. The team should follow the same procedure for each feature. The procedure can be summarized as:

1. Design feature

2. Review design from a technical, experience, and visual perspective

3. Update design

4. Implement

5. Go back to 2 until it is perfect

The advantage of this process that appeals to me is that I have a clear and concise design to work from. There will be very few surprises, since I had a chance early in the process to provide developer feedback on design issues. From a management perspective, having many small milestones allows the team to show progress, allows the client to adjust to design or technical limitations, and reduces surprises for everyone.

Showing off the Platform

When working with designers, it is a good idea to get a sense of how familiar they are with the target platform. As every developer knows, each platform has a different set of limitations. For example, if you are developing an application in HTML and JavaScript, then complex animations might be off the table, but if you allow applets or Flash in your application, animations are very doable.

If your design team is working with a new technology, it is important to sit down with them and explain some of the limitations from a technical perspective. This will save them a lot of time if they know they should throw out an idea before spending any time on it.

Conversely, it is also worth showing off what a platform can do. When first using JavaFX, the designers I worked with were very concerned about this new technology. They thought JavaFX meant applets from the late 1990s. They had a misguided sense of what JavaFX could do, and as such they were afraid to explore what they could do with the platform. After I sat down with the designers and showed them bunch of examples from Sun, they were much more confident about this new platform. They even noticed a few examples that they thought would be impossible on the platforms they were most familiar with.

Setting Realistic Expectations

While it is important to show off what a platform can do, it is equally important to demonstrate reasonable limitations. All platforms are constrained by performance; computers can only do so much work. As the languages we use to describe an application become more and more high level, we have less and less control over things like memory management and performance. For example, in JavaFX there is really only one way to draw a circle on the screen; if JavaFX can't draw that circle fast enough, there is really nothing the developer can do to speed it up.

So when making cool demo applications to show off what JavaFX can do, make sure to show the application on both a high-end workstation and an older laptop. Impress upon everyone that while fancy graphics are important to an application, they must be used sparingly and where they provide most impact.

JavaFX

JavaFX provides a number of features that makes it an excellent environment for developing complex graphical applications. It can be considered a domain-specific language for the creation of animated graphics. A domain-specific language is simply a language that focuses on solving a particular task. For example, SQL is a domain-specific language for working with data in a database. The following sections explore some of the features in JavaFX and how they help mitigate the concerns of designers mentioned earlier in this chapter.

Scene Graph

There are basically two types of graphics libraries, raster and vector. Raster graphics libraries typically just provide a set of utility functions, like drawCircle or drawImage, for setting the values of pixels. A function like drawCircle probably just takes an array of values (pixels) and changes just the right ones to make a circular pattern when the values are drawn to the screen. An application using this library does not necessarily maintain a record that a circle was drawn; the intent of a circle is lost. For example, consider two scenarios, in the first an image has a circle drawn on it and then the image is scaled up. In the second scenario, an image is scaled up and then a circle is drawn on it. Figure 1-8 shows the result of these two scenarios.

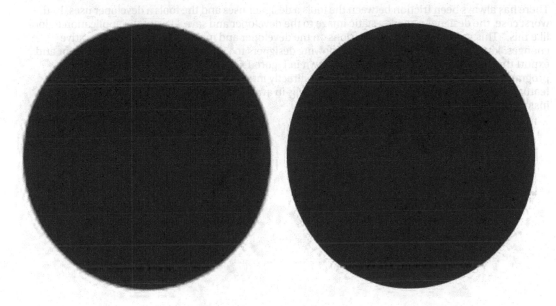

Figure 1-8. *Fuzzy circle, crisp circle*

In Figure 1-8, the circle on the left is the result of the first scenario; the circle on the right is the result of the second scenario. As you can see, the circle from scenario one is fuzzy. This is because when a circle is drawn to a rectangular grid of pixels, the edge of the circle is anti-aliased—there is not a clean separation of pixels. When the image is scaled up, these partially drawn pixels at the edge of the circle are scaled as well, which produces the fuzziness around the circle.

Now if we know our application is going to be scaling an image with a circle on it, we can write it in such a way as to just store the fact that we want a circle drawn. Our application can then be smart enough to always draw the circle after any scaling is performed on the pixels, guaranteeing a nice, crisp circle. This is basically what a vector graphics library like JavaFX does; it provides a way to describe the content of the scene, which is called a scene graph. The scene can then be drawn to any size without a loss in fidelity.

The quality of the finished rendering is very important and makes having a scene graph worthwhile, but there is another advantage as well. Since the scene graph allows you to describe the image on the screen in a non-destructive way, it allows you to make changes to the graph during runtime to create high-quality animations. With a raster library, it is up the developer to figure out how to draw each frame of the animation. This is hard, error-prone work. It is much nicer for the developer to simply say, here is a rectangle at this point, and in 5 seconds it needs to be over here. Since the developer is able to program an animation in much the same way as a designer describes one, the quality of the animation produced by the developer is much better. It is really very nice to be able to spend my development time getting an animation just right, versus getting to work at all. This is the advantage of a domain-specific language.

Designer Tools

There has always been friction between the tools a designer uses and the tools a developer uses. In the worst case, the designer e-mails a static image to the developer and says, "I want the application to look like this." This puts a lot of design decisions on the developer and makes it hard to make iterative changes. JavaFX helps solve this issue by allowing designers to create content in Adobe Illustrator and export their work as a JavaFX resource (as shown in Figure 1-9). This allows the developer to programmatically import the work of designers directly into the code base of the application. This feature is added to Adobe Illustrator through a plug-in available at javafx.com. Simply download and install the JavaFX Production Suite.

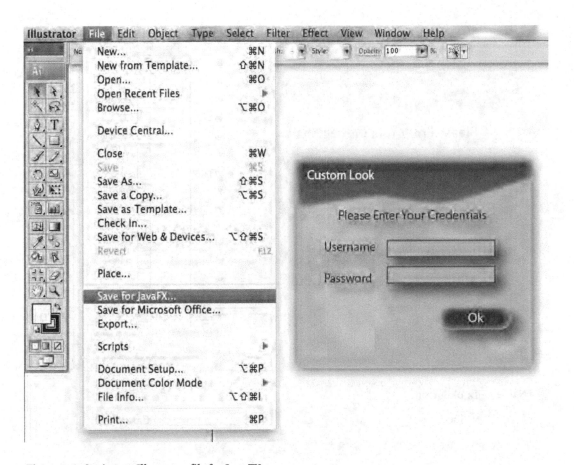

Figure 1-9. Saving an Illustrator file for JavaFX

Figure 1-9 shows the new export menu item in Adobe Illustrator. When this menu item is selected, a dialog appears that allows the user to save the content of an Adobe Illustrator file as an fxz file. An fxz file is a zipped file that contains JavaFX source code describing the scene; it may also contain images and other resources required to reproduce the Adobe file in JavaFX. Each item in an Adobe Illustrator file is called an object, so for each piece of text or shape in the Adobe file, a JavaFX node is created of the appropriate type. While this allows for a smooth workflow from Adobe Illustrator to JavaFX, it is not the whole story. As shown in Figure 1-9, the designer has created a login dialog. This includes elements that are more complicated than just graphics; it also contains controls, like the button and the text fields. To further streamline the designer/developer workflow, the designer can name each layer in a way that allows the developer to programmatically pull out nodes and work with them.

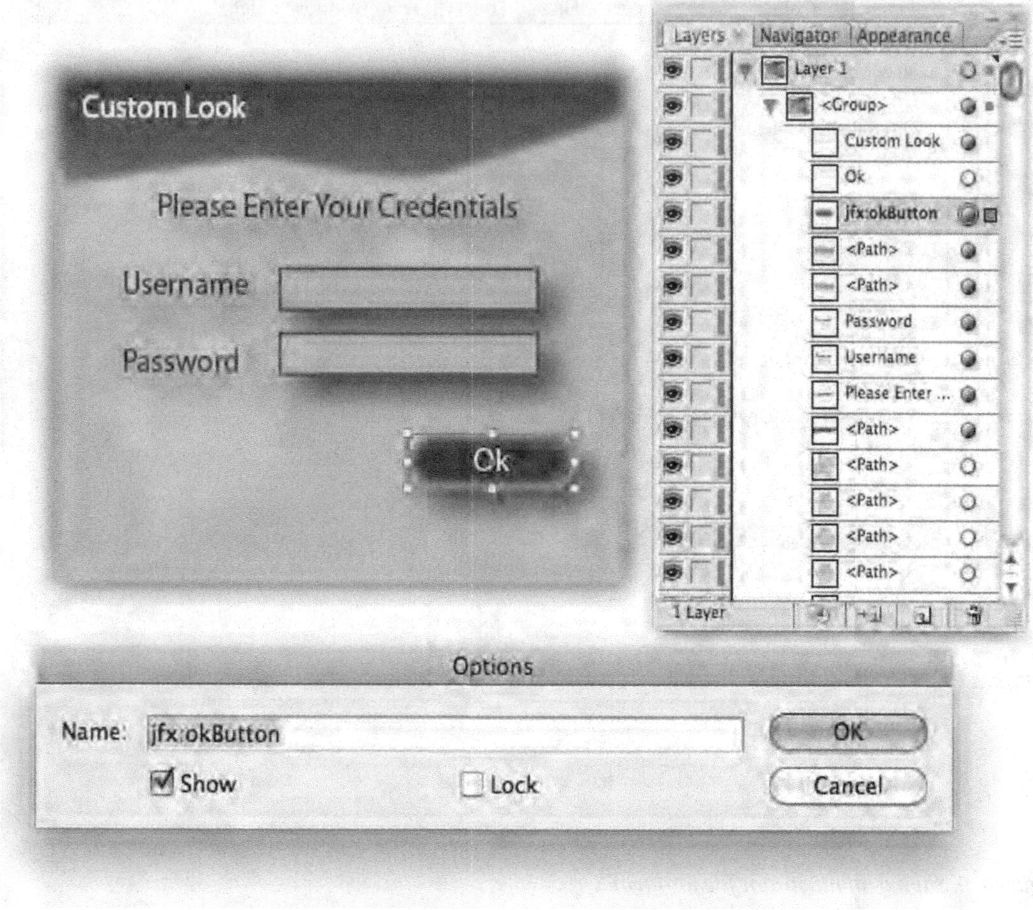

Figure 1-10. *Naming layers*

Figure 1-10 shows the OK button selected and being renamed. By prefixing the layer's name with "jfx:", you can tell the export tool to set the id attribute of the selected layer to okButton. In this way the developer can then easily write code to find exactly the right node and make it act like a button. It can be made to act like a button by adding a mouse listener function to it.

Sun's NetBeansIDE provides a utility to simplify the work for the developer. From NetBeans, you can right-click on an fxz file and have NetBeans create a stub class for that file. This stub class is handy as it allows you to simply create a Node that contains the content of an fxz file. Listing 1-1 shows an example stub class.

Listing 1-1. Stub Class

```
/*
 * Generated by JavaFX Production Suite NetBeans plugin.
 * CustomLookAndFeelUI.fx
 *
 * Created on Tue Oct 27 15:19:14 EDT 2009
 */
package org.lj.jfxe.chapter1;

import java.lang.*;
import javafx.scene.Node;
import javafx.fxd.FXDNode;

public class CustomLookAndFeelUI extends FXDNode {

        override public var url = "{__DIR__}CustomLookAndFeel.fxz";

        public-read protected var okButton: Node;

        override protected function contentLoaded() : Void {
            okButton=getNode("okButton");
        }

        /**
         * Check if some element with a given id exists and write
         * a warning if the element could not be found.
         * The whole method can be removed if such warning is not required.
         */
        protected override function getObject( id:String) : Object {
            var obj = super.getObject(id);
            if ( obj == null) {
                    System.err.println("WARNING: Element with id {id} not found in
{url}");
            }
            return obj;
        }
}
```

Listing 1-1 shows the class `CustomLookAndFeelUI` that extends `FXDNode`. When this node is instantiated, the variable `okButton` points to the node that represents the layer, which was named `jfx:okButton`. Once this stub class is created and used in the application, the designer can feel free to update the look of the dialog panel and submit her changes without developer intervention. If the designer changes the name of the `okButton`, a warning will be generated when this class is instantiated. This warning creates a contract between the designer and developer that will help catch errors between the two workflows.

When working with Eclipse or another IDE that does not yet support the creation of these stub files, you can create them by hand or just use NetBeans to create them and copy them into your IDE of choice.

Deployment

One of the features that sets JavaFX apart from other graphics libraries is its great flexibility when it comes to deployment. JavaFX is designed to be Sun's next generation content delivery language, and as such it has inherited the best parts of deploying Java applications. JavaFX can be deployed as applets in a web page, as desktop applications, as mobile applications, and even to set-top boxes. To manage this complex deployment story, the Java Network Launching Protocol (JNLP) is poised to become the standard way of describing the deployment of JavaFX applications. JNLP is the protocol used in Sun's Web Start application, so these names are often interchangeable.

From the developer's perspective, a JNLP file is an XML file that describes the application. It includes information about the name of the application, a description, as well as function information like the location of JAR files, the level of security required, and a number of other details.

For any evaluation of JavaFX to be complete, I urge you to explore all of the features of JNLP; there are many online resources available.

NetBeans

The JavaFX SDK comes with command-line tools for compiling and running JavaFX applications, and it is probably worth your time to explore how these tools work. However, for day-to-day work, I find that an IDE helps me be productive.

NetBeans is Sun's IDE and currently the best choice for developing JavaFX apps. This is not meant to be a religious statement favoring one IDE over another—I am thrilled to have so many excellent choices when it comes to IDEs. But JavaFX is so new and so very much the child of Sun, the other tools simply have not put in the equivalent time to construct a compelling JavaFX development environment. But, please, go check out the support for you IDE of choice.

Creating a JavaFX project in NetBeans is just a matter of choosing New Project... from the File menu and selecting JavaFX Script Application from the New Project Dialog, as shown in Figure 1-11.

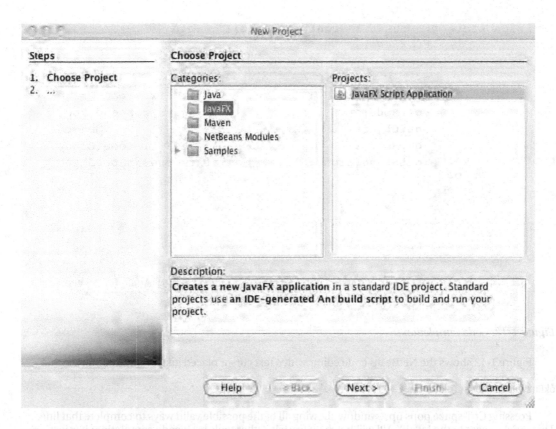

Figure 1-11. *New JavaFX project in NetBeans*

Once a JavaFX project is created, it can be run by pressing F6. The project explorer on the left side of the application provides access the project's source files, while the main display area shows the source code of the file you are editing. What really makes NetBeans a good platform for JavaFX is the code completion feature.

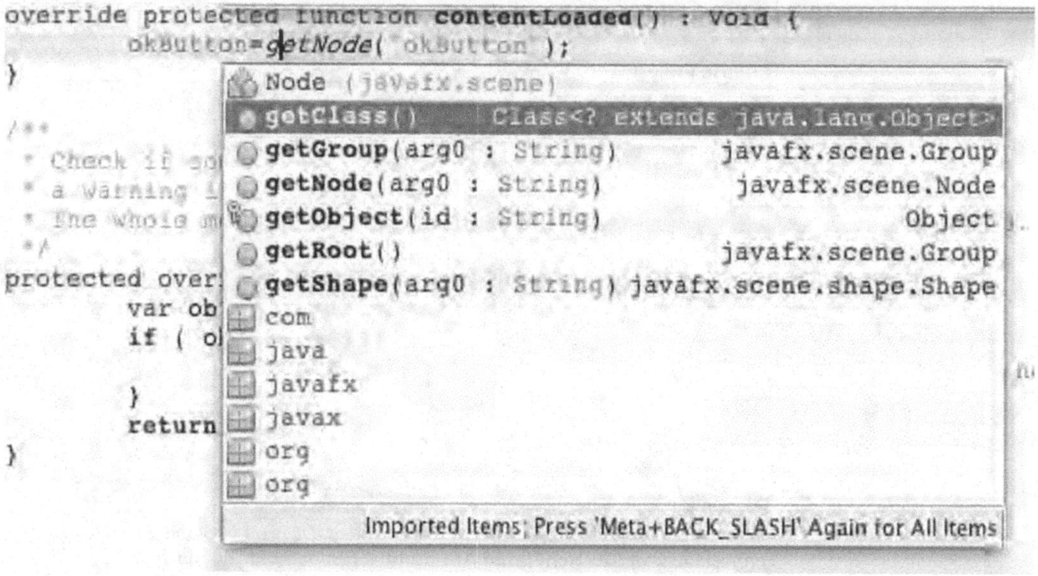

```
override protected function contentLoaded() : Void {
        okButton=getNode( "okButton" );
}

/**
 * Check if so
 * a warning i
 * The whole m
 */
protected over
        var ob
        if ( o

        }
        return
}
```

Node (javafx.scene)	
getClass()	Class<? extends java.lang.Object>
getGroup(arg0 : String)	javafx.scene.Group
getNode(arg0 : String)	javafx.scene.Node
getObject(id : String)	Object
getRoot()	javafx.scene.Group
getShape(arg0 : String)	javafx.scene.shape.Shape
com	
java	
javafx	
javax	
org	
org	

Imported Items; Press 'Meta+BACK_SLASH' Again for All Items

Figure 1-12. *Code completion*

Figure 1-12 shows the NetBeans code editor with a text cursor placed just after the "g" on the line:

```
okButton=getNode("okButton");
```

Pressing Ctrl-space pops up a window showing all of the possible valid ways to complete that line. This quick access to the JavaFX API will help you learn it. Other tools have code completion; it is just their JavaFX support that is missing at this point.

Open Source Tools

While Adobe's tools have been mentioned as ways of creating content for JavaFX applications, there are a number of excellent open source tools that can be used as well. Open source tools can be a great way to get work done on the cheap. Here are a few tools, what they do, and how they contribute to JavaFX development.

GIMP

An open source image-manipulation tool, GIMP runs on a huge number of platforms and has a feature set similar to Adobe's Photoshop. It lacks a few features that make Photoshop users look down at GIMP. However, for a beginner or someone who does not require the "missing" features, this image-editing tool is simply invaluable. While there is no support for exporting JavaFX scene data directly, it does a great job with PNG files, which JavaFX does a great job of rendering.
Download at http://www.gimp.org/.

ImageMagick

ImageMagick is a command-line tool available on most platforms and is used for batch image manipulation. If you have 300 images of different formats and you want to scale them all by 12% and apply a drop shadow, ImageMagick is the tool for you. Again, this tool does not have any JavaFX-specific features; it is just a very useful item to have in your toolbox. Since it is command-line, it can fit nicely into many automated tasks. Download at http://www.imagemagick.org.

Blender

Blender is a tool for creating 3D content. It is feature-rich and has been used to create a number of community-driven animated movies. Though JavaFX does not currently support 3D content, Blender is still useful for creating 2D content that looks unapologetically 3D. I use this tool to create 3D-looking sprites in my video games. Download at http://www.blender.org/.

Inkscape

Inkscape is a vector-based drawing tool and is most often compared to Adobe Illustrator. Content created in Inkscape can be saved directly to JavaFX source code. While the workflow is a little different from the JavaFX Production Suite and Adobe's tools, a fantastic designer/developer workflow can be created with this tool. Download at http://www.inkscape.org/.

Audacity

Audacity is a tool for recording and editing sounds. While this book focuses heavily on graphics and animations, some applications require sound effects. Give this tool a try before spending money on a commercial product. Download at http://audacity.sourceforge.net/.

Summary

I started this chapter by describing the design decisions that must go into creating a graphical interface. The role of designers—and how that relates to developers—was explored within the context of creating an application. Specific features of the JavaFX development tools were highlighted to show how the platform supports a streamlined designer/developer workflow. Lastly, I briefly touched on a number of open source tools that can be helpful for creating a graphics-rich application.

CHAPTER 2

■ ■ ■

Effect: Particle Systems

Particle systems are used in many video games and other animations. A particle system is a general term for any visual effect that uses a large number of small, simple, animated nodes to create a larger, complex effect. This technique produces animations that are hard to reproduce using a single vector, raster image, or other method. Examples of particle systems include fire, magic spells, sparks, and moving water. This chapter covers the basic principles of particle systems in 2D space, and how they are implemented in JavaFX. There are a number of examples, each building on the previous one. You'll find it very helpful to have the example code on hand when reading this chapter.

Basic Principles

A particle system is composed of a single emitter node and many short-lived nodes called particles. In general, an emitter defines where and at what rate particles are created. The particles themselves determine how they will move and when they should be removed from the scene. The visual impact is determined by how they are emitted, as well as the appearance of a given particle.

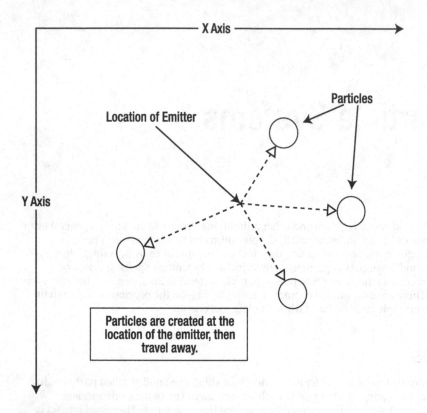

Figure 2-1. Particle basics

Figure 2-1 illustrates a scene with an emitter. The particles are created at the location of the emitter and then travel away from that point. The emitter node is not visible. The particles are the children of the emitter node and are visible.

To achieve a particular visual effect, you need to understand a number of concepts that will help coordinate your code with the visual effect being implemented.

Attributes That Dictate The Appearance of a Particle System

- The location of the emitter.
- The rate at which the particles are emitted.
- The direction or path the particles travel.
- A particle's duration in the scene.
- The visual attributes of a particle such as the color, shape, or transparency.
- Changes to the visual appearance of a particle during its life cycle.

Visual Density

When creating a particle system, it is important to consider the visual density of the particles being emitted, that is, the proportion of a screen area that is dedicated to particles. To create visual effects that look good, you need to be aware of the factors that affect the visual density of a particle system.

Changing the rate at which particles are emitted controls how dense the effect looks. An emitter that creates a new particle every second will look sluggish and empty, while one that emits particles every hundredth of a second will rapidly produce a thick collection of particles. Of course, the speed at which particles travel away from the emitter also affects visual density. Fast-moving particles require an emitter with a high emission rate to avoid appearing sparse. Similarly, slow-moving particles benefit from an emitter with a slow emit rate to avoid over-saturating an area with particles.

The size of the particles is also significant. As the emit rate and animation speed of the particles contribute to the visual density of a particle system, so too can the size of each particle be adjusted to achieve just the right density.

Particle Appearance and Behavior

While visual density describes how the effect will look as a whole, the eye naturally picks out individual particles as they travel across the scene. Controlling the attributes of each particle helps achieve the desired look.

The simplest particles travel in straight lines and then vanish after some time. But there can be many variations in this behavior. For example, particles might start out fast and then slow as they reach the end of their life cycle. Particles could also fade to transparent or change color as they age.

Creating particles that do not travel in a straight line can be a powerful tool when creating an effect. One option is to have particles that "fall" toward the ground, like the sparks of an aerial fireworks display. Or you could have particles that travel erratically, like air bubbles in water racing to the surface.

One of the most important aspects of particles' appearance is how they interact with each other. The first example just uses opaque particles, but later examples show how partially transparent particles, or particles that are combined with a blend effect, create eye-catching results.

Animation Implementation

JavaFX provides powerful techniques for creating animations through its KeyFrame and Timeline classes. In our implementation, we will use a single Timeline with a single KeyFrame to coordinate the animation of all of the particles. To achieve this coordination, our KeyFrame calls a function that updates the location of each particle.

Example 1: Core Classes

This example introduces the basic classes you need to implement a particle system. The code will create a scene with a number of red circular particles being emitted from the center of the visible area, shown as small gray circles in Figure 2-2. You can find the code in the package org.lj.jfxe.chapter2.example1 of the companion source code. There are two implementation classes, Emitter and Particle, as well as a Main class that simply creates a Stage and displays a single Emitter. This example focuses on the pattern used to implement a particle system; later examples look at ways to refine the visual experience. To see this example in action, run the file Main.fx.

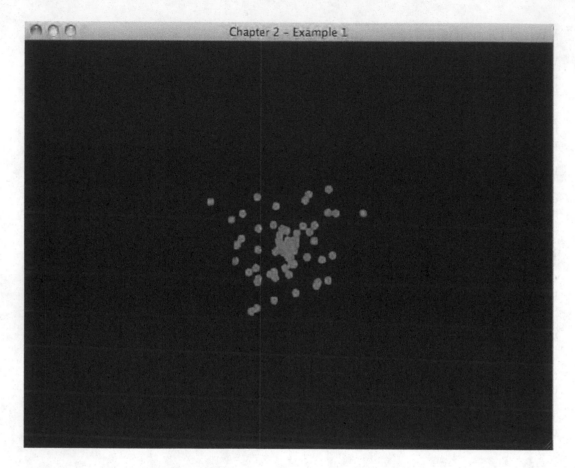

Figure 2-2. *Example 1, emitting particles*

Listing 2-1. *Emitter.fx*

```
package org.lj.jfxe.chapter2.example1;

import javafx.scene.Group;
import javafx.animation.Timeline;
import javafx.animation.KeyFrame;

public class Emitter extends Group{

    //specifies when a new particle should be added to the scene
    var emitTimeline = Timeline{
        repeatCount: Timeline.INDEFINITE;
        keyFrames: KeyFrame{
                    time: .05*1s
```

```
                    action: emit
                }
    }
    //animates the particles.
    var animator = Timeline{
    repeatCount: Timeline.INDEFINITE;
    keyFrames: KeyFrame{
        time: 1.0/30.0*1s
        action:function(){
            for (p in content){
                (p as Particle).doStep();
                }
            }
        }
    }

    init{
        //start emitting
        emitTimeline.play();
        animator.play();
    }

    //called when a new particle should be added.
    function emit():Void{
        insert Particle{} into content;
    }
}
```

In Listing 2-1, the first thing to notice about the class Emitter is that it extends the class Group, so that particles can be added and removed from the content of the Emitter and thus be added and removed from any Scene the Emitter is part of.

Each Emitter has an attribute called emitTimeline of type Timeline, which is used to schedule when particles are added to the scene. The repeatCount is set to INDEFINITE and the single KeyFrame calls the method emit after .05 seconds. The emit method adds a single Particle every time it is called. In this way, a Particle is added to the Scene 20 times a second for the life of the Emitter.

The init method of the class Emitter is called when a new Emitter object is created. This method simply starts the emitTimeline if it is not started already.

The class Emitter does not do much without the class Particle. The code in Listing 2-2 shows a simple implementation.

Listing 2-2. *Particle.fx*

```
package org.lj.jfxe.chapter2.example1;

import javafx.scene.shape.Circle;
import javafx.scene.paint.Color;
import javafx.scene.Group;

//provide random numbers for direction of particle
var random = new java.util.Random();
public class Particle extends Circle{
```

```
var initialSteps = 100;//number of steps until removed
var deltaX;//change in x location per step
var deltaY;//change in y location per step

init{
    radius = 5;
    fill = Color.RED;

    //Set radnom direction, squere technique.
    deltaX = 1.0 - random.nextFloat()*2.0;
    deltaY = 1.0 - random.nextFloat()*2.0;
}

package function doStep(){

    //remove particle if particle has expired
    if (--initialSteps == 0){
        delete this from (parent as Group).content;
    }

    //advance particle's location
    translateX += deltaX;
    translateY += deltaY;
}
}
```

In this example, Particle extends Circle so its visual appearance is that of a red dot with a radius of 5. Particle has three attributes, duration, deltaX, and deltaY. The attribute duration tracks how long a Particle has been in the scene. The attributes deltaX and deltaY describe how the Particle moves. We will look at these last two attributes again after we examine how particles are animated.

As stated above, each Particle is responsible for determining how it travels. The implementation of how a Particle travels is captured in the method doStep, which updates the location of the Particle for a single step of its animation.

In order to animate the Particle, the doStep function will be called 30 times a second. For performance reasons, a single static Timeline called animator is used to animate all particles in the scene. The static sequence named particles keeps track of which particles are still in the scene and should be animated.

When a Particle is created, it sets deltaX and deltaY to a random value in the range of -1.0 to 1.0. The Particle also inserts itself into the sequence particles so that the Timeline animator will call the doStep function. Lastly, animator is started if it is not already running.

The doStep function first decreases the value of duration by one and checks to see if the new value is equal to zero. If so, the Particle has reached the end of its life cycle and should be removed. To remove a Particle, it must be removed from its parent and also from the sequence particles. Removing the Particle from its parent removes the particle from the scene, while removing the Particle from particles stops doStep from being called.

Lastly, the doStep method updates the location of the Particle by incrementing translateX and translateY by deltaX and deltaY respectively. The attributes deltaX and deltaY were set to a random value, causing each Particle to travel linearly away from the Emitter in a random direction. The method for generating the random values of deltaX and deltaY in Listing 2-2 has a few limitations. One limitation is that Particles traveling diagonally appear to be moving faster than particles moving vertically and horizontally. Another limitation is that the particle system will take on a square shape as the visual density increases. I'll discuss other methods for generating these delta values in a later example.

Listing 2-3 shows the code that actually gets the Emitter on the screen.

Listing 2-3. *Main.fx*

```
package org.lj.jfxe.chapter2.example1;

import javafx.stage.Stage;
import javafx.scene.Scene;
import javafx.scene.paint.Color;

Stage {
    title: "Chapter 2 - Example 1"
    width: 640
    height: 480
    scene: Scene {
        fill: Color.BLACK
        content: [
            Emitter{
                translateX: 320
                translateY: 240
            }
        ]
    }
}
```

This very simple snippet of code creates a Stage and adds a single Emitter to a Scene. This is the file that should be run to view Example 1.

Example 2: Adding Some Controls

Building on the previous example, we'll add a few UI controls to the scene that will allow for real-time adjustments of several attributes of an Emitter. To enable these controls, the class Emitter must be refactored to expose the attributes to be adjusted. Figure 2-3 shows the scene, including one Emitter and a number of Sliders that can be used to control the Emitter.

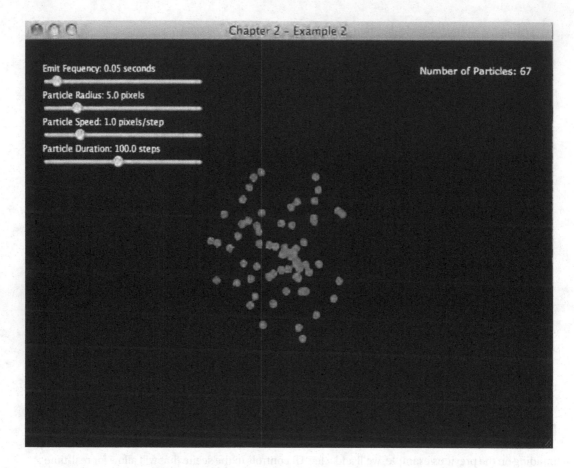

Figure 2-3. *Example 2, adding controls*

Playing with the sliders can help illustrate the concepts discussed in the previous section, especially visual density. By dragging the frequency slider all the way to the right, the rate at which particles are added to the scene drops considerably. Notice how less of the screen displays particles. Conversely, dragging the particle size slider to the right creates a very dense effect.

Listing 2-4. *Emitter.fx (partial)*

```
public var particleRadius = 5.0;
public var particleSpeed = 1.0;
public var particleDuration = 100;
public var frequency  = .05s on replace {
    emitTimeline.playFromStart();
}

///... Rest of class omitted for brevity
```

```
function emit():Void{
insert Particle{
        speed: particleSpeed;
         duration: particleDuration;
          radius: particleRadius;
          } into content;
}
```

The code in Listing 2-4 shows four new attributes of the class Emitter. The attributes particleRadius, particleSpeed and particleDuration are used when creating a new Particle in the emit function. The attribute frequency describes how often the Emitter emits a Particle. Note the on replace function that resets emitTimeline; this avoids some unpredictable behavior in the Timeline class. These exposed attributes are then bound to controls defined in the expanded Main.fx in Listing 2-5.

■ **Note** The attribute radius in the class Particle is inherited from Circle, so there's no reference to radius in the class Particle.

Listing 2-5. *Main.fx*

```
var particleCountLabel = Label{
    translateX: 480
    translateY: 26
    text: bind "Number of Particles: {sizeof emitter.content}"
    textFill: Color.WHITESMOKE
    width: 200
}

var frequencySlider = Slider{
    vertical: false;
    translateX: 20
    translateY: 40
    min: 0.01
    max: 0.5
    value: 0.05
    width: 200
}
var frequencyLabel = Label{
    translateX: 22
    translateY: 26
    text: bind "Emit Fequency: {frequencySlider.value} seconds";
    width: 200
    textFill: Color.WHITESMOKE
    font: Font{
      size: 10;
      }
}
```

31

```
var radiusSlider = Slider{
    vertical: false;
    translateX: 20
    translateY: 40 + 30
    min: 1.0
    max: 20.0
    value: 5.0
    width: 200
}
var radiusLabel = Label{
    translateX: 22
    translateY: 26 + 30
    text: bind "Particle Radius: {radiusSlider.value} pixels";
    width: 200
    textFill: Color.WHITESMOKE
    font: Font{
      size: 10;
    }
}
var speedSlider = Slider{
    vertical: false;
    translateX: 20
    translateY: 40 + 60
    min: .1
    max: 4.0
    value: 1.0
    width: 200
}
var speedLabel = Label{
    translateX: 22
    translateY: 26 + 60
    text: bind "Particle Speed: {speedSlider.value} pixels/step";
    width: 200
    textFill: Color.WHITESMOKE
    font: Font{
      size: 10;
    }
}
var durationSlider = Slider{
    vertical: false;
    translateX: 20
    translateY: 40 + 90
    min: 10
    max: 200
    value: 100
    width: 200
}
var durationLabel = Label{
    translateX: 22
    translateY: 26 + 90
    text: bind "Particle Duration: {durationSlider.value} steps";
```

```
        width: 200
        textFill: Color.WHITESMOKE
        font: Font{
          size: 10;
        }
    }

var emitter = Emitter{
        particleRadius: bind radiusSlider.value;
        particleSpeed: bind speedSlider.value;
        particleDuration: bind (durationSlider.value as Integer);
        frequency: bind frequencySlider.value * 1s;
        translateX: 320
        translateY: 240
}
Stage {
        title: "Chapter 2 - Example 2"
        width: 640
        height: 480
        scene: Scene {
            fill: Color.BLACK
            content: [
                emitter,
                particleCountLabel,
                frequencyLabel,
                frequencySlider,
                radiusLabel,
                radiusSlider,
                speedLabel,
                speedSlider,
                durationLabel,
                durationSlider
            ]
        }
}
```

Listing 2-5 shows four Sliders, each controlling one of the four attributes exposed in the class Emitter. Notice in the declaration of the Emitter that the four new attributes are set using the keyword 'bind'. In this way, when a user adjusts a slider, the value of the attribute adjusts automatically.

There are a number of labels describing the controls, and one that shows the number of particles in the scene. This number is important when fine-tuning an effect, as too many particles can cause performance issues and dropped frames.

The last class to change is Particle, as shown in Listing 2-6.

Listing 2-6. *Particle.fx (partial)*

```
public class Particle extends Circle{
    public-init var initialSteps:Integer;//number of steps until removed
    public-init var speed:Number;//pixels per step
```

```
    var deltaX;//change in x location per step
    var deltaY;//change in y location per step

    init{
        //radius = 5;
        fill = Color.RED;


        //radom direction in radians
        var theta = random.nextFloat()*2.0*Math.PI;


        deltaX = Math.cos(theta)*speed;
        deltaY = Math.sin(theta)*speed;
    }

    package function doStep(){

        //remove particle if particle has expired
        if (--initialSteps == 0){
            delete this from (parent as Group).content;
        }

        //advance particle's location
        translateX += deltaX;
        translateY += deltaY;
    }
}
```

The Particle class has changed only slightly: the attribute duration is now public and a new attribute called speed was added. The attribute speed is used in the init method to calculate deltaX and deltaY. The rest of class is unchanged.

It is worth looking at how deltaX and deltaY are calculated. A random angle is generated that represents the direction the Particle will travel, and this angle is used to calculate deltaX and deltaY. The following code shows how this is implemented.

```
var theta = random.nextFloat()*2.0*Math.PI;
deltaX = Math.cos(theta)*speed;
deltaY = Math.sin(theta)*speed;
```

The change in *X per step* (deltaX) is simply the *cosine* of the angle theta multiplied by speed. The change in *Y per step* (deltaY) is the *sine* of the angle theta, multiplied by speed. The diagram in Figure 2-4 shows these relationships.

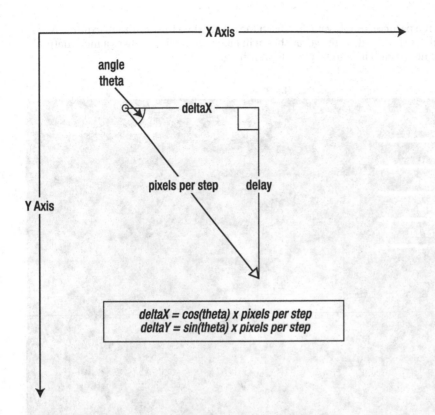

Figure 2-4. *Calculating a random direction*

■ **Performance Consideration** The number of particles can grow very quickly in a scene, and while particle systems are easy ways to spiff up an application, too many particles will bring any computer to its knees.

Example 3: Transparency

The previous examples used very simple particles, just red circles. Now that the framework for a particle system is in place, it is time to start customizing the particles to produce some remarkable effects. In this example, we will continue to use simple circles, but we will modify how the circles are drawn.

Particle systems show their strengths when the particles mix together on the screen. To achieve a rudimentary mixing effect, we can adjust the transparency of the particles. This creates a more compelling visual effect as the partially transparent particles overlap in random ways to produce regions of random shape and color density.

Until this example, the particles simply vanished from the scene when their duration expired. A nice effect is to have the particles slowly fade with age, as shown in Figure 2-5. This produces a more natural look, as the eye does not notice each individual particle vanishing.

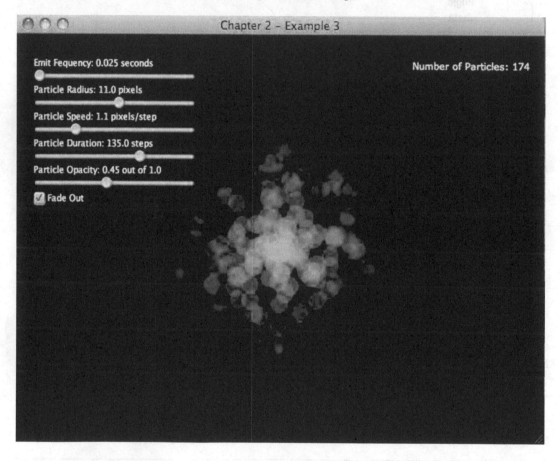

Figure 2-5. Example 3, fading

When running the example, the slider labeled "Particle Opacity" controls the starting opacity of each particle. The checkbox labeled "Fade Out" controls whether or not the particles will fade at the end of their lives. The code in Listing 2-7 shows how to add these two transparency features to the particles.

___

■ **Note** While this text uses the word transparency to describe nodes that can be seen through, the actual attribute on the class Node is called opacity. Opacity is simply the opposite of transparency, so an opacity value of 1.0 has no transparency and an opacity value of 0.2 is mostly transparent.

___

Listing 2-7. *Particle.jx (Partial)*

```
public class Particle extends Circle{

    public-init var initialSteps:Integer;//number of steps until removed
    public-init var startingOpacity = 1.0;
    public-init var speed:Number;//pixels per step
    public-init var fadeout = true;

    var deltaX;//change in x location per step
    var deltaY;//change in y location per step
    var stepsRemaining = initialSteps;

    init{
        //radius = 5;
        fill = Color.RED;
        opacity = startingOpacity;
        //radom direction in radians
        var theta = random.nextFloat()*2.0*Math.PI;
        deltaX = Math.cos(theta)*speed;
        deltaY = Math.sin(theta)*speed;
    }

    package function doStep(){
        //remove particle if particle has expired
        if (--stepsRemaining == 0){
            delete this from (parent as Group).content;
        }
        //advance particle's location
        translateX += deltaX;
        translateY += deltaY;
        if (fadeout){
            opacity = startingOpacity*(stepsRemaining as Number)/(initialSteps as Number);
        }
    }
}
```

The attributes of the class Particle have changed to accommodate the transparency features. A new attribute called startingOpacity sets the opacity of the particle as it is created. The Boolean attribute fadeout controls whether the particle should fade as it animates. The doStep function is reconfigured a little to support the transparency. Instead of decrementing duration on each call, a new attribute called stepsRemaining is decremented. The ratio of stepsRemaining to duration describes how far along the Particle is in its life cycle.

If fadeout is set to true, the opacity of the Particle is set to a fraction of its startingOpacity based on how old it is. This provides the fadeout effect for each particle.

■ **Performance Consideration** While transparency is not as costly as the effects described in the next section, having a hundred or so transparent nodes in a scene can cause performance issues. Keep in mind when designing an application that transparent nodes in general are more expensive than completely opaque nodes.

Example 4: Blend Mode

Transparency is an excellent means of producing a smooth visual effect. Another technique, setting the blend mode of the emitter (the parent node to each particle) can create the types of effects seen in video games and other high-end animations.

To understand blend modes, it is best to consider how nodes are drawn in general. When two nodes overlap in the scene, usually one is drawn and then the other is drawn "over" the first. In other words, the pixels that make up the second node replace the pixels that make up the first. If the second node is partially opaque, the pixels from the first node and the pixels from the second are combined to produce a third value.

This is basically how blend modes work. Instead of simply replacing the value of one pixel with another, a function takes the two pixel values and produces a third value. Remember that a pixel's color is composed of four values, red, green, blue and alpha, so the functions can produce some surprising results.

There are several blend modes that come with JavaFX, but they do not all lend themselves to particle systems. In the example code, the blend effect can be set to ADD, MULTIPLY, SCREEN, and, of course, no blend effect.

For Example 4, the color of the Particle was changed to an orange-like color by adding a little green and a little blue to the red. The blendMode of the Emitter was then set to BlendMode.ADD. This causes the pixels with the greatest amount of overlap to be completely white, as in the center of the cluster of nodes in Figure 2-6. Where there is no overlap the pixels are the normal orange color. Combining the red, green, and blue values of each pixel produces the white color. If the nodes were completely red, this blend mode would not do anything.

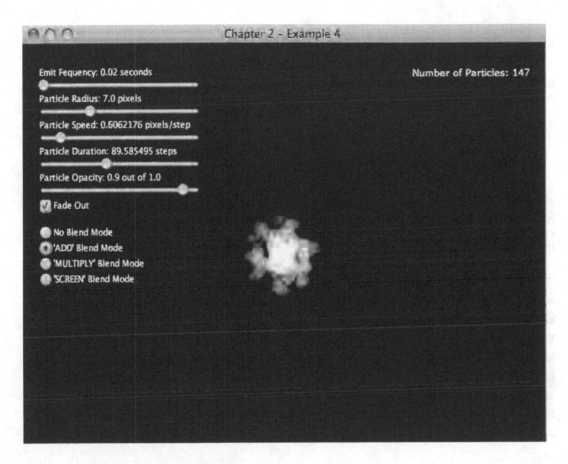

Figure 2-6. *Example 4, Add Blend Mode*

The code in Listing 2-8 shows how the classes have been modified to enable the blend effects.

Listing 2-8. *Main.fx (partial)*

```
var emitter = Emitter{
        blendMode: bind blendMode;
        particleRadius: bind radiusSlider.value;
        particleSpeed: bind speedSlider.value;
        particleDuration: bind (durationSlider.value as Integer);
        particleOpacity: bind opacitySlider.value;
        particleFadeout: bind fadeCheckbox.selected;
        frequency: bind frequencySlider.value * 1s
        translateX: 320
        translateY: 240
    }
```

In the file Main.fx, the `Emitter` is initialized and in this case the `blendMode` is bound to the variable `blendMode`. The variable `blendMode` is of type `BlendMode` and is set by the UI components.

The class `BlendMode` provides constants, so it is as simple as:

```
blendMode = BlendMode.ADD;
```
As mentioned above, the color of the nodes was changed. Here is the code that does this:

```
fill = Color{
        red: 1.0
        green: 0.4
        blue: 0.2
    }
```

Again, a completely red node was not used because blend effects look a lot better when there are multiple colors to work with. In fact, blend modes look the best when the nodes are much more complicated than a simple circle. The following section looks at using simple raster images to produce even more interesting effects.

■ **Performance Considerations** By playing with the example application, it becomes clear that using blend effects is not a computationally cheap operation. The number of nodes that can be involved is considerably lower than when no blend mode is used. When designing an application that uses this technique, be sure to use this feature wisely. It can produce stunning effects—but it can also bring the application to a halt. One strategy for controlling performance degradation might be keeping track of the total number of blended particles in the application, and simply adding no more when a preset limit is reached. Particles are almost always decoration in a scene, so will the user notice if there are only four sparks instead of ten?

Example 5: Nonuniform Nodes

The previous examples all used circular particles, and it is easy to imagine those same examples using rectangles, stars, or some other shape. To explore such options, simply have `Particle` extend the desired shape. This example will explore the benefits of using raster images with nonuniform transparency as the basis of a particle.

The best bitmaps to use are small, have no hard edges, have some transparency, and are not a single color. These features are important because they make it easier to blur the particles together into a seamless visual effect. Modeling a firework explosion does not require that that the particles blend together, but modeling things like fire, smoke, or water works better when each particle is not visually distinguishable.

The image used in this example has all of the features listed above.

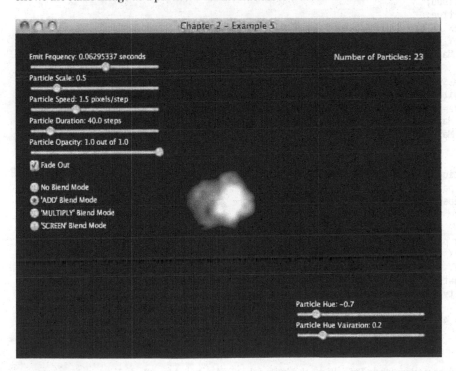

Figure 2-7. *Cloud.png*

Though the image is predominantly red in color (shown in Figure 2-7 as a gray cloud surrounded by a lighter halo), JavaFX provides a mechanism to convert the hue of this image at runtime. Figure 2-8 shows the same image as a particle with the hue set to a bluish color.

Figure 2-8. *Example 5, bit maps*

The code in Listing 2-9 shows how the preceding effect is created.

Listing 2-9. *Particle.fx (Partial)*

```
var cloud = Image{

    url: "{__DIR__}cloud.png"
}

public class Particle extends ImageView{

    public-init var initialSteps:Integer;//number of steps until removed
    public-init var startingOpacity = 1.0;
    public-init var speed:Number;//pixels per step
    public-init var fadeout = true;

    var deltaX;//change in x location per step
    var deltaY;//change in y location per step
    var stepsRemaining = initialSteps;

    init{
        image = cloud;
        smooth = true;
        translateX -= cloud.width/2.0;
        translateY -= cloud.height/2.0;
        rotate = Math.toDegrees(random.nextFloat()*2.0*Math.PI);

        opacity = startingOpacity;
        //radom direction in radians
        var theta = random.nextFloat()*2.0*Math.PI;
        deltaX = Math.cos(theta)*speed;
        deltaY = Math.sin(theta)*speed;
    }

    package function doStep(){
        //remove particle if particle has expired
        if (--stepsRemaining == 0){
            delete this from (parent as Group).content;
        }
        //advance particle's location
        translateX += deltaX;
        translateY += deltaY;
        if (fadeout){
            opacity = startingOpacity*(stepsRemaining as Number)/(initialSteps as Number);
        }
        rotate += 4;
    }
}
```

The Particle class now extends ImageView; the image that is displayed is called cloud and is a static variable. In the init function the attribute smooth, which is defined in the parent class, is set to true, thus asking JavaFX to use a nicer (though more costly) algorithm when rotating the image. The Particle is also rotated a random amount.

In the doStep function, the rotation of the Particle is incremented by four in each step, imparting a gentle rotation to the Particle. Obviously, this is yet another feature of a particle that could be exploited to produce specific effects.

■ **Tip** Load images just once and keep only one copy.

Listing 2-10. *Emitter.fx (Partial)*

```
public var particleScale = 1.0;
public var particleSpeed = 1.0;
public var particleDuration = 100;
public var particleOpacity = 0.5;
public var particleFadeout = true;
public var particleHue = 0.0;
public var particleHueVariation = 0.0;

function emit():Void{
        insert Particle{
            scaleX: particleScale;
            scaleY: particleScale;
            startingOpacity: particleOpacity;
            speed: particleSpeed;
            duration: particleDuration;

            fadeout: particleFadeout;
            effect: ColorAdjust{
                    hue: normalizeHue(particleHue +
randomFromNegToPos(particleHueVariation));
                }
        } into content;
    }

 public function normalizeHue(value:Number):Number{
        var result = value;
        while
        (
        result > 1.0){
            result -= 1.0;
        }
        while
        (
        result < - 1.0){
            result += 1.0;
        }
```

```
        return result;
    }

    public function randomFromNegToPos(max:Number):Number{
        if (max == 0.0){
            return 0.0;
        }
        var result = max - random.nextFloat()*max*2;
        return result;
    }
```

Listing 2-10 shows there are two new attributes to the class Emitter: particleHue and particleHueVariation. The attribute particleHue can be used to adjust the color of the Particles and the attribute particleHueVariation determines how much to randomly adjust the color of each Particle.

The emit function of class Emitter is slightly changed. Now, the attributes scaleX and scaleY are set to control the size of the particle. The attribute effect is set on the Particle to a ColorAdjust effect. This effect alters the color of the node it is attached to; in this case, we adjusting the hue of the Particle. This is what changed the color of the Particles in Example 5 from red to blue.

The function normalizeHue simply makes sure that the value passed to hue is of the correct range, -1.0 – 1.0. When dealing with random numbers it is easy to accidentally set a bad value.

The function randomFromNegToPos is a utility function for generating random numbers from a negative max to a positive max.

Example 6: Direction

When trying to reproduce some effects, it becomes clear that having the particles free to travel in any direction is undesirable. For example, when simulating a candle's fire, the particles should move upward. However, a candle's fire also flickers a little; adding a slight variation to each particle's direction will help simulate that effect. The following example explores how to set the general direction of each particle, as well as dictate the range of variation. The screenshot in Figure 2-9 shows a fire effect.

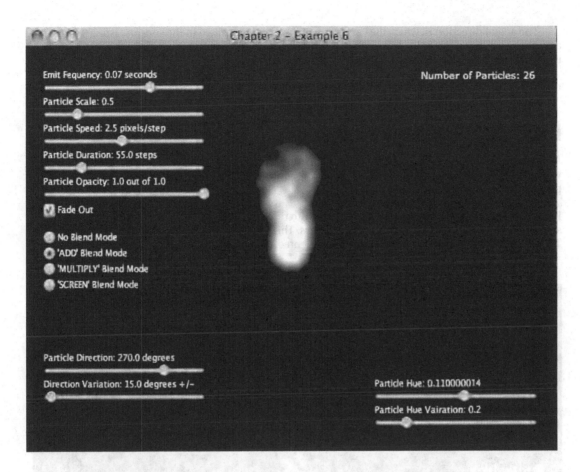

Figure 2-9. *Example 6, fire*

Listing 2-11. *Particle.fx (partial)*

```
//New attributes, other attributes omitted.
public-init var direction = 270.0;
public-init var directionVariation = 10.0;

init{
    //other code omitted.
    var startingDirection = direction + Main.randomFromNegToPos(directionVariation);
    var theta = Math.toRadians(startingDirection);//random.nextFloat()*2.0*Math.PI;
    deltaX = Math.cos(theta)*speed;
    deltaY = Math.sin(theta)*speed;
    //other code omitted.
}
```

The actual direction in which the Particle will travel is determined in the code in Listing 2-11 by adding the attribute direction to a random value based on directionVariation. Once the final direction is calculated, the deltaX and deltaY values are calculated as before.

Using the values above, the Particles will travel mostly straight up, with deviations of up to 10 degrees both clockwise and counterclockwise.

Example 7: Nonlinear Paths

A particle's path is as interesting as how the particle looks. This example explores a particle system where the particles travel as if pulled by gravity. This is accomplished by changing the amount each particle moves in the Y direction on each step.

Utilizing a new star shaped particle, a very festive effect can be created. The screenshot in Figure 2-10 shows how the particles are first shot into the air and then fall. What is not evident from a still shot is the parabolic curve each particle follows. This causes the particle to accelerate downward. The code in Listing 2-12 shows how this is implemented.

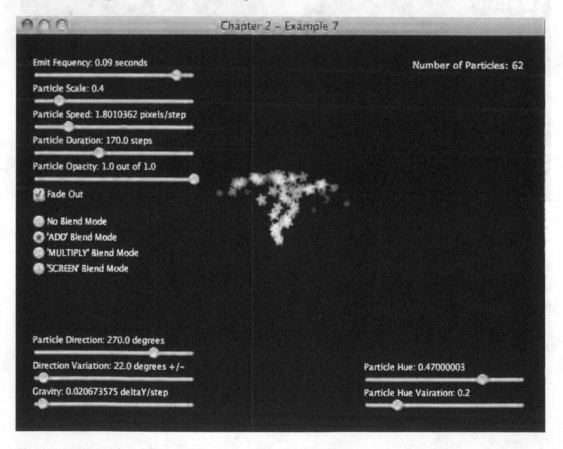

Figure 2-10. *Example 7, falling stars*

Listing 2-12. *Particle.fx (partial)*

```
//Other attributes ommited
public-init var gravity = 0.1;

function doStep(){
      //remove particle if particle has expired
      if (--stepsRemaining == 0){
          delete this from (parent as Group).content;
      }
      //advance particle's location
      translateX += deltaX;
      translateY += deltaY;
      deltaY += gravity;

      if (fadeout){
          opacity = startingOpacity*(stepsRemaining as Number)/(initialSteps as Number);
      }
      rotate += 4;
}
```

A new attribute called gravity is added. This attribute is used in the modified doStep function to increase the value of deltaY for every step.

Further Considerations

The examples in this chapter show how to implement a basic particle system by taking advantage of some of the graphics features of JavaFX. These examples could be used in many games or other visually interesting applications. However, the attributes of emitters and particles can be combined in innumerable ways to produce unique visual effects. Here are a number of other features that could be added to a particle system to produce even more options.

Heterogeneous Particles: There is no reason why all of the particles have to be the same. Combining particles of different shape, color, or even duration can open the door to many new possibilities. Varying the proportion of each particle type is another way of customizing the look of an effect. For example, consider a campfire, where the dominant particle is the fire. It is easy to imagine sprinkling in a second particle to represent the sparks of a popping log.

Moving Emitter: Since the emitter is a node, it can be moved and animated like any other node. Moving an emitter that produces slow-moving or even still particles will produce a snake-like effect. A moving emitter that emits fast-moving particles can be used to create a comet-like effect.

Nonlinear Changes: In the previous examples the rate at which the particles became transparent was linear. Using JavaFX's Interpolator class, it would be simple to implement a particle that only starts to fade during the last 80 percent of its life. This would produce an effect with greater visual density than the previous examples, but will maintain the soft edge provided by the fading effect.

Animate Emitter's Attributes: The implementation in this chapter provides a number of attributes on the Emitter class that define the attributes of each new particle. Changing the attributes on the emitter over time would produce some interesting results. For example, increasing the size of the particles for short periods of time will produce a pulsing effect. You could also slowly adjust the color of the particles to reflect some event in the application. In the context of the game, for instance, a particle system could turn from blue to red as the player loses health.

Summary

This chapter explored how to implement a particle system in JavaFX, and how the features of a particle system affect its look. The first examples provided a simplistic implementation that focused on the organization of the key classes—Emitter and Particle. Later examples added features such as transparency, blend modes, nonlinear motion, and using bitmaps as particles. Combining some or all of these features allows you to implement a wide range of particle effects. However, for performance reasons, it is important to keep the number of particles to a minimum and be wary of some of the more expensive features like transparency and blend modes.

■ ■ ■

CHAPTER 3

Effect: Visual Transitions

Visual transitions are animations that introduce a new visual component to the scene, usually by replacing a component already in the scene. A good example of a visual transition is a fade-out on TV—it is a visual effect that informs the viewer that something is ending and something new has started.

Application designers take advantage of visual transitions to inform the user that new content is on the screen, perhaps because of a navigation choice made by the user. This chapter explores how visual transitions are implemented in JavaFX by setting up a scene where the transitions can be viewed and the details of each transition inspected.

While this book uses the term "transition" to describe a change in an application, the JavaFX API does have a class called javafx.animation.transition.Transition. This is not what we mean here by transition, though the classes contained in the package javafx.animation.transition could certainly be used when implementing a visual transition.

Getting Started

The visual transitions in the following sections all work on the same principle: They are functions that take a node in the scene and replace it with another node. An animation is also involved to make the replacement interesting to the user. It is important when implementing these functions that at the end of the animation, the nodes are left in a predictable state. For example, if a node passed into the transition function has its opacity set to .6 and the transition adjusts that value, at the end of the transition, the opacity should be set back to .6. This will cut down on unwanted side-effects.

The code in Listing 3-1 implements a simple scene containing a node to be transitioned and a number of buttons that trigger each transition type covered in this chapter.

Listing 3-1. Main.fx

```
package org.lj.jfxe.chapter3;

import javafx.stage.Stage;
import org.lj.jfxe.chapter3.example1.*;
import org.lj.jfxe.chapter3.example2.*;
import org.lj.jfxe.chapter3.example3.*;
import org.lj.jfxe.chapter3.example4.*;
import org.lj.jfxe.chapter3.example5.*;
import javafx.scene.Scene;
```

```
import javafx.scene.control.Button;
import javafx.scene.paint.Color;
import javafx.scene.Node;
import javafx.scene.layout.VBox;

/**
 * @author lucasjordan
 */

var nodeA = ExampleNodeA{
    translateX: 320 - 160
    translateY: 240 - 120
}
var nodeB = ExampleNodeB{
    translateX: 320 - 160
    translateY: 240 - 120
}

var displayed:Node = nodeA;
var notDisplayed:Node = nodeB;

var disabled = false;

var fadeButton = Button{
    text: "Fade Transition"
    action: function(){
        disabled = true;
        FadeReplace.doReplace(displayed, notDisplayed, doAfter);
    }
    disable: bind disabled;
}

var slideButton = Button{
    text: "Slide Transition"
    action: function(){
        disabled = true;
        SlideReplace.doReplace(displayed, notDisplayed, doAfter);
    }
    disable: bind disabled;
}

var flipButton = Button{
    text: "Flip Transition"
    action: function(){
        disabled = true;
        FlipReplace.doReplace(displayed, notDisplayed, doAfter);
    }
    disable: bind disabled;
}
var wipeButton = Button{
    text: "Wipe Transition"
    action: function(){
```

```
            disabled = true;
            WipeReplace.doReplace(displayed, notDisplayed, doAfter);
        }
        disable: bind disabled;
}
var burnButton = Button{
    text: "Burn Transition"
    action: function(){
        disabled = true;
        BurnReplace.doReplace(displayed, notDisplayed, doAfter);
    }
    disable: bind disabled;
}

Stage {
    title: "Chapter 3"
    scene: Scene {
        width: 640
        height: 480
        fill: Color.BLACK
        content: [
            VBox{
                spacing: 10
                translateX: 25
                translateY: 30
                content: [fadeButton,slideButton,flipButton,wipeButton,burnButton]
            },
            nodeA
        ]
    }
}

function doAfter():Void{
    var temp = notDisplayed;
    notDisplayed = displayed;
    displayed = temp;
    disabled = false;
}
```

The stage contains a scene with a VBox, which contains the buttons and the node—nodeA. The nodes, nodeA and nodeB, represent the content that we will be switching in and out as the buttons are pressed. The variables displayed and notDisplayed record which node is displayed or not; thus when nodeA is visible, the variable notDisplayed points to nodeB. After each transition, the values of displayed and notDisplayed are switched to reflect the content of the scene. This business of tracking which node is displayed or not is a sort of bookkeeping that facilitates this demonstration. Other applications that use these transitions may or may not keep track of the visible content in this way.

The code in Listing 3-2 is the implementation of the example class ExampleNodeA. This code is also not critical to the transitions themselves, but provides a somewhat realistic demonstration. The implementation of ExampleNodeB is very similar to that of ExampleNodeA, but I'll leave it to you to look to the source code for the details.

Listing 3-2. *ExampleNodeA.fx*

```
package org.lj.jfxe.chapter3;

import javafx.scene.Group;
import javafx.scene.shape.Rectangle;
import javafx.scene.layout.*;
import javafx.scene.paint.*;
import javafx.scene.control.*;
import javafx.geometry.HPos;

/**
 * @author lucasjordan
 */

public class ExampleNodeA extends Group{

    init {
        insert
            Rectangle{
                width: 320
                height: 240
                stroke: Color.BLUE
                strokeWidth: 6
                arcHeight: 24
                arcWidth: 24
            } into content;
        insert
            VBox{
                spacing: 15
                translateX: 30
                translateY: 30
                hpos: HPos.CENTER
                content: [
                    Label{text:"Please Enter Your Personal Information",
                        textFill: Color.WHITESMOKE},
                    Tile{
                        vgap: 7
                        columns: 2
                        content: [
                        Label{text:"First Name", textFill: Color.WHITESMOKE},
                        TextBox{},
                        Label{text:"Last Name", textFill: Color.WHITESMOKE},
                        TextBox{},
                        Label{text:"Email Address", textFill: Color.WHITESMOKE},
                        TextBox{},
                        Label{text:"Home Phone", textFill: Color.WHITESMOKE},
                        TextBox{},
                        Label{text:"Cell Phone", textFill: Color.WHITESMOKE},
                        TextBox{},
                        ]
```

```
                    }
                ]
            } into content;
    }
}
```

The classes presented create a scene that looks like the screenshot in Figure 3-1. There is a large rectangle with rounded corners in the middle of the scene that contains a number of controls. When a button on the left is pressed, the rectangle is replaced with a different but similar rectangle. Each button will demonstrate one of the five example transitions presented in this chapter.

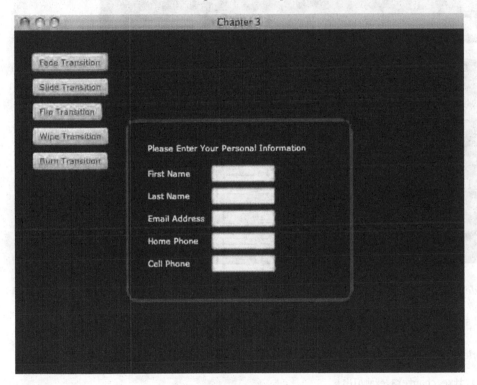

Figure 3-1. *Transition demo*

The following sections will cover the how each visual transition is implemented.

Example 1: Fade Replace

The fade replace is a simple transition where one node fades out to reveal a second. The general strategy is to make the second node transparent and place it behind the first node, then create an animation that simultaneously decreases the opacity of the first node while increasing the opacity of the second node. When the animation is complete, the first node, now transparent, is removed from the scene.

The screenshot in Figure 3-2 shows the animation halfway through. In this state both the old node and the new node are visible.

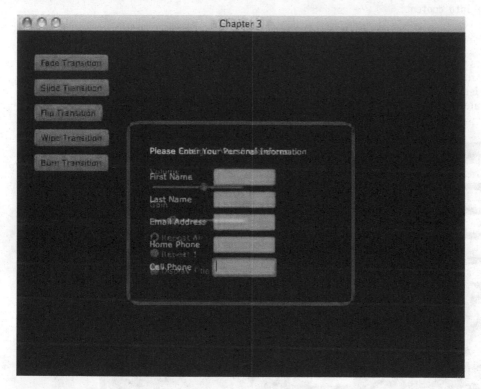

Figure 3-2. *Fade replace in action*

Listing 3-3 shows how this transition is implemented.

Listing 3-3. *FadeReplace.fx*

```
package org.lj.jfxe.chapter3.example1;

import javafx.scene.Node;
import javafx.animation.*;
import javafx.scene.Group;
import javafx.util.Sequences;

/**
 * @author lucasjordan
 */

public function doReplace(nodeToReplace:Node,replacementNode:Node,doAfter:function()):Void{
    var parent:Group = (nodeToReplace.parent as Group);
```

```
        var origNodeToReplaceOpacity = nodeToReplace.opacity;
        var origReplacementNodeOpacity = replacementNode.opacity;

    replacementNode.translateX = nodeToReplace.translateX;
    replacementNode.translateY = nodeToReplace.translateY;

        var index = Sequences.indexOf(parent.content, nodeToReplace);
        insert replacementNode before parent.content[index];

        var t = Timeline{
            keyFrames: [
                    KeyFrame{
                        time: 0s
                        values: [
                            replacementNode.opacity => 0.0 tween Interpolator.EASEBOTH
                            ]
                    }

                    KeyFrame{
                        time: 1s
                        values: [
                            nodeToReplace.opacity => 0.0 tween Interpolator.EASEBOTH,
                            replacementNode.opacity => origReplacementNodeOpacity tween
Interpolator.EASEBOTH
                            ]
                        action: function(){
                            delete nodeToReplace from parent.content;
                            nodeToReplace.opacity = origNodeToReplaceOpacity;
                            doAfter();
                        }
                    }
                ]
            }
        t.play();
    }
```

Looking at Listing 3-3, the doReplace function takes two nodes and a function. The first node, nodeToReplace, is replaced by the second node, replacementNode, and function doAfter is called when the animation is complete. The opacity of both nodes is recorded. And since the opacity of these nodes will change over the course of the animations, it is important that the original values be restored, as the user of this function may not expect those values to change.

Next, replacementNode is placed behind nodeToReplace. This is done by finding the index of nodeToReplace in its parent content and then adding replacementNode before that index, since nodes with a higher index are drawn after nodes with a lower index.

Once the nodes are positioned in the scene, a Timeline called t is created with three KeyFrames. The first KeyFrame sets the opacity of replacementNode to zero. The second KeyFrame states that after one second, the opacity of replacementNode should increase to its original value, and that the opacity of nodeToReplace should be at zero at the end of the first second. The last KeyFrame does not alter the visual appearance of the animation, but does call the callback function doAfter when the animation is done.

Having a callback function is important, as it allows the caller of the function to know when the animation is done. In the example presented here, the callback function is used to re-enable the buttons and keep track of which node is currently displayed in the scene. In a more complex application the callback function could be useful in any number of ways.

Example 2: Slide Replace

The slide replace, as the name implies, slides one node into the scene as the current one slides out. This example has a node sliding in from the left as the existing node slides out of the scene to the right. To achieve this effect, a clipped group is created containing both nodes, and the group and the clipped area are then animated.

The screenshot in Figure 3-3 shows the animation halfway done, where the new node is on the left with its left side clipped. The node being replaced is moving to the right and has its right side clipped.

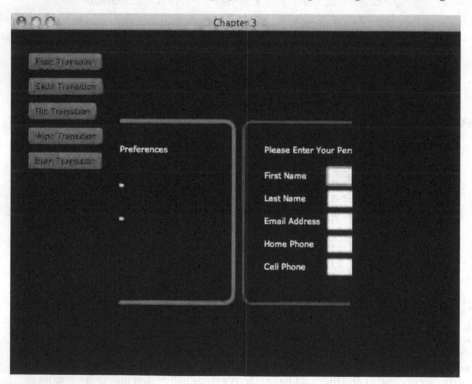

Figure 3-3. Slide replace

Listing 3-4 shows the code that implements this transition.

Listing 3-4. SlideReplace.fx

```
package org.lj.jfxe.chapter3.example2;

import javafx.scene.Node;
import javafx.animation.*;
import javafx.scene.Group;
import javafx.util.Sequences;
import javafx.animation.Interpolator;
import javafx.scene.shape.Rectangle;

/**
 * @author lucasjordan
 */

public function doReplace(nodeToReplace:Node,replacementNode:Node,doAfter:function()):Void{
    var parent:Group = (nodeToReplace.parent as Group);

    var index = Sequences.indexOf(parent.content, nodeToReplace);


    var startingX = nodeToReplace.translateX;
    var startingY = nodeToReplace.translateY;
    var minX = nodeToReplace.boundsInLocal.minX;
    var minY = nodeToReplace.boundsInLocal.minY;
    var totalWidth = nodeToReplace.boundsInLocal.width;
    var totalHeight = nodeToReplace.boundsInLocal.height;

    replacementNode.translateY = -minY;
    replacementNode.translateX = -replacementNode.boundsInLocal.width;


    var clip = Rectangle{
        width: totalWidth;
        height: totalHeight;
    }

    delete nodeToReplace from parent.content;

    var group = Group{
        translateX: startingX + minX;
        translateY: startingY + minY;
        content: [nodeToReplace,replacementNode]
        clip: clip
    }

    nodeToReplace.translateX = -minX;
    nodeToReplace.translateY = -minY;

    insert group before parent.content[index];
```

```
    var t = Timeline{
        keyFrames: [
                KeyFrame{
                    time: 1s
                    values: [
                        group.translateX =>
                            startingX + totalWidth tween Interpolator.EASEBOTH,
                        clip.translateX => -totalWidth tween Interpolator.EASEBOTH
                        ]
                    action: function(){
                        delete group.content;
                        replacementNode.translateX = startingX;
                        replacementNode.translateY = startingY;
                        insert replacementNode before parent.content[index];
                        doAfter();
                    }
                }
            ]
        }
    t.play();
}
```

In Listing 3-4 a new node called group is created that contains both nodeToReplace and replacementNode. We see that nodeToReplace is removed from its parent and replaced with the new Group in the same location, and group also has its clip set to a rectangular area the size of nodeToReplace. Finally, a Timeline is created that simply translates the group containing both nodes to the right while translating the clip area to the left. The effect is that the clip area appears to stay in one place as the two nodes slide to the right. The function in the first KeyFrame does a little bookkeeping, ensuring that the nodes are in a reasonable state when the animation is complete. This includes removing both nodes from the group and placing replacementNode onto the scene where nodeToReplace started out.

Example 3: Flip Replace

The flip replace flips a node to reveal the second node, as if a playing card were flipped to show its backside. This example takes advantage of the JavaFX PerspectiveTransform class to simulate a 3D perspective. However, this is not a real 3D transform, as JavaFX does not currently support 3D content. Instead, the original node is wrapped in a group that is "rotated" in 3D, and when the rotation is halfway done, the original node is replaced with the new node. The screenshots in Figures 3-4 and 3-5 show the animation one-third complete and two-thirds complete.

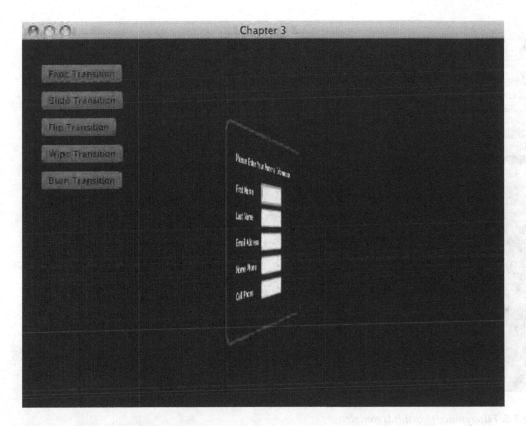

Figure 3-4. *Flip replace one-third complete*

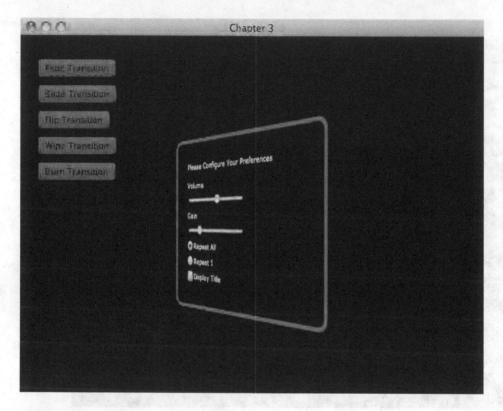

Figure 3-5. *Flip replace two-thirds complete*

Figure 3-4 shows the animation where the first node is rotated about a third of the way. Figure 3-5 shows the replacement about two-thirds through the animation. The code in Listing 3-5 shows how this effect is implemented.

Listing 3-5. *FlipReplace.fx*

```
package org.lj.jfxe.chapter3.example3;

import javafx.scene.Node;
import javafx.scene.Group;
import javafx.util.Sequences;
import javafx.scene.effect.*;
import javafx.animation.*;
import javafx.util.Math;

/**
 * @author lucasjordan
 */
```

```
public function doReplace(nodeToReplace:Node,replacementNode:Node,doAfter:function()):Void{
    var parent:Group = (nodeToReplace.parent as Group);

    var index = Sequences.indexOf(parent.content, nodeToReplace);


    var startingX = nodeToReplace.translateX;
    var startingY = nodeToReplace.translateY;
    var minX = nodeToReplace.boundsInLocal.minX;
    var minY = nodeToReplace.boundsInLocal.minY;

    var startWidth = nodeToReplace.boundsInLocal.width;
    var startHeight = nodeToReplace.boundsInLocal.height;


    delete nodeToReplace from parent.content;

    nodeToReplace.translateX = 0;
    nodeToReplace.translateY = 0;

    var radius = startWidth/2.0;
    var angle = 0.0;
    var back = startHeight/10.0;

    // The following four lines were was inspired by Josh Marinacci
    // http://javafx.com/samples/DisplayShelf/index.html
    var lx = bind radius - Math.sin(Math.toRadians(angle))*radius;
    var rx = bind radius + Math.sin(Math.toRadians(angle))*radius;
    var uly = bind 0 - Math.cos(Math.toRadians(angle))*back;
    var ury = bind 0 + Math.cos(Math.toRadians(angle))*back;


    var perspective = PerspectiveTransform{
        ulx: bind lx
        uly: bind uly
        urx: bind rx
        ury: bind ury
        lrx: bind rx
        lry: bind startHeight + uly
        llx: bind lx
        lly: bind startHeight + ury
    }

    var holder = Group{
        translateX: startingX + minX
        translateY: startingY + minY
        content: [nodeToReplace]
        effect: perspective

    }
```

61

```
    insert holder before parent.content[index];


var timeline = Timeline{
    keyFrames: [
        KeyFrame{
            time: 0s;
            values: [
                angle => 90.0 tween Interpolator.EASEOUT
                ]
        },
        KeyFrame{
            time: 0.5s;
            values: [
                angle => 0.0
                ]
            action: function(){
                delete holder.content;
                insert replacementNode into holder.content
            }

        },
        KeyFrame{
            time: 0.5s+1ms;
            values: [
                angle => 180.0
                ]

        },
        KeyFrame{
            time: 1s;
            values: [
                angle => 90.0 tween Interpolator.EASEIN
                ]
            action: function(){
                delete holder.content;
                replacementNode.translateX = startingX;
                replacementNode.translateY = startingY;
                insert replacementNode before parent.content[index];
                doAfter();
            }
        }
        ]
    }

    timeline.play();
}
```

As shown in Listing 3-5, nodeToReplace is removed from its parent and wrapped with a new Group called holder, which is added to the scene where nodeToReplace was located. A PerspectiveTransform is created, bound to a number of variables that keep track of the left and right x values along with the upper-left and upper-right y values. These variables are lx, ly, ulx, and uly. When the variable angle is updated, lx, ly, uly, and ulx will be updated as well.

The value angle is updated by an animation with four KeyFrames, plus one KeyFrame for the callback function. The first two KeyFrames rotate nodeToReplace from 90.0 degrees to 0.0 degrees, leaving the node as if viewed from the edge; nodeToReplace is then replaced with replacementNode. Next, replacementNode is rotated from 180.0 degrees back to the original 90.0 degrees, leaving replacementNode in the location and orientation as nodeToReplace started.

Though the animation looks as though it performs a 180.0-degree rotation, it does not. As stated previously, the rotation is broken into two steps, from 0.0 to 90.0 and then from 180.0 to 90.0. This is done because applying a 180.0 degree to the final node would leave it displaying its content backwards.

Example 4: Wipe Replace

The wipe replace animates from one node to another by incrementally displaying more and more of the replacement node until the original node is completely covered. This is similar to the star wipe as seen on TV. The star wipe was a way of moving from scene to scene in older TV shows. In this case, however, we are going to use a circle to perform the wipe, as it makes for simpler example code.

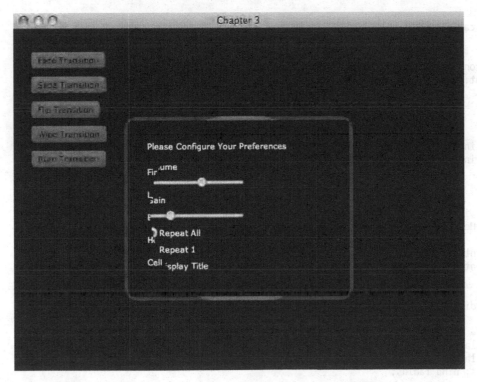

Figure 3-6. Wipe replace

Figure 3-6 shows the transition partway through with the replacement node visible inside the circular cutout shape. The node being replaced is still visible around its edges.

In this effect the new node is wrapped in a group and placed over the existing node. The group has the clip value set to a circle with a radius of 0. As the animation progresses, the radius is increased to expose the new node. And finally, the usual clean-up code is called to leave the scene in the expected state.

Listing 3-6. *WipeReplace.fx*

```
package org.lj.jfxe.chapter3.example4;

import javafx.scene.Node;
import javafx.animation.*;
import javafx.scene.Group;
import javafx.util.Sequences;
import javafx.animation.Interpolator;
import javafx.scene.shape.*;
import javafx.util.*;

/**
 * @author lucasjordan
 */

public function doReplace(nodeToReplace:Node,replacementNode:Node,doAfter:function()):Void{
    var parent:Group = (nodeToReplace.parent as Group);

    var index = Sequences.indexOf(parent.content, nodeToReplace);


    var startingX = nodeToReplace.translateX;
    var startingY = nodeToReplace.translateY;
    var minX = nodeToReplace.boundsInLocal.minX;
    var minY = nodeToReplace.boundsInLocal.minY;

    var startWidth = nodeToReplace.boundsInLocal.width;
    var startHeight = nodeToReplace.boundsInLocal.height;

    replacementNode.translateX = 0;
    replacementNode.translateY = 0;

    var radius = 0.0;
    var maxRadius = Math.sqrt(Math.pow(startWidth/2.0, 2) + Math.pow(startHeight/2.0, 2));

    var clip = Circle{
        translateX: startWidth/2.0;
        translateY: startHeight/2.0;
        radius: bind radius;
    }

    var holder = Group{
        translateX: startingX
```

```
        translateY: startingY
        content: [Circle{
            translateX: startWidth/2.0;
            translateY: startHeight/2.0;
            opacity: 0.0;
            radius: maxRadius;
        },replacementNode]
        clip: clip;
    }

insert holder after parent.content[index];


var t = Timeline{
    keyFrames: [
        KeyFrame{
                time: 0s
                values: radius => 0.0 tween Interpolator.EASEBOTH
            },
        KeyFrame{
            time: 1s
            values: radius => maxRadius tween Interpolator.EASEBOTH
            action: function(){
                delete nodeToReplace from parent.content;
                delete holder.content;
                replacementNode.translateX = startingX;
                replacementNode.translateY = startingY;
                insert replacementNode before parent.content[index];
            }
        },
        KeyFrame{
            time: 1s + 1ms
            action: doAfter
        }

        ]
    }
    t.play();
}
```

In Listing 3-6, the variable holder is used to contain replacementNode. The node holder also contains a second node of type Circle. This Circle is used to expand the bounds of holder to accommodate a clip region that will expand beyond the bounds of replacementNode.

The Timeline in this example is very simple. It adjusts the value of radius from 0.0 to maxRadius, which is the distance from the center of replacementNode to the farthest corner. This ensures that the bounds of clip will be big enough to expose replacementNode entirely.

Example 5: Burn Replace

In this example, the nodes do not move around the screen at all, but an effect is applied to them that makes them look like an increasingly exposed photograph. This is accomplished using the JavaFX classes ColorAdjust and GaussianBlur— classes that come with JavaFX that are instances of the class Effect. The class Effect is an abstract class used to modify the appearance of a Node.

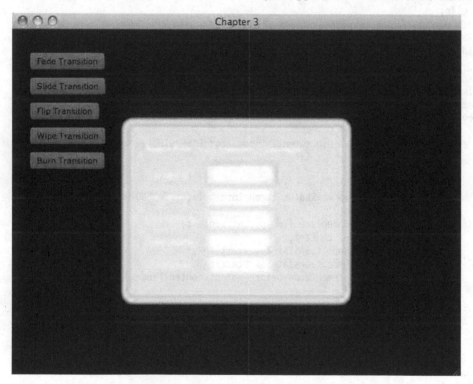

Figure 3-7. *Burn replace*

The screenshot in Figure 3-7 shows the first node almost completely white. The code in Listing 3-7 shows how to implement this simple, but visually interesting effect.

Listing 3-7. *BurnReplace.fx*

```
package org.lj.jfxe.chapter3.example5;

import javafx.scene.Node;
import javafx.animation.*;
import javafx.scene.Group;
import javafx.util.Sequences;
import javafx.animation.Interpolator;
```

```
import javafx.util.*;
import javafx.scene.effect.*;

/**
 * @author lucasjordan
 */

public function doReplace(nodeToReplace:Node,replacementNode:Node,doAfter:function()):Void{
    var parent:Group = (nodeToReplace.parent as Group);

    var index = Sequences.indexOf(parent.content, nodeToReplace);


    var startingX = nodeToReplace.translateX;
    var startingY = nodeToReplace.translateY;
    var minX = nodeToReplace.boundsInLocal.minX;
    var minY = nodeToReplace.boundsInLocal.minY;

    var startWidth = nodeToReplace.boundsInLocal.width;
    var startHeight = nodeToReplace.boundsInLocal.height;

    nodeToReplace.translateX = 0;
    nodeToReplace.translateY = 0;


    var brightness = 0.0;
    var blur = 0.0;

    delete nodeToReplace from parent.content;

    var holder = Group{
        translateX: startingX
        translateY: startingY
        content: [nodeToReplace]
        effect: ColorAdjust{
            brightness: bind brightness;
            input: GaussianBlur{
                radius: bind blur;
            }
        }
    }

    insert holder after parent.content[index];

    var t = Timeline{
        keyFrames: [
            KeyFrame{
                    time: 0s
                    values: [
                        brightness => 0.0 tween Interpolator.EASEBOTH,
```

```
                                    blur => 0.0 tween Interpolator.EASEBOTH
                                    ]
                    },
                    KeyFrame{
                        time: 1s
                        values: [
                            brightness => 1.0 tween Interpolator.EASEBOTH,
                            blur => 6.0 tween Interpolator.EASEBOTH
                            ]
                        action: function(){
                            delete holder.content;
                            replacementNode.translateX = 0.0;
                            replacementNode.translateY = 0.0;
                            insert replacementNode into holder.content;
                            nodeToReplace.translateX = startingX;
                            nodeToReplace.translateY = startingY;
                        }

                    },
                    KeyFrame{
                        time: 2s
                        values: [
                            brightness => 0.0 tween Interpolator.EASEBOTH,
                            blur => 0.0 tween Interpolator.EASEBOTH
                            ]
                        action: function(){
                            delete holder.content;
                            replacementNode.translateX = startingX;
                            replacementNode.translateY = startingY;
                            insert replacementNode before parent.content[index];
                        }
                    },
                    KeyFrame{
                        time: 2s + 1ms
                        action: doAfter
                    }

                ]
        }
        t.play();
}
```

In Listing 3-7, the node nodeToReplace is wrapped by a group called holder. The node holder then has a ColorAdjust applied to it with a GaussianBlur. The Timeline t simply increases the brightness from 0.0 to 1.0, increases the radius of the GaussianBlur to 6.0, swaps the nodes, and then returns the brightness and radius to their original values. The usual clean-up code is executed last.

Further Considerations

Visual transitions are an excellent way to spice up an application, and there are many options to choose from. Some design considerations should be applied when selecting a transition that can be summarized with the following questions:

Is the transition confusing to the user? Sometimes a really great-looking transition can leave a new user confused. For example, consider a panel that travels off the screen to the left when the Next button is pressed. This may look cool, but an inexperienced user might interpret the animation as the panel being thrown out or canceled. However, the slide effect may be perfect for a wizard.

Is a transition too different from other transitions in the application? Some applications will use a different transition for every view or even use a random transition each time. On the other hand, some applications will only use a single transition in all instances. Both cases are probably too extreme. The first example errs on the side of complexity and the second on the side of simplicity. An application is probably best served by having a handful of transitions that are used in a consistent way. The sooner users are exposed to each transition, the sooner they learn what to expect and are less likely to be caught off guard by them.

Does a transition take too long? Even the best applications can suffer from overdoing the duration that a transition takes to complete. In most cases the point of the application is not to show off transitions, but to provide some other service. A user can quickly become tired of transitions that are longer than half a second, so this should be kept in mind as each transition is fine-tuned.

Is a transition required at all? Once a bunch of interesting effects are in the hands of the designers and developers, it can be very easy to use them all of the time. For some applications it may not be appropriate at all to use transitions. Another possibility is that some critical portion of the application should be effect-free to ensure maximum clarity. Take, for instance, a dialog where the user is changing his password—it might be reasonable to not distract that with effects.

Summary

This chapter explored ways to replace one node with another. This was done within the context of one panel containing UI elements being replaced with another. Each transition brought a unique user experience. The implementation made sure that each transition left the scene in a state that would not surprise any developer using the API. Lastly, a few points were addressed concerning how adding graphically rich transitions to an application might affect the user's experience.

CHAPTER 4

■ ■ ■

Effect: Animated Lighting

As you glance around any room, it becomes apparent that though every object is illuminated subtly from many angles, one light source tends to dominate the others. The light from this main source makes one side of an object appear bright and the other side dark, often with a smooth gradient transitioning between the two. The human eye uses this difference between the light and dark to estimate an object's size and shape. When light moves across an object, the eye and brain get a chance to confirm the guesses, providing certainty about the nature of the object.

Simulating light in an application is an old trick; both the beveled corners of the 90s and the over-glossy buttons of the 2000s are ways of simulating light. As animations become increasingly common in everyday computing tasks, the opportunity to take advantage of animated light to produce convincing effects also increases. This chapter explores the basics of lighting in JavaFX and how to animate it.

Lighting Basics

Every node in JavaFX has a property called *effect*. JavaFX comes with a number of built-in effects to give a Node a unique look. Among these is Lighting, which is used to illuminate a Node in a realistic way. The Lighting effect can also give an otherwise flat-seeming node a 3D look. A lighting effect can cast light on a single Node, or all nodes in a Group. Simply placing a light in the scene will not illuminate all Nodes in the scene unless that light is applied to the root Node. When applying a Lighting effect, there are three types of lights to choose from. These three types will be familiar to anyone who has worked with 3D graphics. In fact, two of the three types of lights allow you to specify a Z coordinate, something that is not common in a 2D graphics library.

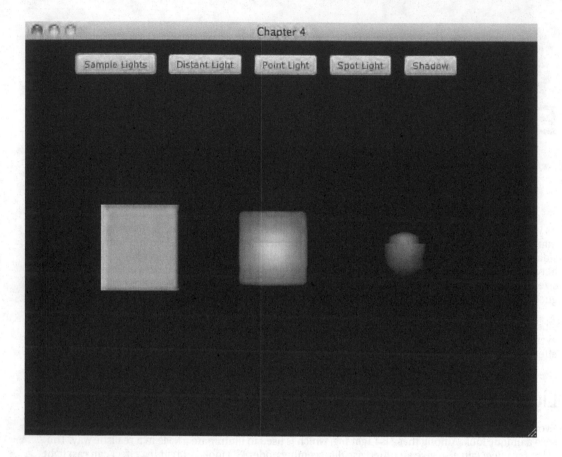

Figure 4-1. *Sample lights*

The screenshot in Figure 4-1 shows three rectangles, the left one illuminated by a DistantLight, the center illuminated by a PointLight and the right illuminated by a SpotLight. Here's how each light works:

DistantLight: A DistantLight is a far-away light and will illuminate a Node evenly from one direction. Much like the Sun, this light will strike every node in a group from the same direction. In JavaFX, how this light hits its target can be specified by setting the properties azimuth and elevation. Azimuth describes the angle from which the light will be coming. An azimuth of 0.0 is to the right of a Node while an azimuth of 90.0 is from the bottom, and so forth.

Elevation describes how directly or obliquely the light will hit the node. An elevation of 0.0 indicates that the DistantLight is shining on the node from the plane of the screen, while an elevation of 90.0 indicates the DistantLight is coming from the perspective of the user.

PointLight: A PointLight is a light that exists someplace in the scene and illuminates Nodes from a specific point in space. This is much like a bare light bulb in a dark room. By specifying an X, Y, and Z coordinate for a PointLight, an object can be illuminated as if it is very close to a light, or very distant.

SpotLight: A SpotLight is much like a PointLight in that an X, Y, and Z location can be specified. However, the SpotLight also has a sense of direction, and a point at which the light is shining can be specified. A SpotLight is like a desk lamp or a flashlight, in that it produces a cone of light. When this cone intersects a surface, it projects a very distinctive light pattern on to the surface.

Animating Light

Each of the light types provides unique opportunities for animation. The examples that follow explore how you can use these light types to produce particular results. There is an additional example at the end that shows how lighting can be combined with shadows to make some interesting animations. The code in Listing 4-1 is the framework in which the examples are run.

Listing 4-1. Main.fx

```
var exampleGroup = Group{};

public function run():Void{

    var sampleButton = Button{
        text: "Sample Lights";
        action: sampleLights;
    }
    var distantButton = Button{
        text: "Distant Light";
        action: distantLight;
    }
    var pointButton = Button{
        text: "Point Light";
        action: pointLight;
    }
    var spotButton = Button{
        text: "Spot Light";
        action: spotLight;
    }
    var withButton = Button{
        text: "Shadow";
        action: withShadow;
    }

    var topBox = HBox{
        translateX: 48
        translateY: 16
        spacing: 32
        content: [sampleButton, distantButton, pointButton, spotButton, withButton]
    }

    Stage {
        title: "Chapter 4"
        width: 640
```

```
            height: 480
            scene: Scene {
                fill: Color.BLACK
                content: [topBox,exampleGroup]
            }
        }
}

function reset(){
    delete exampleGroup.content;
    exampleGroup.scene.fill = Color.BLACK;
}
function sampleLights():Void{
    reset();

    var rect1 = Rectangle{
        width: 100
        height: 100
        fill: Color.WHITE
        effect: Lighting{
            light: DistantLight{azimuth: 180.0, elevation: 45.0, color: Color.RED}
            surfaceScale: 4;
        }
    }

    var rect2 = Rectangle{
        width: 100
        height: 100
        fill: Color.WHITE
        effect: Lighting{
            light: PointLight{x: 50.0, y: 50.0, z: 20.0, color: Color.GREEN}
            surfaceScale: 4;
        }
    }

    var rect3 = Rectangle{
        width: 100
        height: 100
        fill: Color.WHITE
        effect: Lighting{
            light: SpotLight{x: 50.0, y: 30.0, z: 20.0, pointsAtX: 50.0, pointsAtY: 100.0,
color: Color.BLUE}
            surfaceScale: 4;
        }
    }

    var box = HBox{
        translateX: 96
        translateY: 190
        spacing: 64
```

```
        content:[rect1, rect2, rect3]
    }

    insert box into exampleGroup.content;
}
```

Each of the five buttons in Listing 4-1 clears the contents of exampleGroup and then inserts new content. The method that produced the non-animated example from the previous section is also included; it shows how the three rectangles with the different light effect are created. The details of the animated examples follow.

Distant Light Example

This example explores how a distant light can be used to make otherwise 2D text appear 3D. In the screenshots in Figures 4-2 and 4-3, you can see the same text illuminated from two different angles.

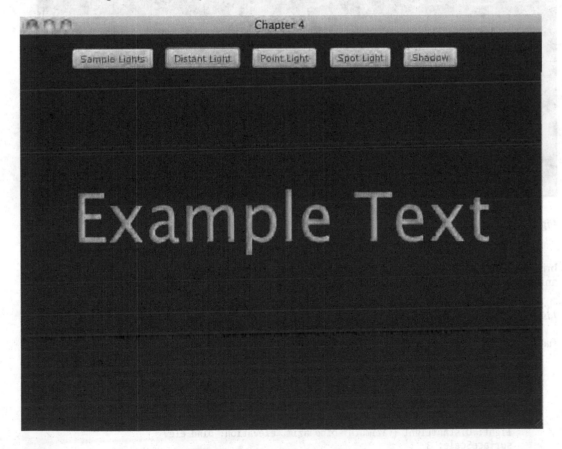

Figure 4-2. *Distant light on the right*

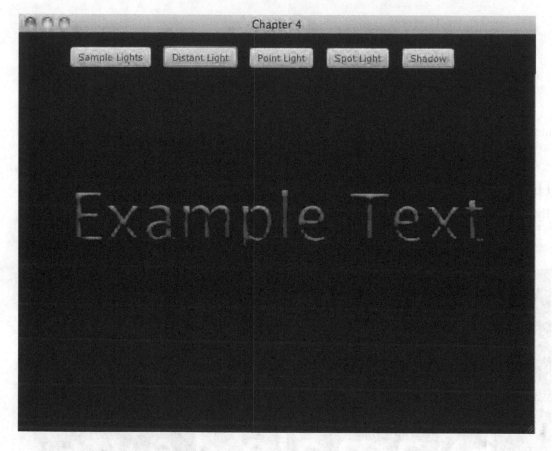

Figure 4-3. Distant light on the top

Figure 4-2 shows the text is being illuminated from the right so that the right side of each letter is brighter than the left side. In Figure 4-3, the letters are lit from the top. The code in Listing 4-2 creates an animation that includes the two scenes.

Listing 4-2. Main.fx (distantLight)

```
function distantLight():Void{
    reset();

    var elev = 0.0;
    var azim = 0.0;

    var lighting = Lighting {
        light: DistantLight { azimuth: bind azim, elevation: bind elev  }
        surfaceScale: 3
    }
```

```
var anim = Timeline{
    repeatCount: Timeline.INDEFINITE
    autoReverse: true
    keyFrames: [
        KeyFrame{time: 0s, values: elev=>0.0},
        KeyFrame{time: 5s, values: elev=>180.0},
        KeyFrame{time: 7.5s, values: elev=>160.0},
        KeyFrame{time: 7.5s, values: azim=>0.0},
        KeyFrame{time: 12.5s, values: azim=>360.0}
    ]
}

var text = Text{
    content: "Example Text"
    font: Font{
        size: 78
    }
    fill: Color.GRAY
}

var group = Group{
    content:text
    effect:lighting
    translateX: 640/2.0 - text.boundsInParent.width/2.0
    translateY: 480/2.0
}

anim.play();
insert group into exampleGroup.content;
}
```

The code creates a lighting effect and applies it to a group containing some sample text. The lighting variable has its light property set to a DistantLight. The properties azimuth and elevation of the DistantLight are bound to the variables azim and elev. A Timeline is created called anim that adjusts the values of elev and azim over a 12.5-second animation. The animation is set to reverse and play forever.

First, the animation increases the elevation of the DistantLight from 0.0 to 180.0, which is like watching the sun rise on the right, travel across the sky, and set on the left. The next part of the animation has the DistantLight move to 160.0 degrees, which is equivalent to the light being raised 30 degrees from the left horizon. Then, the DistantLight is rotated a full 360.0 degrees around the scene.

This example shows how a DistantLight can make text look believably 3D; it also shows how the animation of this light increases the fidelity of the 3D effect.

Point Light Example

In this example, a point light is animated over the surface of a simple rectangle. The screenshot in Figure 4-4 shows one frame of the animation.

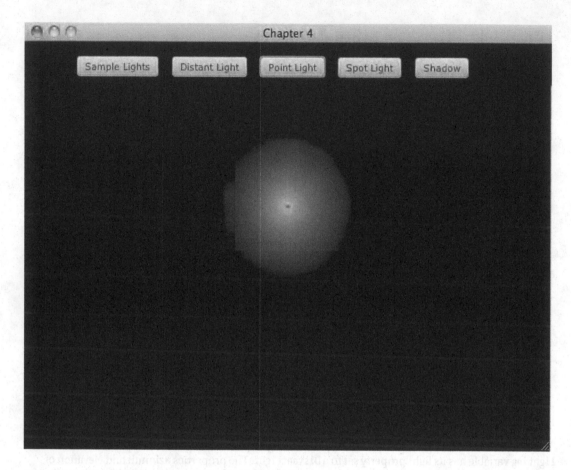

Figure 4-4. *Point light*

The light in Figure 4-4 is located above the rectangle, as if a light was very close to it, creating a circular gradient effect. As the animation progresses, the light on the rectangle will change in accordance with the X, Y, and Z location of the light. Listing 4-3 shows how this animation was produced.

Listing 4-3. *Main.fx (pointLight)*

```
function pointLight():Void{
    reset();

    var rectSize = 300;

    var x = 30.0;
    var y = 60.0;
    var z = 10.0;
```

```
var rect1 = Rectangle{
    width: rectSize
    height: rectSize
    fill: Color.GRAY
    effect: Lighting {
        light: PointLight{
            x: bind x,
            //y: bind rectSize - y + 20, <-- in case of bug. see side bar
            y: bind y,
            z: bind z
        }
        specularConstant: 0.0
        specularExponent: 1.0
        surfaceScale: 0

    }
}

var dot = Circle{
    radius: 2;
    translateX: bind x
    translateY: bind y;
    scaleX: bind 1.0 + (z/50.0);
    scaleY: bind 1.0 + (z/50.0);
    fill: Color.BLUE;
}

var half = rectSize/2.0;

var animation = Timeline{
    repeatCount: Timeline.INDEFINITE
    autoReverse: true;
    keyFrames: [
            KeyFrame{time:0s,values:[x=>0.0,y=>0.0,z=>0.0]},
            KeyFrame{time:2s,values:[x=>0.0,y=>0.0,z=>10.0]},
            KeyFrame{time:4s,values:[x=>half,y=>0.0,z=>10.0]},
            KeyFrame{time:6s,values:[x=>half,y=>half,z=>10.0]},
            KeyFrame{time:7s,values:[x=>half,y=>half,z=>0.0]},
            KeyFrame{time:9s,values:[x=>half,y=>half,z=>100.0]},
            KeyFrame{time:11s,values:[x=>rectSize,y=>half,z=>30.0]},
            KeyFrame{time:13s,values:[x=>rectSize,y=>rectSize,z=>0.0]},
            KeyFrame{time:16s,values:[x=>half,y=>half,z=>100.0]},
            KeyFrame{time:19s,values:[x=>0.0,y=>0.0,z=>0.0]}
        ]
}

var group = Group{
        translateX: 640/2.0 - rectSize/2.0
        translateY: 480/2.0 - rectSize/2.0
        content:[rect1,dot]
}
```

```
    insert group into exampleGroup.content;
    animation.play();
}
```

In this example, a rectangle is created called rect1, which then has a PointLight applied to it. The PointLight has its location bound to the variables x, y, and z. Note that where the y location of the PointLight is set, there's a line of commented-out code above it. At the time of this writing, there is a bug in JavaFX 1.2 that causes PointLight and SpotLight to show up in a weird location.

The rectangle and a circle called dot are included in a group. The dot's coordinates are also bound to the values x and y; the dot's scale is bound to the z value. In this way, as the animation moves the light around, the dot will move with it to indicate its location. The dot will also grow in size as the z value increases, as if it is getting closer to the viewer.

The animation simply starts by setting the x, y, and z values to 0.0, which is the upper left corner of the rectangle. The animation then moves the PointLight to the center of the rectangle where it increases the z value of the PointLight. As the z value increases, the amount of the rectangle that is illuminated increases.

Platform Issue

There is a bug in JavaFX that can cause the light to appear in the wrong location. This may be more of an issue for OS X users. Please see JavaFX bug RT-5579.

Spot Light Example

A spot light is much like a point light when its location and target are on the same z axis, but when a SpotLight is aimed at a point that is not directly under it, the cone of light emitted becomes obvious as it is projected across a surface.

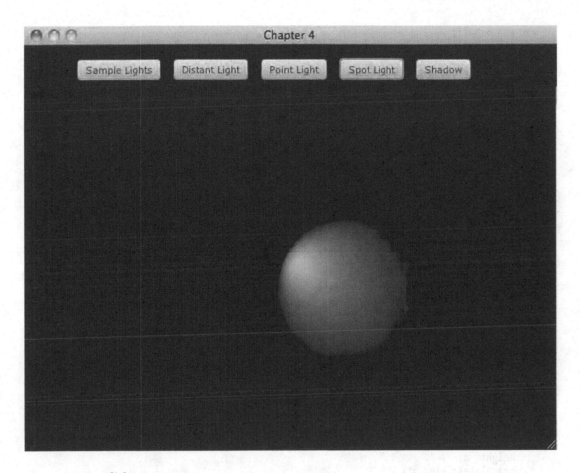

Figure 4-5. Spot light

The light shown in Figure 4-5 is located at the circular dot. The light is configured to point toward the small square dot, and the cone shape of the light can be seen. The source code in Listing 4-4 creates an animation that includes the frame in Figure 4-5.

Listing 4-4. Main.fx (spotLight)

```
function spotLight():Void{
    reset();

    var rectSize = 300;
    var half = rectSize/2.0;

    var x = 30.0;
    var y = 60.0;
    var z = 10.0;
```

```
    var atX = half;
    var atY = half;

    var rect1 = Rectangle{
        width: rectSize
        height: rectSize
        fill: Color.GRAY
        effect: Lighting {
            light: SpotLight{
                    x: bind x,
                    //y: bind rectSize - y + 20, <-- in case of bug. see side bar
                    y: bind y,
                    z: bind z
                    pointsAtX: bind atX;
                    pointsAtY: bind rectSize - atY + 20
            }
            specularConstant: 0.0
            specularExponent: 1.0
            surfaceScale: 0
        }
    }

    var dot1 = Circle{
        radius: 2;
        translateX: bind x
        translateY: bind y;
        scaleX: bind 1.0 + (z/50.0);
        scaleY: bind 1.0 + (z/50.0);
        fill: Color.BLUE;
    }
    var dot2 = Rectangle{
        width: 4;
        height: 4;
        translateX: bind atX - 2
        translateY: bind atY - 2;
        fill: Color.RED;
    }

var animation = Timeline{
        repeatCount: Timeline.INDEFINITE
        autoReverse: true;
        keyFrames: [
            KeyFrame{time:0s,values:[x=>half,y=>half,z=>20.0,atX=>half,atY=>half]},
            KeyFrame{time:2s,values:[atX=>half/2.0,atY=>half]},
            KeyFrame{time:8s,values:[atX=>half/2.0*3]},
            KeyFrame{time:5s,values:[atY=>half/2.0]},
            KeyFrame{time:8s,values:[x=>half,y=>half,z=>20.0,atY=>half/2.0*3]},
            KeyFrame{time:10s,values:[x=>half,y=>half,z=>20.0,atX=>half,atY=>half]},
            KeyFrame{time:12s,values:[x=>half,y=>half,z=>50.0]},
            KeyFrame{time:14s,values:[x=>half/2.0,y=>half,z=>50.0]},
            KeyFrame{time:16s,values:[x=>half/2.0,y=>half/2.0,z=>50.0]},
```

```
            KeyFrame{time:18s,values:[x=>half/2.0*3,y=>half/2.0*3,z=>50.0]}
        ]
    }

    var group = Group{
            translateX: 640/2.0 - rectSize/2.0
            translateY: 480/2.0 - rectSize/2.0
            content:[rect1,dot2,dot1]
    }

    insert group into exampleGroup.content;
    animation.play();
}
```

A rectangle is created with a SpotLight applied to it; the SpotLight has its location properties bound to the variables x, y, z, atX and atY. This is very much like the PointLight example except the two new variables atX and atY. These variables specify where the SpotLight is pointing. A SpotLight can also specify a z coordinate to point at, but this example does not make use of that property. Two dots are used to help visualize what is happening in the animation. The first dot, dot1, is a small circle used to track the location of the SpotLight. The second dot, dot2, is a square that tracks where the SpotLight is pointing. As the animation progresses, the square dot stays approximately in the center of the illuminated area.

The animation moves the SpotLight around the point where the light is shining. Then, the point where the light is shining is kept still, while the light itself moves about.

This animation shows how the illuminated area of a SpotLight is deformed as its location changes, and as its angle to the point at which it is shining changes.

Light and Shadow Example

In the preceding examples we simply moved a light around the scene, showing how each light type works in an animation. However, light is only half of the story when it comes to producing lifelike animations. When a light strikes an object, the eye also notices the shadow of that object. The shadow helps give the object a sense of volume.

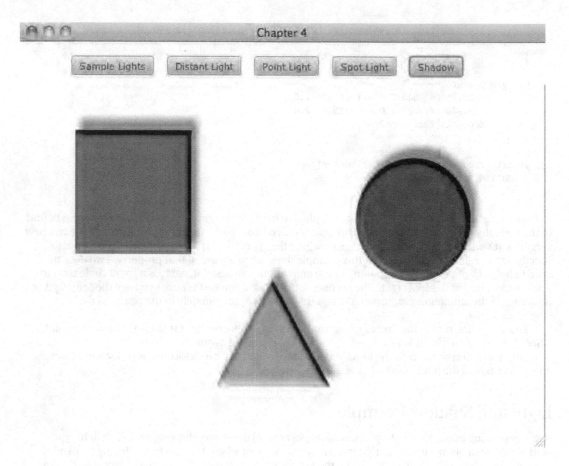

Figure 4-6. *Light and shadow*

The screenshot in Figure 4-6 shows three shapes illuminated by a `DistantLight`. A `DropShadow` is also applied to each shape, so that the shadow is on the opposite side as the light. The code in Listing 4-5 creates an animation where the light rotates around the shapes while the shadows also rotate, always staying on the opposite side of the light.

Listing 4-5. *Main.fx (withShadow)*

```
function withShadow():Void{
    reset();
    exampleGroup.scene.fill = Color.WHITE;

    var size = 140;
    var elev = 45.0;
    var asim = 0.0;
```

```
var rect = Rectangle{
    translateX: 70;
    translateY: 100;
    width: size;
    height: size;
    fill: Color.DARKCYAN
    effect: Lighting{
        light: DistantLight{elevation: bind elev, azimuth: bind asim}
        surfaceScale: 6
    }
}

var circle = Circle{
    translateX:  480;
    translateY:  200;
    radius: size/2.0;
    fill: Color.DARKMAGENTA
    effect: Lighting{
        light: DistantLight{elevation: bind elev, azimuth: bind asim}
        surfaceScale: 6
    }
}

var halfCos30 = Math.cos(Math.toRadians(30.0))/2.0;

var triangle = Polygon{
    translateX:  640/2.0-10;
    translateY:  320/2.0+170;
    points:[0.0, -size*halfCos30, -.5*size, size*halfCos30, .5*size, size*halfCos30]
    fill: Color.GOLD
    effect: Lighting{
        light: DistantLight{elevation: bind elev, azimuth: bind asim}
        surfaceScale: 6
    }
}

var group = Group{
    effect: DropShadow{
        offsetX: bind -Math.cos(Math.toRadians(asim)) * 15.0;
        offsetY: bind -Math.sin(Math.toRadians(asim)) * 15.0;
        color: Color.GRAY
        spread: 0.1
    }

    content:[rect,circle,triangle]
}

var anim = Timeline{
    repeatCount: Timeline.INDEFINITE;
    autoReverse: true;
    keyFrames: [
```

```
                    KeyFrame{
                        time: 0s
                        values: asim => 0.0
                    },
                    KeyFrame{
                        time: 5s
                        values: asim => 360.0
                    },
                    ]
        }

        insert group into exampleGroup.content;
        anim.play();

}
```

In Listing 4-5, each of the three shapes, rect, circle, and triangle are created with a DistantLight applied. Each DistantLight has its elevation set to 45.0 and its azimuth bound to the variable azim. All three shapes are added to a group that has a DropShadow applied. The DropShadow has its offsetX and offsetY properties bound to a simple trigonometric function that converts the angle of the azim to an x and y offset.

The animation anim changes the value of azim from 0.0 to 360.0 and back again; this causes each DistantLight to appear to rotate around each object, while the DropShadow is drawn on the opposite side.

Further Considerations

The examples shown here just touch on what is possible with animated lights. For instance, each light also allows a color to be set or a texture to be used. There is much to explore with lighting, not only with static lights but animated ones as well. Imagine an application, for example, where pressing a button lights up other nearby controls, or where default choices are highlighted by a flickering light.

Once again, designers need to keep in mind the graphics capabilities of the platform they're working on. This in turn will allow their applications to make the most of the platform they run on, whether JavaFX or another.

It is also important to consider that applying a lighting effect is not a cheap operation. Though the implementation of JavaFX is opaque, you can assume that each lighting effect requires JavaFX to rasterize each node the effect is applied to. Platforms where hardware acceleration is present will mitigate this performance issue, but too many lights on a less capable machine will prevent the application from working properly.

Summary

This chapter explored the basics of lighting in JavaFX and showed how lights can be animated to amplify the 3D effect they produce when motionless. Distant light is useful when lighting from a general direction is required, while point and spot lights bring the lights into the scene. Finally, this chapter looked at combining shadows with lights to complete the 3D illusion.

CHAPTER 5

■ ■ ■

Effect: Advanced Interpolators

Animations are pictures that change over time; these changes are composed of transformations and color changes. In either case, the rates at which these changes take place dictate much about the appearance of the animation, and of course, the rates themselves can change over time. Imagine the trivial animation of a rectangle moving from the top of the screen to the bottom. If the box moves down at a constant rate of 2 pixels per second, it would appear to be gently lowering. However, if the box drops 2 pixels the first second, 4 pixels the next second, then 8, 16, and so on, the box would seem to be freely falling. The difference between an object being lowered and an object falling can have a big effect on the impact of the animation.

In the case of keyframe animation, a start position and an end position are defined. In terms of the falling rectangle, the starting position is the top of the screen and the ending position is the bottom of the screen. In order to describe how the box moves from the start position to the end position, you must specify a function that describes that motion. In the case of the lowering box, the function is simply linear, while the falling box is defined by a polynomial function. These functions describe the interpolation between the start and end values. This chapter explores how interpolators are defined and used in JavaFX by providing several examples of custom interpolators.

The Basics

JavaFX comes with a handful of built-in interpolators. Each interpolator gives the developer a chance to tweak her animations in a different way. Though interpolators can be used alone, they are most often used in conjunction with Timelines and KeyFrames. The easiest way to see how interpolators are used is with a quick example, as shown in Listing 5-1.

Listing 5-1. *SimpleExample.fx*

```
function run():Void{
    var dot = Circle{
        radius: 10;
        translateX: 140
        translateY: 240
    }
    var anim = Timeline{
        repeatCount: Timeline.INDEFINITE
        keyFrames: KeyFrame{
```

```
                    time: 5s
                    values: dot.translateX => 440 tween Interpolator.EASEBOTH;
            }
    }

    anim.play();
    Stage {
        title: "Chapter 5 - Simple Example"
        width: 640
        height: 480
        scene: Scene {
            fill: Color.WHITE
            content: [dot]
        }
    }
}
```

In this example, a Circle named dot is added to the scene. The dot starts at the location (140,240) and an animation moves the dot to the location (440,240), over 5 seconds. This very simple animation is made slightly more interesting by using an interpolator. The KeyFrame above describes that the dot's translateX value will be at 440 at the end of 5 seconds. But it also describes where the dot will be between the beginning of the animation and the 5-second mark. This is described by the keyword tween followed by an Interpolator, in this case, the built-in interpolator called EASEBOTH.

If the animation had a KeyFrame at time 10s, that KeyFrame would describe the animation between 5s and 10s. Each KeyFrame's interpolator describes the period of time from the KeyFrame preceding it to the specified time. In our example, there is only one KeyFrame defined. When an animation does not specify a KeyFrame for time 0s, the developer should assume an implicit KeyFrame exits at time 0s.

Visualizing Interpolators

The example code included with this chapter contains a class that can be used to visualize an interpolator. This class is shown in Listing 5-2.

Listing 5-2. InterpolatorViewer

```
public class InterpolatorViewer extends Group{
    public var interpolator:Interpolator = Interpolator.LINEAR on replace{
        draw();
    }

    public var currentFraction:Number = 0.0 on replace{
        currentValue = interpolator.interpolate(0.0, 1.0, currentFraction) as Number;
    };

    var currentValue:Number = 0.0;

    var animation = Timeline{
        repeatCount: Timeline.INDEFINITE;
        autoReverse: true;
```

```
        keyFrames: [
                KeyFrame{
                    time: 0s
                    values: currentFraction => 0.0
                },
                KeyFrame{
                    time: 3s
                    values: currentFraction => 1.0
                },
            ]
    }

init{
    draw();
    animation.playFromStart();
}

public function draw():Void{
    delete content;

    var width = 256.0;
    var height = 256.0;

    var border = Rectangle{
        width: width;
        height: height;
        fill: null;
        stroke: Color.GRAY
        strokeWidth: 3
    }
    insert border into content;

    insert Text{
        translateX: width/2.0 - 40
        translateY: height - 2;
        content: "<- fraction ->"
        fill: Color.DARKGRAY
    } into content;
    insert Text{
        translateX: -39
        translateY: height/2.0
        content: "<- 0.0 - 1.0 ->"
        fill: Color.DARKGRAY
        rotate: -90.0
    } into content;

    var samples = 64.0;

    for (i in [0..samples]){
        var fraction:Number = i/samples;
        var value = (interpolator.interpolate(0.0, 1.0, fraction) as Number);
```

```
        var dot = Circle{
            translateX: i*(width/samples);
            translateY: height-value*height;
            radius: 2;
            fill: Color.BLUE
        }
        insert dot into content;
    }

    var playhead = Line{
        startX: bind currentFraction * width;
        startY: 0;
        endX: bind currentFraction * width;
        endY: height;
        stroke: Color.RED
    }

    insert playhead into content;

    var topLine = Line{
        startX: 0.0
        startY: 0.0
        endX: 10.0
        endY: 0.0
        stroke: Color.GRAY
        strokeDashOffset: 10
    }

    var bottomLine = Line{
        startX: 1.0
        startY: height
        endX: 10.0
        endY: height
        stroke: Color.GRAY
        strokeDashOffset: .5
    }

    var vball = Circle{
        radius: 4
        fill: Color.GREEN
        translateX: 5
        translateY: bind height - currentValue*height;
    }

    var vetical = Group{
        translateX: width + 20
        content: [topLine, bottomLine, vball]
    }

    insert vetical into content;
```

```
    var rotate = Rectangle{
        translateX: width + 80
        translateY: 90;
        width: 70
        height: 70
        fill: Color.MAGENTA
        rotate: bind currentValue*360.0
    }

    insert rotate into content;
    }
}
```

Listing 5-2 shows the class `InterpolatorView`, which extends `Group`. Setting the property `interpolator`, which populates the content by calling the function `draw`, controls the visual appearance of this Node.

The function `draw` creates a graph that displays an `Interpolator` as a function of time. The function `draw` also creates several animated components. The first is a red line that moves across the graph to show which value of the Interpolator is being expressed by the other components.

The other two components are a green dot that moves vertically with the value `currentValue` and a rotating square, which is also synchronized with the `currentValue`.

Built-In Interpolators

The interpolators that come with JavaFX are just enough to whet the appetite. All of the built-in interpolators can be accessed by static calls to the class Interpolator, as shown in the first example. A description of each interpolator follows and is demonstrated in the companion code.

Linear

The linear interpolator is the default interpolator used by `KeyFrame`. It is not much of an `Interpolator`, as it simply returns the value passed to it. A node being animated with a linear interpolator starts moving and travels at a constant speed until it suddenly stops at its destination. For the sake of completeness, Figure 5-1 shows a graph describing the motion over time.

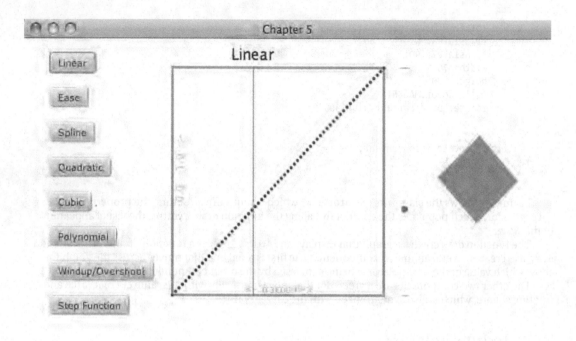

Figure 5-1. *Linear interpolation*

Ease Out, Ease In, Ease Both

The Ease family of interpolators is used to create more natural animations than simply linear animations. In real life, objects don't suddenly stop, nor do they transition from stopped to moving without a period of acceleration. An object being animated with an EASEIN interpolator starts out slow, speeds up for a short period, then travels at a constant speed for the remainder of the animation. Conversely, a node being animated with an EASEOUT interpolator starts moving much like a linear interpolation, but just before the end of the animation the node slows to a stop.

The interpolator EASEBOTH combines these two periods of acceleration and deceleration into a single animation, so a node will start slowly, travel at a constant speed, then slow to a stop. The screenshot in Figure 5-2 presents the EASEBOTH interpolator, showing the slight curves at the beginning and end of the interpolation.

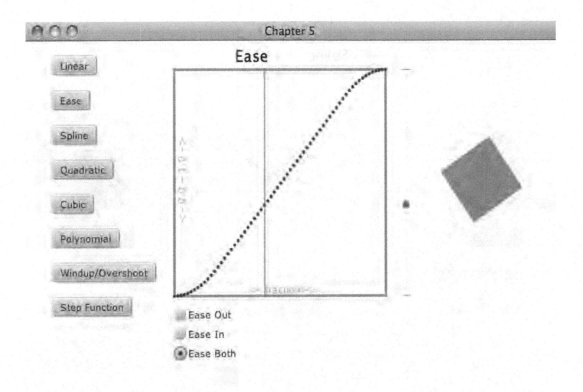

Figure 5-2. *The EaseBoth interpolator*

Spline

A spline Interpolator can be used to create a number of different animations, by specifying different parameters. In general a spline is a type of curve that is described by four points, a start point, an end point, and two control points. For the sake of interpolation, the start and end points are considered fixed, and what is specified when creating a spline interpolator are the control points.

Many drawing applications have a tool that allows the user to create a line and then adjust the curve by moving the control points.

Figure 5-3 shows a spline curve that can be modified.

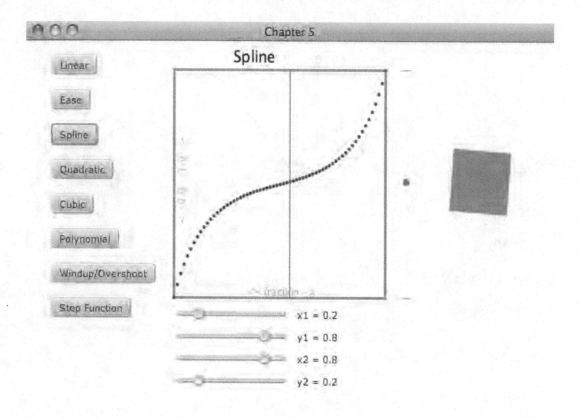

Figure 5-3. *Spline interpolator*

By moving the sliders at the bottom of the screen, the control points can be relocated to create a number of different curves. One considerable limitation of the spline is its inability to create curves that extend beyond 1.0 or below 0.0. This limitation is a characteristic of the JavaFX API, not an inherent limitation of splines in general.

Custom Interpolators

The default interpolators are a good start, but eventually a designer will want more control over the animations. For example, the default set of interpolators provides no way of creating an animation that extends beyond the start and end values. Creating an interpolator is very simple; creating an interpolator that looks good is a bit more complex. The following section describes how to implement an interpolator and provides a number of examples.

Extending Interpolator

You can extend the class `Interpolator` to create a custom interpolator. `Interpolator` has one method that must be overridden. The code in Listing 5-3 provides a trivial example.

Listing 5-3. *TrivialInterpolator.fx*

```
public class TrivialInterpolator extends Interpolator{
    public override function interpolate(start:Object,end:Object,fraction:Number):Object{
        var s:Number = (start as Number);
        var e:Number = (end as Number);
        return s + (e-s)*fraction;
    }
}
```

The `TrivialInterpolator` class in Listing 5-3 implements a single function called `interpolate`. The function `interpolate` takes three arguments, `start` and `end`, which are both of type `Object`, and `fraction`, which is of type `Number`. The idea is that the function will return a value, which is a certain value between `start` and `end`. The example in Listing 5-3 is the same as the linear interpolator. If 10.0 and 20.0 are passed in for `start` and `end`, and 0.7 is passed in for the `fraction`, then the function is being asked for an appropriate value for an animation that is 70% complete. In this case, the value would be 17.0.

After implementing a number of interpolators, it becomes obvious that the preceding code, which finds the value between `start` and `end`, is boilerplate code, and the interesting part is figuring out what to do with the fraction. For example, how does the `EASEBOTH` interpolator create those slopes at either end of the line? It is best to think of an interpolator as a function that takes a value between 0.0 and 1.0 and generally returns value within the same range. The function should probably return 0.0 for 0.0 and 1.0 for 1.0. To facilitate this concept, JavaFX provides a utility class that can be extended instead of Interpolator; this class is called `SimpleInterpolator`. The example in Listing 5-3 can be rewritten as in Listing 5-4.

Listing 5-4. *TrivialSimpleInterpolator.fx*

```
public class TrivialSimpleInterpolator extends SimpleInterpolator{

    public override function curve(fraction:Number):Number{
        return fraction;
    }
}
```

Since the examples in this book will be focusing on interpolating numbers, the function curve makes a lot more sense—for starters it returns a Number, which all of these examples will return.

■ **Tip** Interpolators work with values besides Numbers, such as Colors.

Quadratic Interpolator

While the spline interpolator can produce a large range of curves, sometimes it is desirable to create an interpolator that uses a quadratic function to describe this curve. For example, the effect of gravity on a falling body is best modeled with a quadratic function. A quadratic function has the form:

$ax^2 + bx + c = 0$

Since it is expected that interpolators produce curves that intersect with 0,0 and 1,1, the formula above can be simplified to the following:

$ax^2 + bx = 1$

The variable c can be removed since we always want the curve to pass through the origin, as c describes where the curve intersects with the y axis. Now, changing a and b will change the shape of the curve, but the curve must pass through the point 1,1, so only one of the two coefficients can be set by the application. The other must be calculated based on the value of the other, in order to keep the equation balanced. This example assumes that a can be set by the application and b will be solved for.

Listing 5-5 shows how a quadratic function is expressed in code.

Listing 5-5. *QuadraticInterpolator.fx*

```
public class QuadraticInterpolator extends SimpleInterpolator {
    public var a = 1.0 on replace{
        b = 1.0 - a;
    }
    var b:Number = 1.0 - a;

    public override function curve(fraction:Number):Number{
        return (a*fraction*fraction + b*fraction);
    }
}
```

In Listing 5-5, the function curve takes a fraction and calculates a value based on the values of a and b. This function will always return 0.0 for the fraction 0.0 (since anything times 0 is 0) and will also return 1.0 for 1.0, since as a changes, b will be recalculated to balance the equation. The screenshot in Listing 5-4 shows this interpolator in action.

The slider at the bottom of Figure 5-4 allows the value of a to be set, and the calculated value of b is displayed. Note the parabolic curve produced.

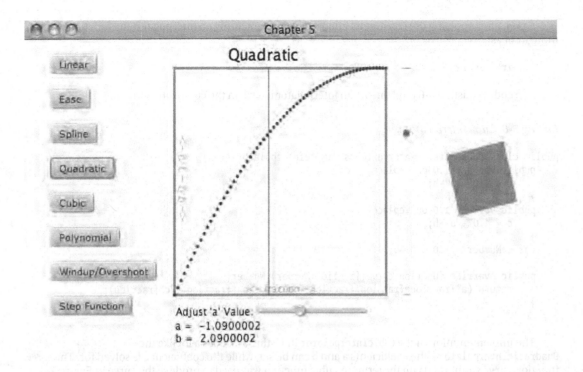

Figure 5-4. *Quadratic*

Cubic Interpolator

Like the quadratic interpolator, the cubic interpolator is based on a polynomial expression. Cubic functions can produce more complex curves than quadratic functions, and are characterized by having a vertical point of inflection. That is to say, they go up, then down, then back up again.

Cubic functions are of the form:

$$ax^3 + bx^2 + cx + d = 0$$

Again, after applying the constraints imposed by implementing an interpolator, the function can be thought of as:

$$ax^3 + bx^2 + cx = 1$$

The code in Listing 5-6 implements an interpolator based on the cubic function.

Listing 5-6. *CubicInterpolator.fx*

```
public class CubicInterpolator extends SimpleInterpolator {
    public var a = 1.0 on replace{
        c = 1.0 - a -b;
    }
    public var b = 1.0 on replace{
        c = 1.0 - a -b;
    }
    var c:Number = 1.0 - a -b;

    public override function curve(fraction:Number):Number{
        return (a*fraction*fraction*fraction + b*fraction*fraction + c*fraction);
    }
}
```

The implementation of the CubicInterpolator in Listing 5-6 looks a lot like the QuadraticInterpolator—the coefficients a and b can be set, while the coefficient c is solved for. The function curve simply adds up the terms. A cubic function was used to produce the curve in Figure 5-5, which shows the signature up and down wave pattern that identifies a cubic function.

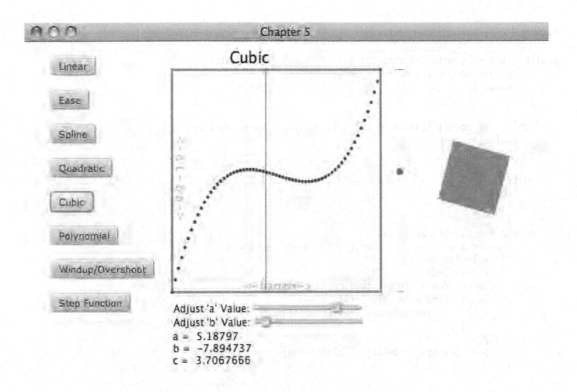

Figure 5-5. *Cubic interpolator*

Polynomial Interpolator

The QuadraticInterpolator allows the creation of nice, clean curves, while the CubicInterpolator can create curves of more complexity. It follows that the more terms in the function, the more complex the curve that can be expressed. So creating a function with 4, 5, or even more terms will generate increasingly interesting curves.

The general term for functions like the quadratic and cubic functions is *polynomial*. While a quadratic function has a term with a power of 2 and a cubic function has a term with the power of 3, a polynomial can have the highest power of any value. Specifically, the form the polynomial is:

$$ax^n + bx^{n-1} + cx^{n-2} \ldots ix^2 + jx + k = 0$$

The implementation of the quadratic and cubic interpolators suggests that an interpolator could be created that implements any number of terms. The code in Listing 5-7 shows how this is done.

Listing 5-7. PolynomialInterpolator.fx

```
public class PolynomialInterpolator extends SimpleInterpolator{
    public var solveFor = 0 on replace{
        solve();
    }

    public var coefficients:Number[] = [1.0, 1.0, 1.0] on replace{
        solve();
    }

    init{
        solve();
    }

    public function solve():Void{
        //given a + b + c = 1, then c = 1 - b - c, or a = 1 - c - b
        if (solveFor != -1){
            var solvedValue = 1.0;
            for (index in [0..(sizeof coefficients)-1]){
                if (index != solveFor){
                    solvedValue -= coefficients[index];
                }
            }
            coefficients[solveFor] = solvedValue;
        }
    }

    public override function curve(fraction:Number):Number{
        var power = fraction;
        var total = 0.0;
        for (coeff in coefficients){
            total += coeff*power;
            power *= fraction;
        }
        return total;
    }

}
```

Instead of specifying a, b, c, and so on, the implementation above uses a Sequence called coefficients to store an arbitrary number of terms. It should be pointed out that coefficients stores in the sequence in the reverse order of the function in Listing 5-7. So, coefficients[0] is the least significant term.

The variable solveFor is used to keep track of which coefficient must be solved for when one of the others changes. This is an improvement over the previous versions, where the least significant coefficient was always solved for.

The function solve is called every time the Sequence coefficients changes and once during init time. The function solve calculates a value for one of the coefficients to make sure the function always creates a curve that passes through the origin and the point 1,1.

The function curve simply adds up each term, increasing the power with each term. The screenshot in Figure 5-6 shows just how interesting the curves can get.

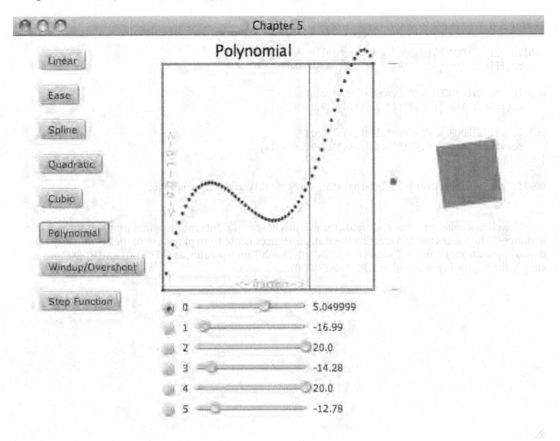

Figure 5-6. *Polynomial interpolation*

Windup-Overshoot Interpolator

The custom interpolators defined up to this point allow a developer so specify a huge number of different interpolations and this flexibility is wonderful. However, when designing an application, it is desirable to have a few well-defined interpolators that are used over and over again. This example shows how to take a powerful interpolator and create a handful of good choices, which can then be reused whenever needed.

The ease in/out interpolators are examples of this kind of simplification; they are probably implemented with the spline interpolator, but the API hides the details. All the designer and developer know is that there are a number of pre-built interpolators that produce nice results. This makes the developer's life easier and allows the designer to make a choice from a reasonably small set of good options. The Interpolator presented in Listing 5-8 is an example of this type of simplification.

Listing 5-8. *WindupOvershootInterpolator.fx*

```
public var WINDUP_OVERSHOOT = PolynomialInterpolator{
    coefficients: [-1.25564,6.842106,-4.586466]
}
public var OVERSHOOT = PolynomialInterpolator{
    coefficients: [0.6992483,2.581203,-2.1804514]
}
public var WINDUP = PolynomialInterpolator{
    coefficients: [-0.95488644,4.135338,-2.1804514]
}

public class WindupOvershootInterpolator extends PolynomialInterpolator{
}
```

The class WindupOvershootInterpolator extends PolynomialInterpolator and provides three static instances. The values used in creating the static instances came from playing with the accompanying demo application. Figure 5-7 shows the WINDUP_OVERSHOOT interpolator, as OVERSHOOT and WINDUP are simply the beginning and end of WINDUP_OVERSHOOT.

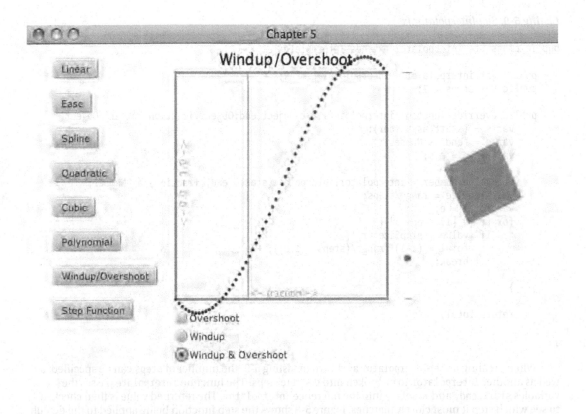

Figure 5-7. The Windup Overshoot interpolator

As you can see, this interpolator is designed to animate nodes beyond the bounds of the start and end. This gives a certain amount of enthusiasm to an animation and works well with popup menus and other animated UI controls.

Step Interpolator

While most things in the world move with smooth curves, there are human-made things that may appear to move instantly from one place to another. For example, the second hand on some analog clocks appears to jump from second to second. Of course, the hand simply moves very quickly from second to second, but in order to capture that tick-tick-tick feeling, an interpolator that jumps from value to value can be used.

The code in Listing 5-9 creates an interpolator that takes another interpolator and breaks it up into a number of steps.

Listing 5-9. *StepInterpolator.fx*

```
public class StepInterpolator extends Interpolator{

    public var interpolator = Interpolator.LINEAR;
    public var steps = 7;

    public override function interpolate(start:Object,end:Object,fraction:Number):Object{
        var s = (start as Number);
        var e = (end as Number);
        var range = e-s;

        var value:Number = interpolator.interpolate(start, end, fraction) as Number;
        var stepSize = range/steps;
        var total = e;
        for (r in [1..steps-1]){
            if (value < stepSize*(r)){
                total = (r-1)*(range/(steps - 1.0));
                break;
            }
        }

        return total;
    }
}
```

When creating a StepInterpolator as shown in Listing 5-9, the number of steps can be specified, as well as another Interpolator to be broken into discrete steps. The function interpolate passes the variables start, end, and fraction into the reference interpolator. The returned value is then checked to see which step it most closely matches. Figure 5-8 shows the step function being applied to the default linear interpolator, and Figure 5-9 shows a step interpolator applied to the polynomial interpolator used earlier.

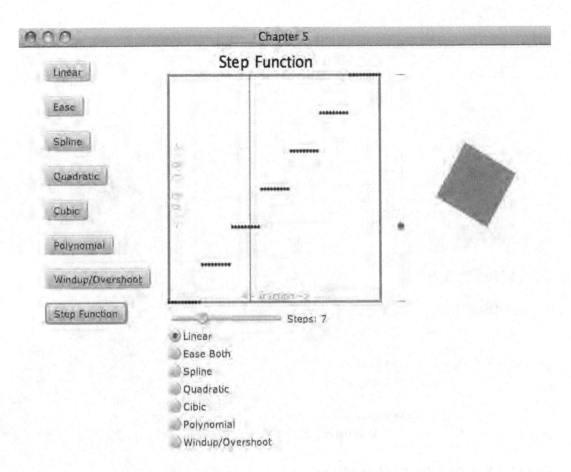

Figure 5-8. *Step plus linear interpolation*

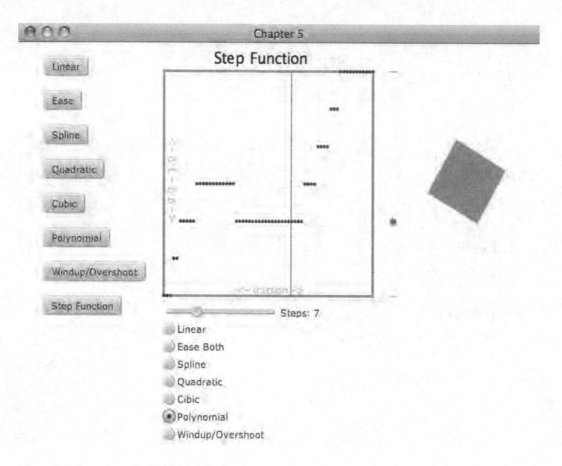

Figure 5-9. *Step plus polynomial interpolation*

Now that the implementation of the step interpolator has been described, let's explore how it can be useful. Taking the clock example again, consider the code in Listing 5-10.

Listing 5-10. *ClockExample.fx*

```
function run():Void{
    var clock = Group{
        translateX: 320
        translateY: 230
    }
    for (i in [0..59]){
        var dot = Group{
            content: Circle{
                translateX: 200
                radius: 1
```

```
                fill: Color.BLACK
            }
            transforms: Transform.rotate(i/60.0 * 360.0, 0, 0);
        }
        insert dot into clock.content;
    }
    for (i in [0..11]){
        var bigDot = Group{
            content: Circle{
                translateX: 200
                radius: 3
                fill: Color.BLACK
            }
            transforms: Transform.rotate(i/12.0 * 360.0, 0, 0);
        }
        insert bigDot into clock.content;
    }

    var rotation = 0.0;
    var hand = Rectangle{
        width: 190
        height: 1
        fill: Color.RED
        transforms: bind Transform.rotate(rotation, 0, 0);
    }

    insert hand into clock.content;

    var anim = Timeline{
        repeatCount: Timeline.INDEFINITE
        keyFrames: KeyFrame{
            time: 60s
            values: rotation => 360.0 tween StepInterpolator{steps: 61}
        }
    }
    anim.play();
    Stage {
        title: "Chapter 5 - Clock Example"
        width: 640
        height: 480
        scene: Scene {
            fill: Color.WHITE
            content: [clock]
        }
    }
}
```

In the code, a number of dots are drawn in a circular pattern, like the tick marks for seconds on an analog clock. A rectangle called hand is rotated 360 degrees over 60 seconds. A StepInterpolator is used make the second hand snap from tick to tick. The StepInterpolator uses 61 steps, since in this case we don't want the last step to be the same as the first step. The code from Listing 5-10 creates the image in Figure 5-10.

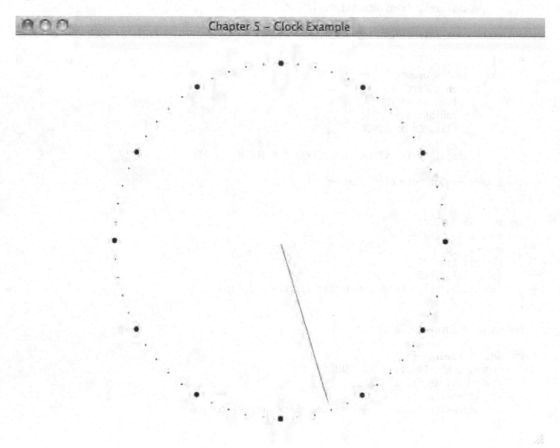

Figure 5-10. Clock with a second hand

Transition Example

Looking back at Chapter 3 we can see that transitions are a great place to use different interpolators. Each of the transitions could be combined with an interpolator to make a large number of different transitions with different feels. Figure 5-11 shows what some of these combinations look like. The source code containing this example is in the package com.lj.jfxe.chapter5.transitions. A few of the interpolators used in this example can represent lots of different transitions, such as the spline and polynomial transitions. I have hard coded the default values to provide a talking point about a particular effect.

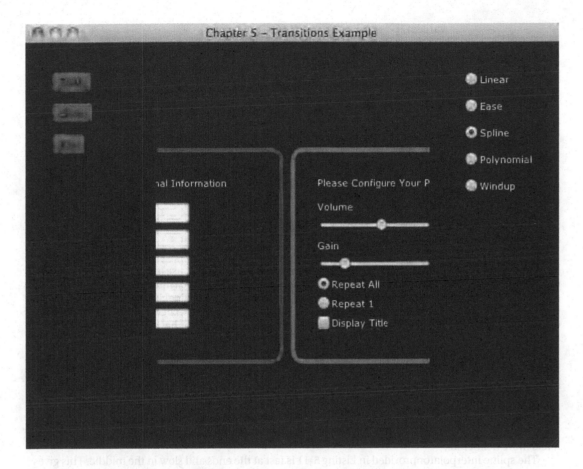

Figure 5-11. *Transitions and interpolators*

In Figure 5-11 we see the transitions example running. Clicking one of buttons on the left triggers the transition, and the radio buttons on the right select which interpolator should be used. The transitions require a little modification to take an interpolator as an argument. Listing 5-11 shows how SlideReplace is modified.

Listing 5-11. *Modified Parts of SlideReplace*

```
public function
doReplace(nodeToReplace:Node,replacementNode:Node,inter:Interpolator,doAfter:function()):Voi
d{
//…
var t = Timeline{
        keyFrames: [
                KeyFrame{
                    time: 1s
```

```
                values: [
                    group.translateX => startingX + totalWidth tween inter,
                    clip.translateX => -totalWidth tween inter
                    ]
                action: function(){
                    delete group.content;
                    replacementNode.translateX = startingX;
                    replacementNode.translateY = startingY;
                    insert replacementNode before parent.content[index];
                }
            },
            KeyFrame{
                time: 1s + 1ms
                action: doAfter
            }
        ]
    }
```

In Listing 5-11 we can see that only three lines need to be modified to use an Interpolator; the lines that are different are shown in bold. Obviously the signature of the function must be changed to take an Interpolator. The other change is that Interpolator inter is used in the Timeline to tween the values of the animation. The other transitions have been modified in a similar way—check out the source code for details. Let's take a candid exploration of the visual effect each interpolator has on each transition.

Fade Transition

The fade transition simply fades out one node while fading in another, and by applying different interpolators, the rate at which the fade takes place is altered. The linear and ease interpolators are pretty similar, and it would not be obvious which one is being used if you did not know. That said, I do think the ease interpolator is slightly nicer than the linear, and the way the ease interpolator ends makes it feel more deliberate.

The spline interpolator provided in Listing 5-11 is fast at the ends and slow in the middle. This gives a sense of hesitation, or that the transition is in some way difficult. This effect could be used when the user makes a final decision about something, as it might reinforce the sense of finality.

I deliberately selected a polynomial interpolator that is sort of weird. When used with the fade transition it is hard to find any value in it at all. This is partly due to the fact that this interpolator extends beyond the 1.0 range value, and a node with opacity greater than 1.0 or less than 0.0 has no meaning.

The windup interpolator has the same limitation as the polynomial interpolator. The first and last parts of this interpolator create values that make no sense for opacity. Hence the transition seems to be shorter than the others, since only the middle range of the interpolator provides any visual changes.

So while the exotic interpolators didn't do much for this transition, there was something to be learned regarding the built-in interpolators. They offer two very different experiences.

Slide Transition

The slide transition animates one node to the right, while the new node follows it. A clipping area around the starting location of the first node makes it look like one node is sliding out to make room for the new node. Again, the linear and ease interpolators are similar, but still a little different. The linear interpolator is very mechanical—it's like watching a subway go by. The ease interpolator gently slows the animation at the end, which gives a sense of the node settling into place like a subway stopping. Either choice is a good choice, but selecting one over the other should be deliberate.

The spline interpolator provides the same sense of hesitation as it did with the fade transition, but for some reason I find it annoying in this context. Maybe it annoys me because part of the new node is visible and part of it is not.

The polynomial interpolator is similar to the spine interpolator in that it only shows part of the controls. But there is something about the back-and-forth action that redeems it. I could see using a transition like this in a game, as long as the game was sufficiently silly and involved rubber in some way.

I think I like the windup interpolator the best. It combines the back-and-forth motion of the polynomial interpolator with the certainty of the ease interpolator.

I find it interesting that some interpolators work so much better with one transition over with another.

Flip Transition

The flip transition uses a sheering effect to make it look like the nodes are on two faces of a card being spun about its middle. In this case I much prefer the linear interpolator to the ease interpolator, as the ease interpolator makes the animation feel broken. The broken feeling might come from the fact that when you watch something spin, the amount of the scene that changes is different depending on the angle. For example, when the animation is halfway complete, the amount that the scene changes per degree is very high. But when the animation is almost done, those last few degrees don't change the scene all that much, so having the rate that the angle changes seems unnatural.

The spline interpolator produces a robotic motion, like there is something that has to be adjusted before the rotation can complete. I find this interesting because the linear interpolator usually strikes me as the most robotic, but in this case it is not.

The polynomial interpolator looks like the animation is just broken; I don't see any point in using this one.

The windup interpolator gives a real nice wiggle at the end; it makes me want to create an interpolator with a few additional wiggles.

Further Considerations

Interpolators provide an excellent API for describing animation as well as any other change in the scene. It is a good idea to spend time creating a set of excellent interpolators, as they can quickly add life to an application without adding to the complexity of the animation code.

It is worth emphasizing the value of creating demo software to help express ideas to designers. JavaFX is a powerful graphics library and is capable of some truly amazing animations, but a lot of the power of JavaFX is locked into its API. If a developer creates a demo application that shows off a handful of interpolators and how they work with different types of animations, such as scaling and rotation, a designer can immediately start adding those capabilities to her bag of tricks.

Remember that interpolators are called many times a second to produce smooth animations. It is worth the time to make sure the implementation of the interpolator is as efficient as possible.

Summary

This chapter looked at the basics of what an interpolator is and provided a method for visualizing interpolators through the class `InterpolatorView`. Further, a number of custom interpolators were implemented, showing how `Interpolators` are defined. The complex polynomial interpolator was used to create a general-purpose interpolator that can be reused in many projects. Lastly, a concrete example of using interpolators with transitions was explored.

CHAPTER 6

■ ■ ■

Effect: Physics

A physics engine is a software library that simulates how objects move in the real world. Adding physics to an application provides a way to create animations that appeal to the user's sense of realism. While it is possible to create animations that have a life-like quality without implementing physics, cracking open that high school physics book will provide consistency throughout your application. However, if the thought of implementing "real life" in your application feels a little out of scope, you can make use of a third-party library. This chapter will explore what a physics engine can do, and how to use an excellent open-source library to add physics-based effects to a JavaFX application.

The most obvious use of physics is in video games, but you can create animations for use in any application. The last example in this chapter shows how physics can be used to create a UI transition.

Simulation

Computers have been used to simulate the real world from the very beginning. Whether calculating the motion of an artillery shell or the path of a hurricane, the basic idea is the same. Find a way to express how the world works in code, setup a scenario, run the program, display the output.

Expressing how the world works in code is the hardest part of the problem. To simplify this problem, a subset of physics, known as *rigid body dynamics*, is used. Rigid body dynamics describes how objects or bodies interact when they move about or collide, but does not consider how a body might deform as it impacts another body, or how a body might weaken over time. Nor does this subset include any details about fluids, electromagnetism or other phenomena. This might sound like a large limitation, but remember the goal is to create eye-catching animations, not actually replicate the real world. Producing animations where objects fall and collide in a realistic way can produce some amazing results; you can see this in modern video games that increasingly take advantage of realistic physics, even to the point where some companies offer specialized hardware to perform these physics calculations.

In addition to limiting the calculations to rigid body dynamics, the examples in this chapter also limit the simulations to 2D space. This limitation makes sense in the current implementation of JavaFX, as JavaFX is primarily a 2D drawing library at this time.

In general, a simulation works by defining the *bodies* that exist in the simulated *world*, each body has shape, mass, location, rotation, velocity, and an angular velocity. There may also be a number of attributes that can be used to fine-tune a simulation, such as friction or bounciness. The world in which these objects reside can also have attributes, such as the force/direction of gravity or a dampening on the movement of objects.

Bodies have:

1. Shape

2. Mass

3. Location

4. Rotation

5. Velocity

6. Angular Velocity

Once the bodies and the world are defined in a suitable data structure, the rules of motion are applied to each body. The location and orientation of each is advanced for a small amount of time, usually called a *step*. A step is often the target frame rate of the application, 1/30th of a second. So bodies with a velocity are moved, bodies with an angular velocity are rotated, and all objects are moved in the direction of gravity, but only as much as they would for the amount of time in a single step.

When the new location of the bodies is determined, each body is checked to see if it now overlaps any other body. If bodies overlap, that is to say, if a collision is detected, then the velocity and angular velocity are adjusted based on how the bodies collided. After each body has its location and rotation updated, the application applies any other changes to the world that makes sense for that app—perhaps bodies that collide with each other are removed or change color. Lastly, the scene that is displayed to the user is updated to reflect these changes. Once the new scene is drawn, the world is advanced by another step.

Third-Party Implementation

As noted earlier, implementing your own physics engine is a lot of work. Not to dissuade an inspired developer, but the intricacy of handling complex shapes, efficiently checking for collisions, and generally getting the math right are all good reasons to use someone else's hard work. The following examples use a physics engine called Phys2D, an open source physics library implemented in Java. Phys2D is the work of Kevin Glass, an active member of the Java Gaming Community who ported the Box2D library from C to Java. Phys2D can be downloaded from http://code.google.com/p/phys2d/. It is available under the terms of the New BSD License, which is pretty liberal—but worth reading up on to make sure you conform to the terms.

Phys2D works much as described above—a World object is created and a number of Body objects are added. Then the function step is called on the World object and the location and rotation of each body is updated. Phys2D is a Java library, not a JavaFX library, but this is of little concern as Phys2D is easily called from JavaFX. In general there will be one JavaFX node for each Body in the world, and the location and rotation of the Node will be updated based on the location and rotation of its Body object after each step. The application will do something like the following:

1. Add Bodies to the World and corresponding Nodes to the Scene.

2. Call World.step().

3. Apply application logic.

4. Update the location and rotation of each Node.

5. Go back to step 2.

The following examples will show how to set up a JavaFX application to use Phys2D, as well as how to use a number of features in Phys2D.

Simple Example

For this first example, the Phys2D jar file must be downloaded and included in the projects classpath. Once Phys2D is on the classpath, the classes in that library may be instantiated in a JavaFX application in the same way as any Java class is instantiated in JavaFX, by simply calling the constructor. The code in Listing 6-1 shows how to set up the basic components of a JavaFX application using Phys2D.

Listing 6-1. *Main.fx*

```
var random = new Random();

var worldNodes:WorldNode[];
var group = Group{}
var world = new World(new Vector2f(0,1200), 1);

var worldUpdater = Timeline{
    repeatCount: Timeline.INDEFINITE
    keyFrames: KeyFrame{
        time: 1.0/30.0*1s
        action: update;
    }

}
public function update():Void{
    world.<<step>>();
    for (worldNode in worldNodes){
        worldNode.update();
    }

}
public function addWorldNode(worldNode:WorldNode):Void{
    insert (worldNode as Node) into group.content;
    insert worldNode into worldNodes;
    for (body in worldNode.bodies){
        world.add(body);
    }
    for (joint in worldNode.joints){
        world.add(joint);
    }

}
public function reset():Void{
```

```
        world.clear();
        delete worldNodes;
        delete group.content;
    }
public function run():Void{
        var button0 = Button{
            text: "Simple";
            action: simpleBalls;
        }
        var button1 = Button{
            text: "Falling Balls";
            action: fallingBalls;
        }
        var button2 = Button{
            text: "Pendulum";
            action: pendulum;
        }
        var button3 = Button{
            text: "Teeter Totter";
            action: teetertotter;
        }

        var vbox = VBox{
            translateX: 32;
            translateY: 64;
            spacing: 16
            content: [button0,button1,button2,button3]
        }

        Stage {
            title: "Chapter 6"
            width: 640
            height: 480
            scene: Scene {
                fill: Color.BLACK
                content: [group, vbox]
            }
        }

        worldUpdater.play();
}
function simpleBalls():Void{
    reset();

    addWorldNode(Ball{translateX: 320, translateY: 10});

    addWorldNode(Wall{width: 100, height: 16, translateY: 200, translateX: 320, rotate:
30});
    addWorldNode(Wall{width: 100, height: 16, translateY: 370, translateX: 430, rotate: -
30});
}
```

This code shows that the strategy is to create a Phys2D World and then mirror the Bodies in that World with JavaFX Nodes. In order to mirror the Bodies, a new class called WorldNode is created—a simple JavaFX class that contains two sequences and an abstract function called update. In this way, a Node will be created that extends WorldNode so that each Node in the Scene maintains a reference to its corresponding Bodies in the World. Looking at the variables in the code, we can see that worldNodes maintains a reference to all WorldNodes in the application, world is a Phys2D World and maintains a reference to the bodies in each WorldNode, and group contains all WorldNodes in the scene. The function addWorldNode shows these relationships, as this method is how content is added to the application. Note that there is a reference to something called a Joint in the code, which will be described in a later example.

The function simpleBalls shows how addWorldNode is called, which produces a scene like the one in Figure 6-1.

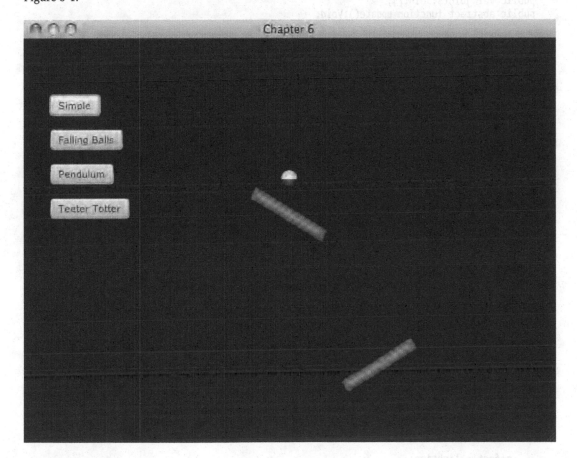

Figure 6-1. *One falling ball*

Figure 6-1 shows a ball that is above two walls. When the application is run, the ball will fall and bounce off the top wall first, then the bottom wall. To understand how this animation works, consider the variable worldUpdater in Main.fx. This variable is of type Timeline and is used to drive the animation; it does this by calling the function update 30 times a second. The function update does two things—first it asks the world object to advance the location of all of the bodies by one step, then it asks each WorldNode to update itself based on any changes to their associated bodies.

Listing 6-2 illustrates how bodies in the world drive nodes in the scene.

Listing 6-2. *WorldNode.fx*

```
public mixin class WorldNode {
    public var bodies:Body[];
    public var joints:Joint[];
    public abstract function update():Void;
}
```

Listing 6-3. *Ball.fx*

```
var lighting = Lighting {
    light: DistantLight { azimuth: -135 elevation: 85  }
    surfaceScale: 5
}
public class Ball extends Group, WorldNode{
    public var radius = 10.0;
    var arcs = Group{};

    init{
        var arc1 = Arc{
            radiusX: radius
            radiusY: radius
            startAngle: 0;
            length: 180
            fill: Color.WHITE
            }

        var arc2 = Arc{
            radiusX: radius
            radiusY: radius
            startAngle: 180;
            length: 180
            fill: Color.BLUE
            }

        insert arc2 into arcs.content;
        insert arc1 into arcs.content;

        effect = lighting;

        bodies[0] = new Body(new net.phys2d.raw.shapes.Circle(radius), radius);
        bodies[0].setPosition(translateX, translateY);
```

```
    bodies[0].setRestitution(1.0);
    bodies[0].setCanRest(true);
    bodies[0].setDamping(0.2);

    insert arcs into content;
  }
  public override function update():Void{
    translateX = bodies[0].getPosition().getX();
    translateY = bodies[0].getPosition().getY();
    arcs.rotate = Math.toDegrees(bodies[0].getRotation());
  }
}
```

Listing 6-4. *Wall.fx*

```
public class Wall extends Group, WorldNode{
  public var width:Number;
  public var height:Number;

  init{
    var rectangle = Rectangle{
      width: width;
      height: height;
      translateX: width/-2.0;
      translateY: height/-2.0;

      fill: Color.RED
    }
    effect = lighting;

    var shape = new net.phys2d.raw.shapes.Box(width,height);
    bodies[0] = new StaticBody(shape);
    bodies[0].setRotation(Math.toRadians(rotate));
    bodies[0].setPosition(translateX, translateY);
    bodies[0].setRestitution(0.5);

    insert rectangle into content;
  }
  public override function update():Void{
    //do nothing, walls don't move.
  }
}
```

The class Ball shown in Listing 6-3 implements the classes Group and WorldNode. In this way, instances of Ball will contain both the Phys2D representation and the JavaFX representation of a ball. (WorldNode is shown in Listing 6-2.) As you can see in the init function of Ball, two Arcs are used to represent a ball; we use two arcs of different color instead of a JavaFX Circle so rotation can be seen. A Body is also created with the shape of a circle, with the same radius as the two arcs. Phys2D has its own representation of shapes outside of JavaFX, so some work must be done to coordinate the two different APIs. The update method of Ball shows how the location of the Ball in the scene is updated based on the location of the Body. Remember that update is called each time step is called on the world, so the visual position of the Ball is updated with each step. The rotation of the node is similarly updated.

In the case of the class Ball, both the JavaFX representation of the two arcs and the Phys2D representation of a circle assume that the center of the circle is at the location (0,0). However, if we look at the Phys2D class Box and compare it to the JavaFX class Rectangle, we can see that the same assumption was not made. While Box is centered at (0,0), the class Rectangle assumes the upper left corner is at (0,0). So while the implementation of Wall shown in Listing 6-4 is similar to Ball, the location of the representing Rectangle must be shifted up and to the left in order to be displayed in the correct spot. Figure 6-2 shows the differences in the origins between Phys2D and JavaFX.

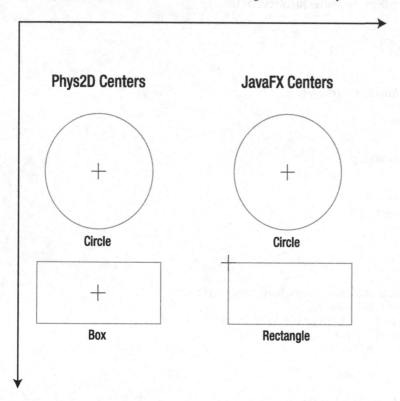

Figure 6-2. *Centers of different shapes in Phys2D (left) and JavaFX (right)*

Also note in the class Wall that a StaticBody was used, not a Body. A StaticBody is a special type of Body that does not move in the world. As a result, the update method of Wall does nothing, as it will never move. A later example will show how StaticBodies and Bodies can be mixed to create some interesting results.

Now that we know how this first simple example works, we can see how the function in Listing 6-5 can quickly create a more interesting effect.

Listing 6-5. *Main.fx (partial)*

```
function fallingBalls():Void{
    reset();

    addWorldNode(Ball{translateX: 128, translateY: 50});
    addWorldNode(Ball{translateX: 128+32*1, translateY: 50});
    addWorldNode(Ball{translateX: 128+32*2, translateY: 50});
    addWorldNode(Ball{translateX: 128+32*3, translateY: 50});
    addWorldNode(Ball{translateX: 128+32*4, translateY: 50});
    addWorldNode(Ball{translateX: 128+32*5, translateY: 50});
    addWorldNode(Ball{translateX: 128+32*6, translateY: 50});
    addWorldNode(Ball{translateX: 128+32*7, translateY: 50});
    addWorldNode(Ball{translateX: 128+32*8, translateY: 50});
    addWorldNode(Ball{translateX: 128+32*9, translateY: 50});
    addWorldNode(Ball{translateX: 128+32*10, translateY: 50});
    addWorldNode(Ball{translateX: 128+32*11, translateY: 50});
    addWorldNode(Ball{translateX: 128+32*12, translateY: 50});

    addWorldNode(Wall{width: 100, height: 16, translateY: 200, translateX: 128, rotate: 45});
    addWorldNode(Wall{width: 100, height: 16, translateY: 200, translateX: 128*2, rotate: -45});
    addWorldNode(Wall{width: 100, height: 16, translateY: 220, translateX: 128*3, rotate: 45});
    addWorldNode(Wall{width: 100, height: 16, translateY: 180, translateX: 128*4, rotate: -45});

    addWorldNode(Wall{width: 500, height: 16, translateY: 350, translateX: 350, rotate: -20});
}
```

The code in Listing 6-5 adds a number of balls to the scene, as well as a number of walls. Once this animation starts, it will look like the screenshot in Figure 6-3, in which a number of balls are falling onto walls placed about the scene. What starts out orderly quickly turns into a complex and dynamic animation.

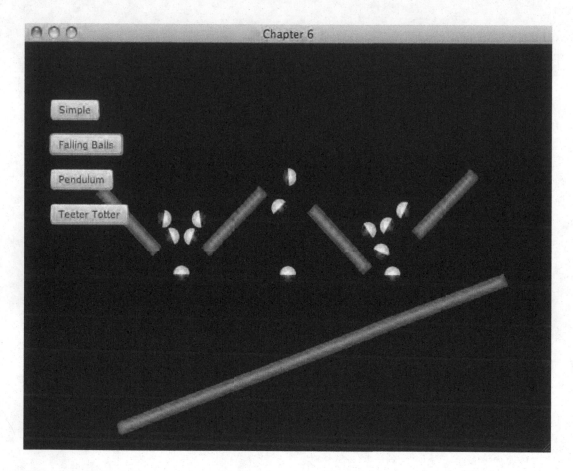

Figure 6-3. *Falling balls*

Pendulum Example

This example explores some addition features of Phys2D, such as the Joint class and how to combine Bodies with StaticBodies. The screenshot in Figure 6-4 shows a simulation of a popular toy. In the figure, a number of balls are suspended with equal length string. When one ball is raised and released, it swings down and collides with the other balls, causing the ball on the opposite side to be knocked upward while leaving the middle balls relatively still. When the newly raised ball falls, it knocks the original ball back up, and the action repeats until entropy and friction bring the entire system to a halt.

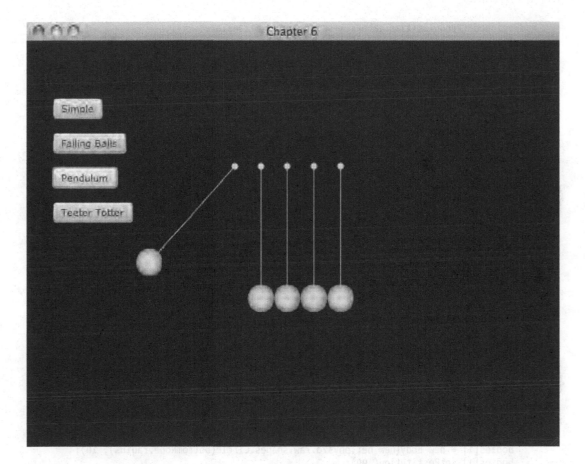

Figure 6-4. *Pendulum*

Using the framework from the first example, we can create this pendulum with the code in Listing 6-6.

Listing 6-6. *Main.fx*

```
function pendulum():Void{
    reset();

    var x = 250;
    var y = 140;
    var separation = 32;

    addWorldNode(Pendulum{translateX: x, translateY: y, angle: -70});
    addWorldNode(Pendulum{translateX: x+seperation*1, translateY: y});
    addWorldNode(Pendulum{translateX: x+seperation*2, translateY: y});
    addWorldNode(Pendulum{translateX: x+seperation*3, translateY: y});
```

```
        addWorldNode(Pendulum{translateX: x+seperation*4, translateY: y});
}
```

Listing 6-6 shows that adding the new nodes is pretty easy—you simply create each one and add it with the function addWorldNode. It is the implementations of the new class Pendulum that shows how the Bodies are created to behave like pendulums.

Listing 6-7. Pendulum.fx

```
public class Pendulum extends Group, WorldNode{

    public-init var distance = 150.0;
    public-init var angle = 0.0;

    var topNode = Circle{
        radius: 4
        fill: Color.AQUA;
    }
    var bottomNode = Circle{
        radius: 16
        fill: Color.SILVER;
        effect: lighting;
    }
    var shaft = Line{
        fill: Color.CORAL;
        stroke: Color.CORAL;
    }

    init{
        bodies[0] = new StaticBody( new net.phys2d.raw.shapes.Circle(topNode.radius));
        bodies[0].setPosition(translateX, translateY);
        bodies[1] = new Body(new net.phys2d.raw.shapes.Circle(bottomNode.radius), 10);
        bodies[1].setRestitution(.99);
        var a = Math.sqrt((distance*distance)/2.0);

        var x = Math.sin(Math.toRadians(angle))*distance;
        var y = Math.cos(Math.toRadians(angle))*distance;
        bodies[1].setPosition(translateX+x, translateY+y);

        joints[0] = new DistanceJoint(bodies[0], bodies[1], new Vector2f(0,0), new
Vector2f(0,0), distance);

        shaft.startX = bodies[0].getPosition().getX() - translateX;
        shaft.startY = bodies[0].getPosition().getY() - translateY;

        insert shaft into content;
        insert topNode into content;
        insert bottomNode into content;
        update();
    }
}
```

```
public override function update():Void{
    shaft.endX = bodies[1].getPosition().getX() - translateX;
    shaft.endY = bodies[1].getPosition().getY() - translateY;

    bottomNode.translateX = bodies[1].getPosition().getX() - translateX;
    bottomNode.translateY = bodies[1].getPosition().getY()  - translateY;
}
}
```

In the init method of the class Pendulum in Listing 6-7, two bodies are created. The first Body stored in bodies[0] is a StaticBody that defines the top, fixed circle. The second Body, stored in bodies[1] is the big ball at the bottom. Since the class Pendulum allows the caller to specify the distance between the top and bottom bodies and the starting angle for the bottom Body, a little math is required to find the starting position of the bottom Body, as shown in Figure 6-5.

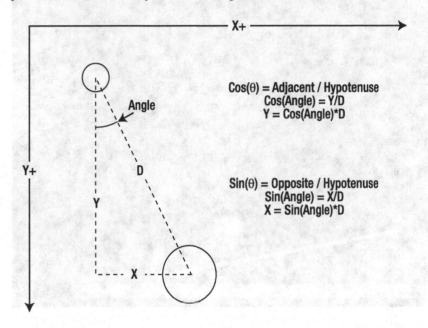

Figure 6-5. Starting positions

Here we introduce the concept of a Joint. A Joint in Phys2D is an object that defines a constraint between two Bodies. In this case, we want the two bodies to stay a particular distance from each other to simulate that the lower body is hung from the upper body by a string or wire. In this way, the lower Body will swing around the upper Body when it is pulled by gravity or impacted by another object.

There are three JavaFX Nodes that are used to draw each Pendulum, one for each body and a Line used to draw the connection between the two. The position of these Nodes is updated in much the same way as the other WorldBodies defined in this chapter—simply update the location for each step. For this class we are ignoring rotation.

Teeter Totter Example

The previous example used a StaticBody to "hang" a ball from a fixed point. In this example we will use a StaticBody to fix a rectangular Body in place to make a sort of Teeter Totter or lever.

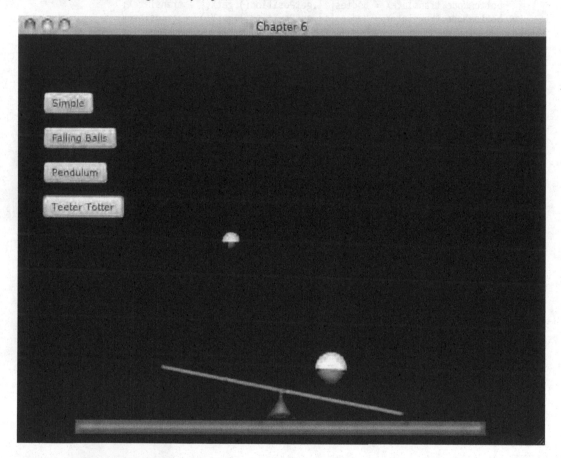

Figure 6-6. *Teeter Totter*

Figure 6-6 shows the scene, where the triangle at the bottom is the static body, holding the center of the long rectangle in place as two balls fall on the rectangle and make it move like a Teeter Totter. In this example the balls are randomly created, so this example is a little different than the other examples because every time it runs, something different happens. This demonstrates how a good physics engine can simplify life for the developer, since the animations simply work, regardless of the particulars in the scene.

Listing 6-8. Main.fx

```
function teetertotter ():Void{
    reset();

    addWorldNode(Ball{translateX: 320-20-random.nextInt(120), translateY:
10+random.nextInt(300), radius: 10+random.nextInt(10)});
    addWorldNode(Ball{translateX: 320+20+random.nextInt(120), translateY:
10+random.nextInt(300), radius: 10+random.nextInt(10)});

    addWorldNode(Wall{width: 500, height: 16, translateX: 320, translateY: 440});

    addWorldNode(TeeterTotter {translateX: 320, translateY: 400});
}
```

The function teetertotter in Listing 6-8 shows how the WorldNodes are added to the application. Again, the interesting part is in the implementation of the class TeeterTotter, shown in Listing 6-9.

Listing 6-9. TeeterTotter.fx

```
public class TeeterTotter extends Group, WorldNode{
    var barWidth = 300.0;
    var barHieght = 5.0;

    var crossbar = Rectangle{
        width: barWidth;
        height: barHieght;
        fill: Color.GREEN;
        arcWidth: 3
        arcHeight: 3
    }

    init{
        bodies[0] = new Body(new net.phys2d.raw.shapes.Box(barWidth,barHieght),50);
        bodies[0].setPosition(translateX, translateY);
        bodies[0].setRestitution(0.5);

        var points:Vector2f[];
        insert new Vector2f(0,0) into points;
        insert new Vector2f(20,30) into points;
        insert new Vector2f(-20,30) into points;

        bodies[1] = new StaticBody(new net.phys2d.raw.shapes.ConvexPolygon(points));
        bodies[1].setPosition(translateX, translateY);

        joints[0] = new DistanceJoint(bodies[0], bodies[1], new Vector2f(0,barHieght/2.0),
new Vector2f(0,0), 0);

        var fulcrum = javafx.scene.shape.Polygon{
```

```
        fill: Color.BLUE;
        translateX: bodies[1].getPosition().getX()-translateX;
        translateY: bodies[1].getPosition().getY()-translateY;
    }
    for (vector in points){
        insert vector.getX() into fulcrum.points;
        insert vector.getY() into fulcrum.points;
    }
    insert fulcrum into content;


    insert crossbar into content;

    effect = lighting;

    update();
}

public override function update():Void{
    crossbar.rotate = Math.toDegrees(bodies[0].getRotation());
    crossbar.translateX = (bodies[0].getPosition().getX() - barWidth/2.0) - translateX;
    crossbar.translateY = (bodies[0].getPosition().getY() - barHieght/2.0) - translateY;

    }
}
```

The init function in Listing 6-9 shows how the Bodies are constructed. The Body in bodies[0] is the 'board' of the teeter totter, which is composed of a simple box, much like the Wall class. The triangular fixed body acts as the fulcrum, and its shape is defined by specifying the points of triangle. The Node that represents the fulcrum in the scene is constructed by iterating over this list points, creating a JavaFX Polygon based on those points. Lastly, the update method makes sure to update the position and rotation of the crossbar as it moves.

Transition Example

Chapter 3 on transitions explored how to transition between two views; this chapter shows how to make realistic animations with JavaFX and the open source library Phys2D. Why not combine the two?

The code in this example takes a Group that contains a number of Control nodes and creates an animation that makes it appear as if the Controls are suddenly affected by gravity. In turn, each Control starts to fall, bouncing off the other Controls. The animation ends when all the Controls have fallen out of the original bounds of their container, then the second Group of Controls fades in.

You'll find this example in a different package from the rest of this chapter. I found trying to combine this transition example with the other examples created code that was not suitable for demonstration. Please find this code in the package org.lj.jfxe.chapter6.transition, and start the example by running the file TransitionExampleMain.

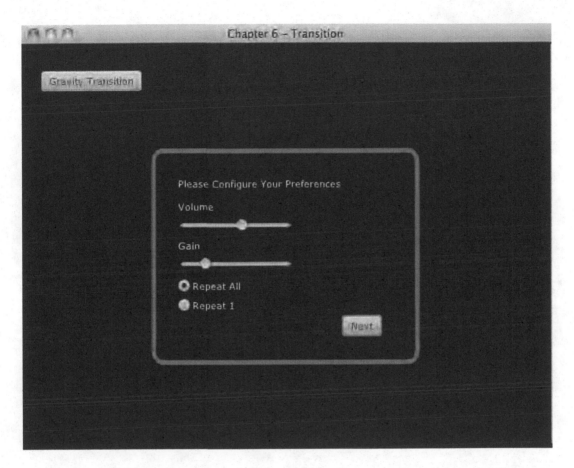

Figure 6-7. Controls before gravity

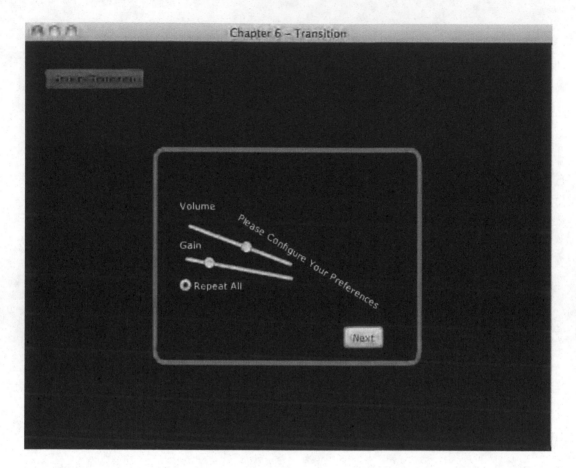

Figure 6-8. *Controls in the process of falling*

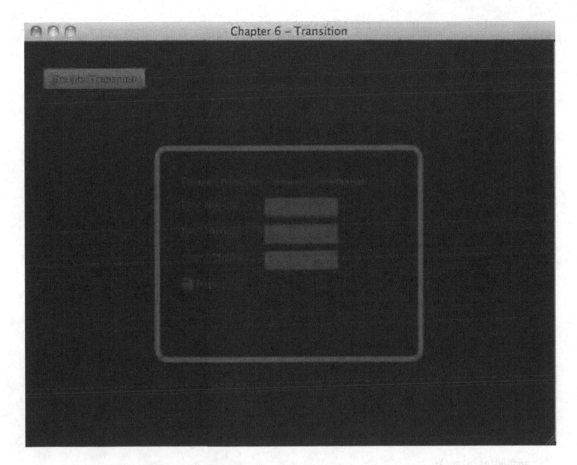

Figure 6-9. *Second set of controls fading in*

Figure 6-7 presents the controls before the transition starts; there are number of Controls contained in a rounded rectangle. Figure 6-8 displays the same controls falling as the force of gravity affects each one. Figure 6-9 shows the second group of controls fading in. The basic strategy is to identify all of the Controls and link their location to a Phys2D Body. As this Body's location is updated, the location of the Control is updated. The code in Listing 6-10 shows how this was implemented.

Listing 6-10. *TransitionExampleMain.fx (partial)*

```
public function
doReplace(nodeToReplace:Group,replacementNode:Group,doAfter:function()):Void{
    var handlers:ControlHandler[];
    var inactives:ControlHandler[];

    var initHeight = nodeToReplace.boundsInLocal.height;
```

```
var world = new World(new Vector2f(0,1200), 1);

for (node in nodeToReplace.content){
    if (node instanceof Control){
        var control:Control = node as Control;
        var handler = ControlHandler{
            control: control
        }
        insert handler into inactives;
        insert handler into handlers;
        world.add(handler.staticBody);
    }
}

inactives = Sequences.shuffle(inactives) as ControlHandler[];


var addBodies = Timeline{
    repeatCount: Timeline.INDEFINITE
    keyFrames: KeyFrame{
        time: .5s
        action: function(){
            if (sizeof inactives > 0){
                var handler = inactives[0];
                delete inactives[0];
                handler.isStatic = false;
                world.remove(handler.staticBody);
                world.add(handler.body);
            }
        }
    }
}

addBodies.play();

var worldUpdater = Timeline{
    repeatCount: Timeline.INDEFINITE
    keyFrames: KeyFrame{
        time: 1.0/30.0*1s
        action: function(){
            world.<<step>>();
            for (handler in handlers){
                handler.update();
            }

        }

    }
}

worldUpdater.play();
```

```
        var cleanup = Timeline{
                keyFrames: KeyFrame{
                    time: 1s
                    action: function(){
                        addBodies.stop();
                        worldUpdater.stop();
                        for (handler in handlers){
                            handler.control.translateX = handler.startingX;
                            handler.control.translateY = handler.startingY;
                            handler.control.rotate = handler.startingRot
                        }
                    }
                }
        }

        var checkCleanup:Timeline = Timeline{
            repeatCount: Timeline.INDEFINITE
            keyFrames: [
                    KeyFrame{
                        time: 1s
                        action: function(){
                            var stop = true;
                            for (handler in handlers){
                                if (handler.body.getPosition().getY() < initHeight){
                                    stop = false;
                                    break;
                                }
                            }
                            if (stop){
                                FadeReplace.doReplace(nodeToReplace, replacementNode, doAfter);
                                cleanup.playFromStart();
                                checkCleanup.stop();
                            }
                        }
                    }
            ]
        }
        checkCleanup.play();
}

class ControlHandler{
    var control:Control;
    var body:Body;
    var staticBody:StaticBody;

    var startingX:Number;
    var startingY:Number;
    var startingRot:Number;
```

133

```
    var isStatic = true;

    init{

        startingX = control.translateX;
        startingY = control.translateY;
        startingRot = control.rotate;

        var box = new net.phys2d.raw.shapes.Box(control.width, control.height);
        body = new Body(box, 10);
        body.setRestitution(.9);
        staticBody = new StaticBody(box);

        staticBody.setPosition(control.translateX + control.width/2.0, control.translateY +
control.height/2.0);
        body.setPosition(control.translateX + control.width/2.0, control.translateY +
control.height/2.0);
    }
    function update(){
        if (not isStatic){
            control.translateX = body.getPosition().getX() - control.width/2.0;
            control.translateY = body.getPosition().getY() - control.height/2.0;
            control.rotate = Math.toDegrees(body.getRotation());
        }
    }
}
```

Listing 6-10 shows a function named doReplace and a helper class called ControlHandler. The function doReplace follows the same pattern as the doReplace functions in the chapter on transitions. It takes two Nodes, in this case Groups, and a function named doAfter that is called when the transition is over.

The function doReplace looks through the contents of the Group nodeToReplace and finds all children that are of type Control. For each Control node found, a ControlHandler is created and added to the Sequence handlers and to the Sequence inactives. The idea here is that handlers will keep a reference to all Controls and Bodies in the animation. The Sequence inactives keeps track of which Controls have not yet started to fall. The staticBody of each handler is also added to the world. If you recall a World object is used to do the actual physics calculations, the staticBody is added at his point so that so that the first few falling bodies will have something to bounce off of.

The Sequence inactives is then shuffled so that the Controls will start to fall in a random order. In my testing I liked the randomness, but this line can easily be commented out to create a reproducible animation.

The Timeline addBodies is created and started; this Timeline pops ControlHandlers from the inactives and activates them. The process of activating a ControlHandler means that it should swap out its StaticBody for a Body. This makes the Control start to fall. The Timeline addBodies activates a new ControlHandler every .5 seconds, so that all of the Controls don't just start dropping all at once.

The Timeline worldUpdater is used to advance the location of each Body. This is basically identical to the Timeline used in this chapter to explore physics. The world object is stepped and each handler is updated. The update function takes the location and rotation of the body and applies it to the location and rotation of the Control Node.

Two more Timelines are created to help manage when the transition is done. The Timeline checkCleanup checks every second to see if all of the Controls have fallen below the original bottom bounds of the Group nodeToReplace. When all the Controls have fallen, the transition FadeReplace from the transitions chapter is used to fade in the replacementNode. Lastly, the Timeline cleanup is started and the Timeline checkCleanup is stopped.

The Timeline cleanup stops the Timeline addBodies and worldUpdater, then restores the location of the each Control as if nothing ever happened.

The class ControlHelper is basically an implementation of the class WorldNode taken from earlier in the chapter. It keeps track of a JavaFX node and two Physics Bodies. This implementation is different from the previous implementation as it switches from representing a StaticBody to a regular Body.

Further Considerations

Adding a physics engine to an application can save a lot of work for a developer creating animations that borrow from the physical world. The sense of weight and motion helps draw the eye, while animations that that fail to convince the user can be distracting. However, a physics engine is a general-purpose tool, and as such, it can be complicated both in implementation and in the amount of work needed to calculate each frame. Sometimes it is better to simply tweak more traditional animations until they look right, rather than trying to make them mathematically correct with a physics engine.

Remember that with a physics engine, the application must check to see if each body has collided with *every other* body in the world. This means that the cost of calculating collisions grows exponentially as bodies are added to the scene. Of course smart engines reduce this cost as best they can, but eventually there is no escaping the math as bodies are added. It is best to include only the objects in your calculations that might actually interact. If a component on the screen will never effect the animation, don't include it your physics calculations.

It is rare when a physics engine gets used outside of a game. It might be interesting, however, to produce some UI controls with physics elements, such as a progress bar that fills with balls and tips over when it is full.

Summary

This chapter looked at what a physics engine is and how you can use the open source engine Phys2D to add animations to an application. The examples showed how to use JavaFX to display the bodies within a simulation. Another example showed how to create a UI transition that took advantage of the physics engine to create a playful animation.

CHAPTER 7

■ ■ ■

Effect: Animated Image Sequences

Not all animations in an application are dynamic. It is often desirable to create the animations in a dedicated tool and then play the animation in the app. JavaFX has good support for video, for example, but sometimes video is too heavy of a solution. Or perhaps you want to have an animation sequence with partial transparency or be able to specify exactly which frames of the animation are visible when. In these cases, animating a sequence of image files can produce desirable results, and as a bonus, most animation software supports exporting image sequences directly.

This chapter discusses strategies for creating images and displaying the sequence as an animation in a JavaFX scene. By displaying one image at a time an animation will be created, much like an old film movie where each frame is a picture on the filmstrip. This will be implemented using a few core JavaFX classes, such as Image and ImageView. The number of images that can be used to create animations like this is surprisingly high, but some effort must be made to do this without ruining the performance of your application. But before we get to the code, let's first discuss how to create the images.

Creating Images

There are excellent tools available for creating animations, and you should feel free to use any tool you are comfortable with. Some are better suited for 2D animations, such as Adobe's After Effects, and other tools are better at 3D. For 3D I can't recommend Blender enough. The learning curve is amazingly steep, but after 20 hours or so you will find yourself able to create any shape you can think of. You will also find video tutorials for all animation tools online, and I find this a good way to learn. Conduct a web search for "Blender tutorial videos," take your pick from the results, and start following along. And check out the Blender web site at http://www.blender.org/education-help/, which contains documentation and videos to assist you.

Figure 7-1 shows a Blender project set up to create an animation. The plethora of buttons on the screen hints at Blender's power and learning curve.

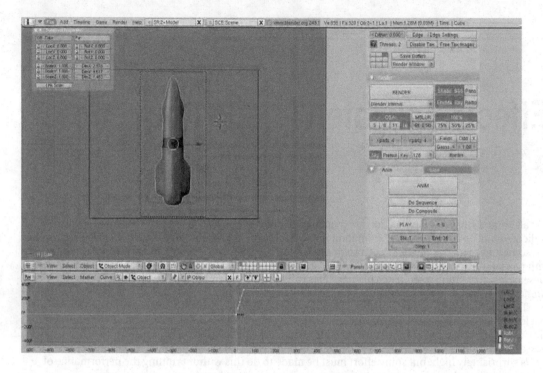

Figure 7-1. *Blender*

If you choose to explore Blender as a tool for creating content in your JavaFX scenes, remember that you can add as much detail as you want. You can also render the animation with the most time-consuming rendering options if you want. This is the real beauty of pre-rendering these animations: Once the work is committed to a sequence of images, it does not matter how complex your 3D scene is. All of that detail is presented to the user in a fluid animation.

If the JavaFX scene you are creating will contain multiple image sequences, then it is best to track how each item is lit. Combining content that looks 3D to the user will be confusing if one item seems to be lit from the left and another is lit from the right. An example of this can be seen in Figure 7-2.

Figure 7-2. *Multiple asteroids with consistent lighting*

Figure 7-2 shows four different asteroid sequences that are all animated with several light sources, but in the same location for each asteroid. This gives them a consistency within the scene. Note that the buildings at the bottom are also illuminated in a way consistent to each other. You can also see that the light on the asteroids might be coming slightly from the left, while on the buildings the light is coming from the right. This is inconsistent, but I think it is close enough for a $1 game.

One criterion for this exercise is that the animation tool must be able to export the frames of the animation as a sequence of images that JavaFX knows how to read. I find PNG files perfect for this task.

The demo code, shown later in the chapter, provides three examples of using images as frames in an animation; the screenshots in Figure 7-3 show each example with a gradient background to highlight the transparency.

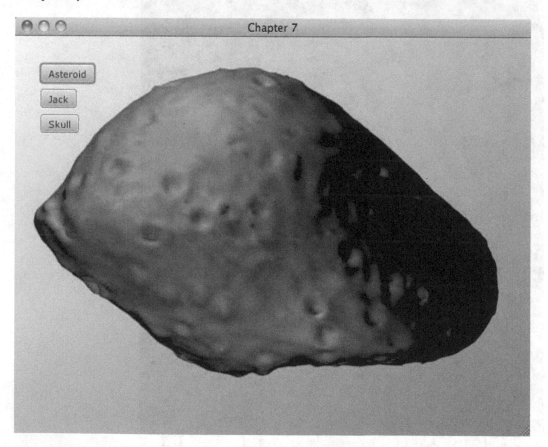

Figure 7-3. *Asteroid*

Figure 7-3 shows an asteroid that was created with Blender. When animated, the asteroid appears to be spinning.

Figure 7-4 shows a jack that I created to be a sort of space bomb in a video game I originally created for the iPhone.

140

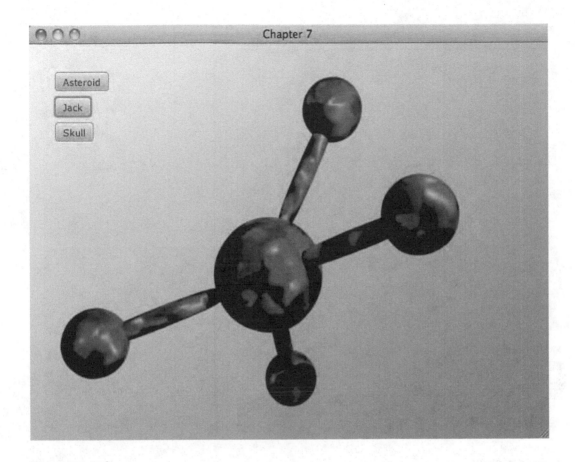

Figure 7-4. Jack

While porting the game to JavaFX, I decided to include it as an example in this book. The jack rotates on two axes, which makes it look like it is falling out of control in the game.

Figure 7-5 is an animation created with Adobe After Effects by my colleague Tim Wood. Tim is a professional designer, and it shows—I think his animation looks a lot more interesting than my examples.

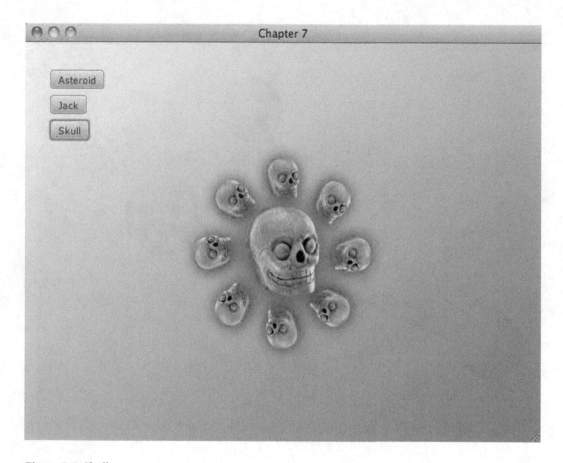

Figure 7-5. *Skulls*

When looking at the image sequence playing in the sample app, it is clear that there are a lot of subtle animations at play. While JavaFX possesses the ability to express this animation, the quick iterations of a dedicated tool make the production of animations much easier. With JavaFX you have to make a change to the code and recompile and run the application. With a dedicated tool, it is much easier to fuss with sliders until the animation is just right.

When creating these animations, it is important that the animation is a loop. That is to say, when the last image in the sequence is replaced with the first image, we want to avoid a visual jump.

Figure 7-6 shows the entire set of asteroid images, starting at the upper left and progressing to the right.

Figure 7-6. *Entire sequence*

As you see, there is only a minor variation between each frame, but there are enough frames to make it look like the asteroid is spinning around. Also note how similar the last asteroid is to the first. This creates animation that is not jerky when going from the last image to the first. But they are not identical either, as that would cause a quick but annoying pause in the animation.

Implementation

To animate a number of images they must first be loaded. It is important to load an image in an application only once, otherwise it is costly in memory and speed. The example code shows a simple way to ensure that images are loaded just one time. It also shows how the images can be loaded at the start of the app, which will remove any pauses later in the running of the app.

The second step is to cycle the images in the scene to create the frames of an animation. Listing 7-1 shows how these two steps—loading and cycling images—are achieved with the provided classes. Further listings will show the details of each class used in this example.

Listing 7-1. *Main.fx*

```
var sequenceView:ImageSequenceView;
var anim = Timeline{
        repeatCount: Timeline.INDEFINITE
        keyFrames: KeyFrame{
            time: 1.0/30.0*1s
            action: function(){
                sequenceView.currentImage++;
            }
        }
    }

function run():Void{
    var seq1 = MediaLoader.imageSequence("/org/lj/jfxe/chapter7/images/asteroidA_64_", 31,
true);
    var seq2 = MediaLoader.imageSequence("/org/lj/jfxe/chapter7/images/bomb-pur-64-", 61,
true);
    var seq3 = MediaLoader.imageSequence("/org/lj/jfxe/chapter7/images/Explosion01_", 35,
true);

    var asteroidButton = Button{
        text: "Asteroid"
        action: asteroid
```

```
            disable: true
    }
    var jackButton = Button{
        text: "Jack"
        action: jack
        disable: true
    }
    var skullButton = Button{
        text: "Skull"
        action: skull
        disable: true
    }
    var buttons = VBox{
        translateX: 32
        translateY: 32
        spacing: 6
        content: [asteroidButton,jackButton,skullButton]
    }
    var progressText = Label{
        text: "Loading Images..."
        translateX: 320
        translateY: 200
        scaleX: 2.0
        scaleY: 2.0
        width: 300
    }

    var stage = Stage {
        title: "Chapter 7"
        width: 640
        height: 480
        scene: Scene {
            fill: LinearGradient{
                    stops: [
                            Stop{
                                offset:0.0
                                color: Color.WHITESMOKE
                            },
                            Stop{
                                offset:1.0
                                color: Color.CHOCOLATE
                            },
                            ]
                        }
            content: bind [progressText, sequenceView, buttons]
        }
    }

    var checkProgress:Timeline = Timeline{
        repeatCount: Timeline.INDEFINITE;
        keyFrames: KeyFrame{
```

```
            time: .7s
            action:function(){
                var totalProgress = seq1.progress() + seq2.progress() + seq3.progress();
                if (totalProgress == 300.0){
                    checkProgress.stop();
                    progressText.text = "";
                    asteroidButton.disable = false;
                    jackButton.disable = false;
                    skullButton.disable = false;
                } else {
                    var progress:Integer = Math.round(totalProgress/300.0*100);
                    progressText.text = "Loading Images...{progress}%";
                }
            }
        }
    }
    checkProgress.play();


}

function asteroid():Void{
    sequenceView = ImageSequenceView{
        translateX: 640/2
        translateY: 480/2
        imageSequence:
MediaLoader.imageSequence("/org/lj/jfxe/chapter7/images/asteroidA_64_", 31, false)
    }
    anim.play();
}
function jack():Void{
    sequenceView = ImageSequenceView{
        translateX: 640/2
        translateY: 480/2
        imageSequence: MediaLoader.imageSequence("/org/lj/jfxe/chapter7/images/bomb-pur-64-
", 63, false)
    }
    anim.play();
}
function skull():Void{
    sequenceView = ImageSequenceView{
        translateX: 640/2
        translateY: 480/2
        imageSequence:
MediaLoader.imageSequence("/org/lj/jfxe/chapter7/images/Explosion01_", 35, false)
    }
    anim.play();
}
```

In Listing 7-1 the main function builds the scene. A couple of buttons are added and an ImageSequenceView called sequenceView is added. There is also a Label used to tell the user that the application is initializing. At the beginning of the function main, three variables called seq1, seq2, and seq3 are created. Each of these three variables holds an ImageSequence created by a call to MediaLoader.imageSequence.

MediaLoader is a class that is used to manage different types of media in an application. The function imageSequence takes a path, a count, and a flag specifying if the function should return before all of the images are loaded. Passing true to the function imageSequence tells the MediaLoader to not wait for all of the images to load. Having the first calls to imageSequence return immediately allows us to set up the scene without waiting for a background thread to load all of the images. This improves the user experience, as the window pops up much sooner.

Since the three ImageSequences are not fully loaded when the application starts, we want to let the user know that the application is loading and give her some sense of progress. The Timeline named checkProgress is used to check if the ImageSequences are fully loaded by checking the progress of each ImageSequence every .7 seconds. If they are not loaded, the Label progressText is updated to let the user know the current progress. If all of the ImageSequences are loaded, then the three buttons are enabled. The Timeline checkProgress knows that the ImageSequences are loaded if the sum of their progress is 300 percent—that's 100 percent per sequence.

Once the buttons are enabled, they can be pressed. Pressing each button sets a different ImageSequenceView to be displayed in the scene. For example, in Listing 7-1 the function asteroid creates a new ImageSequenceView and makes sure the Timeline anim is started. You should note that each of these functions creates a new ImageSequenceView, but its imageSequence attribute is set by a call to MediaLoader. This is done to illustrate a helpful pattern. Since we know MediaLoader will only load a particular ImageSequence once, and if we rely on MediaLoader to always get an ImageSequence, then we know for sure that our application is only loading each ImageSequence once. Granted, in such a simple application this is not really required, but in more complex applications it is very useful.

Before we explore how the ImageSequence and ImageSequenceView classes are implemented, let's explore in more detail the class MediaLoader.

Listing 7-2. MediaLoader

```
def instance:MediaLoader = MediaLoader{};

public function image(classpath:String, background:Boolean):Image{
    instance.getImage(classpath, background);
}

public function imageSequence(classpathBase:String,imageCount:Integer,
background:Boolean):ImageSequence{
    return instance.getImageSequence(classpathBase, imageCount, background);
}

public class MediaLoader {
    var imageMap:Map = new HashMap();
    var sequenceMap:Map = new HashMap();

    public function getImage(classpath:String, background:Boolean):Image{
        var image:Image = imageMap.get(classpath) as Image;
        if (image == null){
            image = Image{
                url: this.getClass().getResource(classpath).toString();
                smooth: true
```

```
            backgroundLoading: background;
        }
        imageMap.put(classpath, image);
    }
    if (image == null){
        println("WARNING: image not found at: {classpath}");
    }

    return image;
}

public function getImageSequence(classpathBase:String,imageCount:Integer,
background:Boolean):ImageSequence{
    var key = "{classpathBase}{imageCount}";
    var sequence:ImageSequence = sequenceMap.get(key) as ImageSequence;

    if (sequence == null){
        sequence = ImageSequence{
            classpathBase:classpathBase
            imageCount:imageCount
            backgroundLoading: background;
        };
        sequenceMap.put(key, sequence);
    }

    return sequence;
}
}
```

In Listing 7-2 we can see on the first line that an instance of MediaLoader is created. This will be the instance used by all subsequent calls to the static functions defined in this class. The static methods image and imageSequence call getImage and getImageSequence on the default MediaLoader respectively. The function image takes two arguments: The first is the path to the image file with the jar, and the second indicates if the image should be loaded in the background. If the parameter background is true, then function getImage will return before the Image is fully loaded. Figure 7-7 shows the path of the application NetBeans.

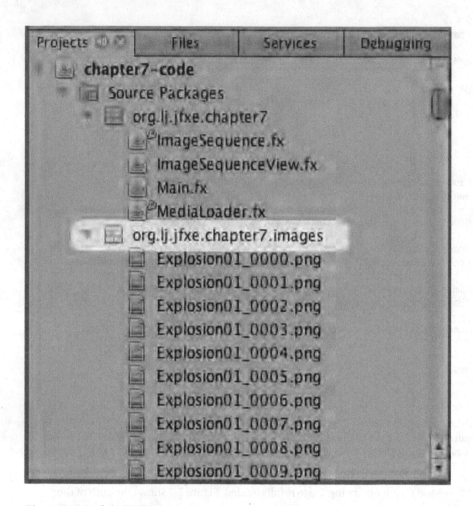

Figure 7-7. *Path in NetBeans*

To load the Image, the function getImage first checks a local Map named imageMap to see if the image was loaded in the past. If the Image was loaded, it is simply returned. If the Image was not loaded, a new Image is created based on the values passed into the function and stored in the Map imageMap before it is returned.

The pattern of loading items only once as seen in the function getImage is used again in the function getImageSequence. It first checks to see if an appropriate ImageSequence was created and hence stored in the Map sequenceMap. If the ImageSequence was already loaded, it is then returned. If it was not previously created, a new ImageSequence map is created, stored, and returned.

When this pattern is implemented in Java, care must be taken to make sure that two threads don't ask for the same resource in such a way as to cause the image to be loaded twice. With JavaFX this is not strictly required, as the JavaFX event thread is effectively single threaded—though it should be noted that someone could write a Java method that could access the MediaLoader in a multi-threaded way. But as long as you only call these methods from JavaFX, you will be OK.

Ultimately MediaLoader allows this application to load Images and ImageSequences, which are used by ImageSequenceViews to animate a number of images in the scene. Let's look at ImageSequence found in Listing 7-3 and see how it is implemented.

Listing 7-3. *ImageSequence*

```
public class ImageSequence {
    public-init var classpathBase:String;
    public-init var imageCount:Integer;
    public-init var backgroundLoading:Boolean = false;

    public var images:Image[];

    init{
        for (i in [1..imageCount]){
            var classpath = "{classpathBase}{numberToString(i)}.png";
            insert MediaLoader.image(classpath, backgroundLoading) into images;
        }
    }

    function numberToString(i:Integer):String{
        if (i < 10){
            return "000{i}";
        } else if (i < 100){
            return "00{i}";
        } else if (i < 1000){
            return "0{i}"
        }
        return "{i}"
    }

    public function progress():Number{
        var totalProgress = 0.0;
        for (i in [0..sizeof(images)]){
            totalProgress += images[i].progress;
        }
        return totalProgress/sizeof(images);
    }
}
```

In Listing 7-3 we see that ImageSequence basically holds a JavaFX sequence of Images called images plus some details about the Images stored in the variables classpath, imageCount, and backgroundLoading. In the init function of the class ImageSequence, each Image is loaded and inserted into the sequence images. Note that ImageSequence used MediaLoader to load each Image, which ensures that even images that might be stored in another ImageSequence are loaded only once.

The function numberToString is used to format a number by padding it with the correct number of zeros. This is somewhat arbitrary, as Blender names the files with four digits by default. Other tools will export images with different formatting, so it might be necessary to either rename all of the files or change how this function works.

The last function in Listing 7-3 is called progress and is used to calculate the total progress of each Image in this ImageSequence. The progress of an image refers to how far along it is in its loading. For an Image, a progress of 0.0 means it is not loaded, and a progress of 100.0 means it is loaded and ready to be displayed. I think that the values should have ranged from 0.0 to 1.0, as that would be more consistent with the rest of the JavaFX API. But since it is out of my power to change this, I decided to make the progress function on ImageSequence consistent with that pattern. It returns a value with the range 0.0 to 100.0—just like Image. Taking advantage of the progress function enabled the Timeline checkProgress from Listing 7-2 to indicate the percentage of images that were loaded.

The last class to look at is ImageSequenceView, which is used to actually put the images on the screen. Listing 7-4 shows the details.

Listing 7-4. *ImageSequenceView*

```
public class ImageSequenceView extends Group{
    public-init var imageSequence:ImageSequence;
    public var currentImage:Integer on replace {
        updateImage()
    }

    var lastImage:Integer = 0;
    init{

        for (i in [0..imageSequence.imageCount-1]){
            var image = imageSequence.images[i];

            var imageView = ImageView{
                image: image;
                translateX: image.width/-2.0
                translateY: image.height/-2.0
                visible: false;
            }

            insert imageView into content;
        }
        currentImage = 0;
        updateImage();
    }

    function updateImage():Void{
        currentImage = currentImage mod imageSequence.imageCount;

        content[lastImage].visible = false;
        var currentImageView = content[currentImage];

        currentImageView.visible = true;

        lastImage = currentImage;
    }
}
```

In Listing 7-4 we see that `ImageSequenceView` extends `Group`, and it takes a single `imageSequence` when created. The `init` function creates an `ImageView` for each `Image` in the `ImageSequence`. Each `ImageView` is translated so its center is at 0.0 of the `ImageSequenceView` and set to be invisible. The `ImageViews` are centered for two reasons: First, I used this class in a game, and knowing the center is more convenient in terms of game logic. Second, if the `Images` are not all the same size, I want them aligned by their centers. The `ImageViews` are set to invisible (`visible: false`) because only one image will be visible at a time, so it makes sense to start them all invisible. Each `ImageView` is then inserted into the `content` of the `ImageSequenceView`.

The last thing `init` does is call the function `updateImage`. Note that `updateImage` is also called when the variable `currentImage` is changed. The function `updateImage` coordinates which `ImageView` in the content is visible. This is done by finding the last `ImageView` that was visible, setting it to invisible, and then setting the `ImageView` at the index of `currentImage` to visible.

Figure 7-8 shows a graph diagram for an `ImageSequenceView`.

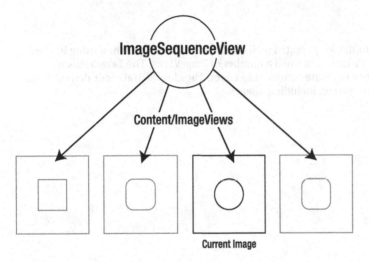

Figure 7-8. *Node graph of an ImageSequenceView*

The circle is the `ImageSequenceView` itself. The big squares are the `ImageViews` that are contained in the content of the `ImageSequenceView`, which extends `Group`. The third big square from the left, shown in a darker color, is the currently displayed `ImageView`.

Further Considerations

In this chapter, `ImageSequenceViews` are used to represent cyclical animations, but this is not their only function. They could also be used to store all of the different images that comprise a sprite in a game, for example. Consider a character from a side-scrolling game: The character will require five or six images to represent the sprite when it is walking, at least one to represent it when it is just standing still, and perhaps three or four more for each action it performs. An `ImageSequenceView` could be used to store all of these images, and changing how the sprite looks would be as simple as setting `currentImage` to the correct value.

The ImageSequenceViews in this chapter store a large number of images to create complex animations. If you have created a compelling animation with only a few frames, the techniques presented can still be used.

When using many ImageSequenceViews with large images, it would be best to spend some time tuning the Java Virtual Machine (JVM) that is running your application. JavaFX, like any Java process, has a large number of options that can be set at a JVM level. Probably the biggest concerns will be running out of memory and the startup time of the app. The option -Xmx can be used to increase the amount of available RAM, and the option -Xms can be used to specify how much RAM the JVM starts with. Increasing the value of -Xms decreases startup time since it reduces how often the JVM has to claim more memory, which takes a little time. I recommend figuring out how much memory your application needs and setting -Xmx and -Xms to the same value. In this way your application will never run out of memory and will never have to waste time growing its memory size.

Summary

This chapter showed how to bring animations created with other tools into JavaFX when using Images. The effect was created using a Group, which contained a number of ImageViews. The ImageViews were made visible and invisible in sequence to create a movie-like effect. The class MediaLoader demonstrated a method for managing numerous resources, including images.

CHAPTER 8

■ ■ ■

Effect: Animated Gradients

Colors are obviously a key component of any graphical application. Modern monitors are able to display millions of colors, and the designers of software have taken advantage of that. One important aspect of colors within an application is how they blend together, and a number of graphical libraries provide a mechanism to display the many grades of colors between any two colors. In general, this feature is called a gradient. Gradients can be used to create remarkable subtlety, be it the shine of a button or a slight sense of depth. While displaying solid colors or gradients is an excellent first step, some remarkable things can happen when these components are animated.

This chapter explores the basics of colors and gradients in JavaFX and how to animate them.

The Basics

To set the color of any of the shape nodes in JavaFX, you set the property fill with a Paint object. This can be surprising to developers new to graphics, as it is not exactly obvious why the property is called fill and why the value being set to is of type Paint. First, shapes actually have two different parts that can have color, so it would be confusing to simply have one property called color. The parts are the fill and the stroke. The fill is the area inside the shape, and the stroke is the line that defines the shape. For example, if you draw a rectangle on a piece of paper with a pencil, the stroke is the pencil line, while the color of the paper is the fill.

The other question—why the two properties fill and stroke are of type Paint and not simply Color—can be answered by looking at the classes that extend Paint. These are the classes Color, LinearGradient, and RadialGradient. Let's take a quick look at each class.

Paint Types

Included here are the current types of Paint available in JavaFX. It would seem logical that in the future there may be more, such as those that mimic physical brushes, give texture to a shape, or any number of possibilities.

153

Color

The class Color is a simple class that allows colors to be described as values of red, green, and blue, plus opacity. This is a standard way to represent color in software and not much of a surprise. It is worth noting that the range for each value is from 0.0 to 1.0.

Color also has a number of static Colors that can be easily referenced, such as Color.ANTIQUEWHITE and standard colors including RED, BLUE, GREEN, and YELLOW.

The class Color also comes with several static utility functions that can be used to create Colors from other methods of representing color. For example, the function Color.hsb can be used to specify a color in terms of hue, saturation, and brightness. There is also the function Color.web, which can be used to construct a Color from a String representation commonly used in cascading style sheets (CSS). For example, calling Color.web("#FF0000") will return a Color object that represents red. Most of these utility functions include a second form where you also specify the opacity of the color.

Linear Gradient

The class LinearGradient is used to describe the transition between two or more Colors across a section of the scene. Imagine a rainbow created by a prism—there are parts that are clearly red and yellow, but there are also colors in-between that are orangey. This is basically how a LinearGradient works: It specifies a number of points along the gradient and says this one is red, and here is yellow, and this states that the space between those points will be an interpolation of those two colors.

Figure 8-1 shows a rainbow-like pattern in grey scale on a number line going from 0.0 to 1.0, plus a number of points that define where the gradient should be a specific color.

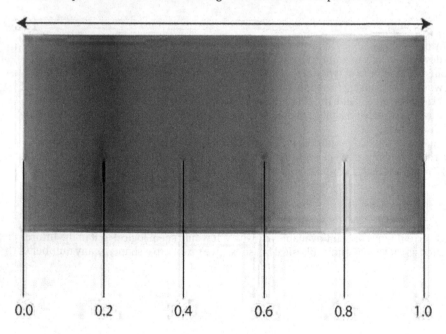

Figure 8-1. *Rainbow-like pattern as a LinearGradient*

LinearGradients store this information in a Sequence called stops, which is composed of objects of type Stop. A Stop is a very simple class; it is composed of an offset and a color and corresponds to the vertical black lines from Figure 8-1.

RadialGradient

RadialGradients work just like LinearGradients, but create a circular pattern. It is as if a line with a linear gradient was rotated around one of its ends. So when specifying the Stops for a linear gradient, the Stop at offset 0.0 is the center of the circle, and the stop at offset 1.0 is the outside of the circle.

Proportional

Each type of gradient works in two different modes. Setting the property proportional on either a LinearGradient or a RadialGradient will toggle the two modes. When proportional is set to false, a region of the shape is specified where the gradient will be drawn. And when proportional is set to true, the gradient is applied to the entire shape. Let's examine the case when proportional is set to false first.

LinearGradient has a set of four coordinate properties—startX, startY, endX, and endY—that are used to describe the region where the gradient should be drawn. Since the region defined by the coordinate properties might be smaller than the shape, there are three ways to color the regions outside of the coordinates. The regions outside of the coordinates will either be the color of the first or last stop depending on the side, simply colored as if the gradient repeated, or colored as if a mirror image of the gradient were applied. These options are controlled by the property cycleMethod.

RadialGradient works similarly to LinearGradient except that a set of coordinates is not used to describe the region drawn by the gradient. The properties radius, centerX, and centerY are used to define a circular region where one cycle of the gradient is drawn. Again, specifying the cycleMethod will dictate what is drawn outside of this region.

When proportional is set to true, JavaFX tries to apply the gradient to the entire shape. For example, a rectangle with a LinearGradient applied to it will be drawn so that the upper left corner is the color at offset 0.0 and the lower right color is that at offset 1.0 as defined by the steps. The properties startX, startY, endX, and endY can be set, but only specify the direction of the gradient. With a RadialGradient, the radius has no effect. However, the centerX and centerY can still be specified to move the center of radial effect.

Figure 8-2 shows four examples of gradients.

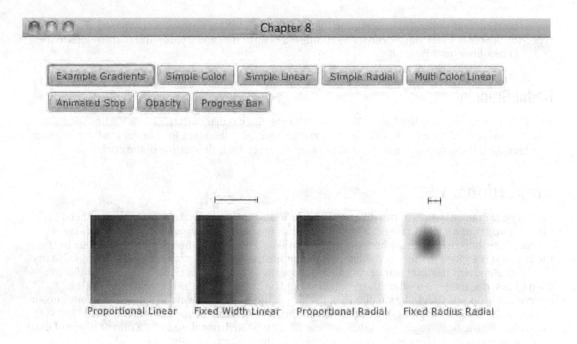

Figure 8-2. *Gradient examples*

Looking at the Proportional Linear example we can see that the gradient spans the entire square. This is compared to the Fixed Width Linear example, which only draws the gradient within the region specified. The two radial examples work in the same way—the proportional draws the gradient over the entire square, while the fixed one is confined to the radius of the circle specified. Listing 8-1 shows the code that created the examples.

Listing 8-1. *Main.fx (partial)*

```
function example():Void{
    delete group.content;
    var rect1 = Rectangle{
        width: 100
        height: 100
        fill: LinearGradient{
```

```
                proportional: true
                stops: [
                        Stop{
                            offset: 0.0
                            color: Color.BLUE
                        },
                        Stop{
                            offset: 1.0
                            color: Color.YELLOW
                        },
                ]
        }
}
var v1 = VBox{
    nodeHPos: HPos.CENTER
    content: [rect1, Label{text:"Proportional Linear"}]
}
var rect2 = Rectangle{
    width: 100
    height: 100
    fill: LinearGradient{
        proportional: false
        startX: 20
        endX: 80
        startY: 0
        endY: 0
        stops: [
                Stop{
                    offset: 0.0
                    color: Color.BLUE
                },
                Stop{
                    offset: 1.0
                    color: Color.YELLOW
                },
        ]
    }
}
var v2 = VBox{
    nodeHPos: HPos.CENTER
    content: [rect2, Label{text:"Fixed Width Linear"}]
}
var rect3 = Rectangle{
    width: 100
    height: 100
    fill: RadialGradient{
        proportional: true
        stops: [
                Stop{
                    offset: 0.0
                    color: Color.BLUE
```

```
                },
                Stop{
                    offset: 1.0
                    color: Color.YELLOW
                },
            ]
        }
    }
    var v3 = VBox{
        content: [rect3, Label{text:"Proportional Radial"}]
    }
    var rect4 = Rectangle{
        width: 100
        height: 100
        fill: RadialGradient{
            proportional: false
            radius: 20
            centerX: 30
            centerY: 30
            stops: [
                Stop{
                    offset: 0.0
                    color: Color.BLUE
                },
                Stop{
                    offset: 1.0
                    color: Color.YELLOW
                },
            ]
        }
    }
    var v4 = VBox{
        content: [rect4, Label{text:"Fixed Radius Radial"}]
    }
    var hbox = HBox{
        spacing: 20
        translateX: 80
        translateY: 200
        content: [v1,v2,v3,v4]
    }
    insert hbox into group.content;
}
```

In Listing 8-1 there are three rectangles created, each with a different fill applied. The rectangle rect1 has a proportional LinearGradient applied and only the most basic information is required—just two stop values. This causes the entire rectangle to have a gradient on it. When the non-proportional LinearGradient is applied to rect2, a region is specified where the gradient is drawn. The RadialGradients work in the same way.

Animations

Now that you've seen the basics of how gradients are created and applied to shapes, it is time to animate them. At first glance it would seem that you would animate colors and gradients the same way as the locations of Nodes. In some ways that is true—the Timeline API can be used to transition from one color to another. However, to achieve a higher level of control over the animations, a few tricks are required because it is impossible to create a Paint object with its properties bound to another value. I don't know if this was implemented in this way for technical reasons or if it was a simple oversight in a young technology.

All of the animation examples use a trick where the fill property of a Shape is bound to a function that creates a new Paint. The parameters to that function are then adjusted by a Timeline to produce the animation. I have no doubt that this is inefficient, but the current limitations of JavaFX require us to implement the code in this way. If you are planning on using lots of animated gradients in your application, I would recommend doing a little performance testing before you get too far along on your design. If you are just going to use a few gradients in your application, the technique presented will not be a performance issue.

Simple Color Example

This example looks at the basics of animating a Paint, in this case just a simple color. The goal here is to look at the technique that enables this to work. Listing 8-2 shows a simple rectangle with a color animation.

Listing 8-2. Animated Color

```
function simpleColor():Void{
    delete group.content;
    var red = 0.0;
    var rect = Rectangle{
        translateX: 640/2-100
        translateY: 480/2-100
        width: 200
        height: 200
        fill: bind createColor(red,1.0,0,1.0)
    }
    insert rect into group.content;
    var anim = Timeline{
            repeatCount: Timeline.INDEFINITE;
            autoReverse: true;
            keyFrames: KeyFrame{
            time: 2s
            values: red => 1.0;
        }
    }
    anim.play();
}
```

In Listing 8-2, the Rectangle named rect is created with its fill property bound to a function called createColor, which is passed to a variable named red and some constant values. The variable red is a Number that is modified by the Timeline named anim. The magic is in the function createColor, as shown in Listing 8-3.

Listing 8-3. *createColor*

```
function createColor(red:Number,green:Number,blue:Number,opacity:Number){
    return Color{
        red: zeroToOne(red)
        green: zeroToOne(green)
        blue: zeroToOne(blue)
        opacity: zeroToOne(opacity)
    }
}
```

In Listing 8-3, the function createColor simply takes the values passed in and creates a new color. The function zeroToOne is a utility function that forces the values to be in the range 0.0 to 1.0. Color will throw an exception if a value is outside of this range. However, I find it a useful technique with animations, as it allows values outside of the legal range to be "modded" into the correct range. Listing 8-4 shows the function zeroToOne.

Listing 8-4. *zeroToOne*

```
public function zeroToOne(number:Number):Number{
    if (number > 1.0){
        var whole:Integer = Math.round(Math.floor(number));
        return number - whole;
    } else if (number < 0.0){
        var whole:Integer = Math.round(Math.floor(number));
        return (number - whole) + 1;
    } else {
        return number;
    }
}
```

The function zeroToOne takes a number and checks if it is geater than 1.0. If it is, it returns just the fractional part of the number. If the number is less than 0.0, then the fractional part plus one is returned. Thus given an input of -1.8, we would take the fractional part (-0.8) and add 1.0 to it, yielding 0.2. If the number is neither greater than 1.0 nor less than 0.0, it is simply returned.

This example shows the basic technique of binding to a function in order to create a new object. The next examples will expand on this technique so it can be used with the two types of gradients.

Simple Linear Gradient

The animations are a little more exciting with the gradients. This example looks at how a LinearGradient can be animated using the same technique as in Listing 8-4. In this case, however, the function that is bound creates a LinearGradient instead of a Color.

Figure 8-3 shows a LinearGradient in two steps of an animation.

Figure 8-3. *Simple linear*

Note how only one end of the rectangle changes. This is because only one of the two Stops is being changed by the animation. Listing 8-5 shows how this is implemented.

Listing 8-5. *simpleLinear*

```
function simpleLinear():Void{
    delete group.content;

    var red = 0.0;

    var rect = Rectangle{
        translateX: 640/2-350/2;
        translateY: 400/2-50
        width: 350
        height: 50
        fill: bind createLinearGradient([
                Stop{color:Color.BLUE, offset:0.0},
                createStop(createColor(red, 0, 0, 1.0), 1.0)
                ]);
    }
    insert rect into group.content;
```

```
var anim = Timeline{
        repeatCount: Timeline.INDEFINITE;
        autoReverse: true;
        keyFrames: KeyFrame{
        time: 2s
        values: red => 1.0;
    }
}

anim.play();
}
```

Listing 8-5 shows a Rectangle that has its fill property bound to the function createLinearGradient, which is a sequence of Stops. The sequence of Stops is composed of a Stop at offset 0.0 and the color Color.BLUE and a second stop defined by the function createStop. The function createStop takes a color and an offset. In this case the Color passed to createStop is also defined by the function createColor, as shown in Listing 8-3. Since LinearGradient, Stop, and Color are immutable classes, these helper functions must be created to allow us to make new ones during the course of the animation. Listing 8-6 shows the function createStop, and Listing 8-7 shows the function createLinearGradient.

Listing 8-6. *createStop*

```
public function createStop(color:Color,offset:Number):Stop{
    return Stop{
        color: color;
        offset: zeroToOne(offset)
    }
}
```

In Listing 8-6 we see that the function createStop simply creates a new Stop from the parameters passed in. Again, the function zeroToOne from Listing 8-4 is used to normalize the offset.

Listing 8-7. *createLinearGradient+*

```
public function createLinearGradient(stops:Stop[]):LinearGradient{
    return LinearGradient{
        startX: 0
        endX: 1
        startY: 0
        endY: 0
        proportional: true
        stops: sortStops(stops);
    }
}
```

Listing 8-7 shows the function createLinearGradient, which creates a LinearGradient from the Stops passed in. The Stops are first sorted to make sure they are in the correct order. When defining an animation where the offset values can change, it is good to know they will be sorted before being used to create a new LinearGradient, as LinearGradient will throw an exception if the Stops are in the wrong order. Listing 8-8 shows the function sortStops. It should also be noted that the LinearGradient created has proportional set to true, making it quick to show the gradient for example purposes. A later example will use a LinearGradient with proportional set to false. This is often desirable, as it allows you to specify exactly which part of the shape has the gradient applied to it.

Listing 8-8. *sortStops*

```
public function sortStops(stops:Stop[]):Stop[]{
    var result:Stop[] = Sequences.sort(stops, Comparator{
        public override function compare(obj1:Object, obj2: Object):Integer{

            var stop1 = (obj1 as Stop);
            var stop2 = (obj2 as Stop);

            if (stop1.offset > stop2.offset){
                return 1;
            } else if (stop1.offset < stop2.offset){
                return -1;
            } else {
                return 0;
            }
        }
    }) as Stop[];

    return result
}
```

Listing 8-8 shows the function sortStops, which takes a sequence of stops and returns a sorted Sequence. To sort the Sequence, a Comparator is passed to the static function Sequences.sort. The Comparator simply compares the offset of the two Stops and returns an Integer value indicating if the first Stop is greater than, equal to, or less than the second Stop. If you are familiar with the Java Collections API you will recognize this pattern, as the class Sequences is an analog of the class Collections.

Simple Radial

Animating a RadialGradient is similar to animating a LinearGradient. The differences are minor, but worth exploring for completeness and to bring home how bind, combined with a function, is used to create these effects.

Figure 8-4 shows two phases of an animation of a RadialGradient, with the Stop at 0.0 being changed from black to yellow.

Figure 8-4. *Animated radial gradient*

Listing 8-9 shows how this is implemented.

Listing 8-9. *simpleRadial*

```
function simpleRadial():Void{
    delete group.content;
    var colorValue = 0.0;
    var rect = Rectangle{
        translateX: 640/2-100
        translateY: 480/2-100
        width: 200
        height: 200
        fill: bind createRadialGradient(0.5,0.5,[
                createStop(animateColor(colorValue, colorValue, 0, 1.0), 0.0),
                Stop{color:Color.BLUE, offset:1.0}
                ]);
    }
    insert rect into group.content;
    var anim = Timeline{
            repeatCount: Timeline.INDEFINITE;
            autoReverse: true;
            keyFrames: KeyFrame{
            time: 2s
            values: colorValue => 1.0;
        }
    }
```

```
    anim.play();
}
```

Listing 8-9 shows a Rectangle with its fill value bound to the function createRadialGradient, which takes a Sequence of Stops. The first stop is defined by the function createStop from Listing 8-6. In turn, createStop is taking a Color defined by the function createColor, which is defined in Listing 8-7. The interesting thing here is the function createRadialGradient shown in Listing 8-10.

Listing 8-10. *createRadialGradient*

```
public function createRadialGradient(centerX:Number, centerY:Number,
stops:Stop[]):RadialGradient{
    return RadialGradient{
        centerX: centerX
        centerY: centerY
        stops: sortStops(stops)
    }
}
```

Listing 8-10 shows the function createRadialGradient, which takes the location of the center as the two arguments centerX and centerY. The last argument is a sequence of Stops called stops that are sorted before being used to create a new RadialGradient.

Multi-Colored Linear

Up to this point only the red portion of a single Color was being changed to create the animations. The following example fleshes out how colors can be animated by using several different values animated by a more complex Timeline. There is little reason to show a screenshot, as it would require many, many shots to show all the different combinations this example creates. But you can run the source code in Listing 8-11 to view this and the other animations.

Listing 8-11. *mutlipleColorsLinear*

```
function mutlipleColorsLinear():Void{
    delete group.content;

    var red1 = 0.0;
    var green1 = 0.0;
    var blue1 = 0.0;

    var red2 = 0.0;
    var green2 = 0.0;
    var blue2 = 0.0;

    var rect = Rectangle{
        translateX: 640/2-350/2;
        translateY: 480/2-50
        width: 350
        height: 50
```

```
        fill: bind createLinearGradient([
                createStop(createColor(red1, green1, blue1, 1.0), 0.0),
                createStop(createColor(red2, green2, blue2, 1.0), 1.0)
                ]);
    }
    insert rect into group.content;

    var anim = Timeline{
            repeatCount: Timeline.INDEFINITE;
            autoReverse: true;
            keyFrames: [
                KeyFrame{
                    time: 1s
                    values: [red1 => 1.0]
                },
                KeyFrame{
                    time: 3s
                    values: [
                            blue1 => 1.0,
                            green2 => 1.0,
                            ]
                },
                KeyFrame{
                    time: 5s
                    values: [
                            red1 => 0.0,
                            red2 => 1.0,
                            ]
                },
                KeyFrame{
                    time: 7s
                    values: [
                            green1 => 1.0,
                            blue2 => 1.0,
                            ]
                },
            ]
        }

    anim.play();
}
```

Listing 8-11 shows a complex animation where each component of the two colors is animated distinctly. This creates an animation that visually flows continuously from one color to another.

Animated Stops

Changing the colors of Stops is a required part of creating animated gradients. The previous examples have focused on changing the color of a stop within a set of Stops with fixed offsets. This example explores how the offsets of the Stops can be animated and how this is implemented. Figures 8-5 and 8-6 show two phases of an animation.

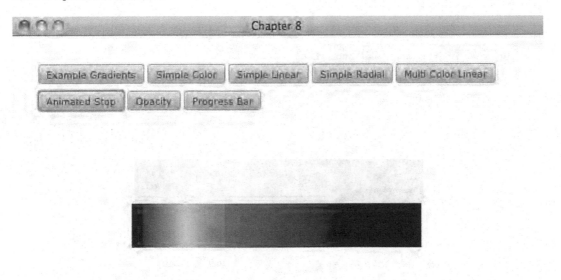

Figure 8-5. *Animated Stops phase1*

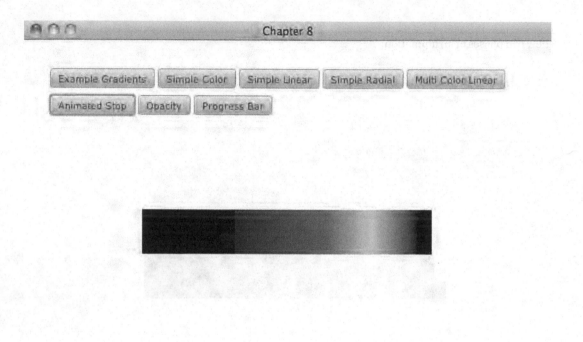

Figure 8-6. *Animated Stops phase 2*

Figure 8-5 shows a LinearGradient with three Stops. The middle Stop is mostly to the left, and in Figure 8-6 it is mostly to the right. The middle Stop cycles back and forth, creating a sort of "Cylon eye" effect, but in this case rendered in yellow and blue. The code in Listing 8-12 shows how this is implemented.

Listing 8-12. *animatedStopLinear*

```
function animatedStopLinear():Void{
    delete group.content;

    var stop = 0.0;

    var rect = Rectangle{
        translateX: 640/2-350/2;
```

```
            translateY: 480/2-50
            width: 350
            height: 50
            fill: bind createLinearGradient([
                    Stop{color:Color.YELLOW, offset:0.0},
                    createStop(Color.CYAN, stop),
                    Stop{color:Color.YELLOW, offset:1.0},
                    ]);
    }
    insert rect into group.content;

    var anim = Timeline{
            repeatCount: Timeline.INDEFINITE;
            autoReverse: true;
            keyFrames: [
                KeyFrame{
                    time: 3s
                    values: [stop => 1.0 tween Interpolator.EASEBOTH]
                }
            ]
        }

    anim.play();
}
```

Listing 8-12 shows a Rectangle being created with the now familiar function createLinearGradient from Listing 8-7 used to set the fill. The only real difference between this example and Listing 8-11 is that there are three Stops in this example instead of two, and the offset of the middle Stop is having its offset changed as the animation progresses. This shows that the functions we have created provide the flexibility required to make increasingly interesting animations.

Animate Opacity and Stops

The nice part about animating gradients is how they generate very smooth effects. Sometimes when looking at an animation where a gradient changes it is not entirely clear how the animation works. I consider this sort of confusion a success for the animators, because we want the audience to focus on the end result, not the details of how it is obtained. This example combines the two techniques of animating a color and animating a stop, and the color in this case will have its opacity value changed.

Figure 8-7 shows an animation in progress.

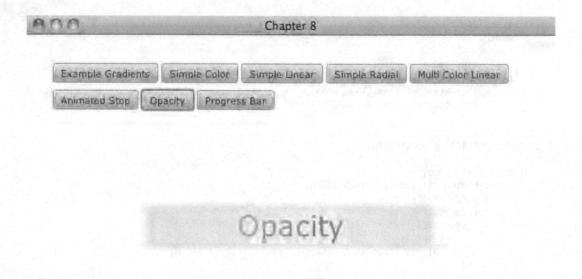

Figure 8-7. *Animated opacity*

The word Opacity is revealed as the middle Stop approaches the center of the image, while at the same time becoming more transparent. The source code in Listing 8-13 shows how this animation is simplified by the animation functions defined earlier in the chapter.

Listing 8-13. *opacity*

```
function opacity():Void{
    delete group.content;

    var offset = 0.0;
    var opacity = 1.0;

    var rect = Rectangle{
        translateX: 640/2-350/2;
```

```
            translateY: 480/2-50
            width: 350
            height: 50
            fill: bind createLinearGradient([
                    Stop{color:Color.YELLOW, offset:0.0},
                    createStop(createColor(1.0, 1.0, 0.0, opacity), offset),
                    Stop{color:Color.YELLOW, offset:1.0},
                    ]);
    }
    insert Label{
            translateX: 300
            translateY: 205
            text: "Opacity"
            scaleX: 3
            scaleY: 3
            } into group.content;
    insert rect into group.content;

    var anim = Timeline{
            repeatCount: Timeline.INDEFINITE;
            autoReverse: true;
            keyFrames: [
                KeyFrame{
                    time: 0s
                    values: opacity => 1.0
                },
                KeyFrame{
                    time: 2s
                    values: opacity => 0.3
                },
                KeyFrame{
                    time: 4s
                    values: [
                        offset => 1.0 ,
                        opacity => 1.0
                        ]
                }
            ]
        }
    anim.play();
}
```

Listing 8-13 again shows a Rectangle with its fill being set. In this case the middle Stop has both its color and offset components set to a value that is animated. The Timeline named anim increases the value of the variable offset from 0.0 to 1.0 in four seconds. The Timeline anim also decreases the value of opacity from 1.0 to 0.3 over two seconds, then increases it back to 1.0 over the last two seconds. In this way, the animated Stop starts out on the left, fully opaque. Then as it moves to the right, it becomes more transparent until it reaches the middle where it becomes more opaque again and continues to the right. While the Stop is partially transparent, the word Opacity is visible. The visible text is just a Text node behind the rectangle.

Progress Bar

This last example takes the animation functions one step further to create a more complex visual effect. If you have used OS X, then you are familiar with the animated progress bars found in that operating system. Now the example here is not a direct clone, but I thought I would mention the inspiration for the example to show that something familiar can be animated with gradients.

Figure 8-8 shows a rounded rectangle with a number of vertical bars that appear to animate to the right.

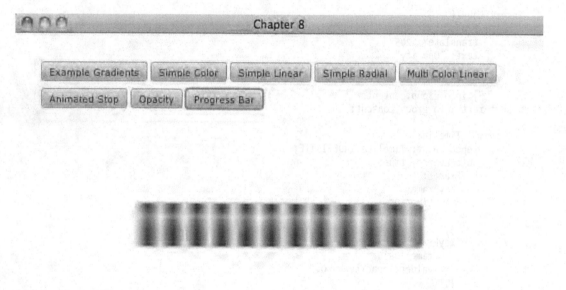

Figure 8-8. *Animated progress bar*

It is true that the OS X progress bar appears to animate to the left, but I found keeping the animation going to the right made for a more readable example. In addition to the animated gradient, two non-animated gradients are used to give the bar a sense of depth. Listing 8-14 shows the implementation.

Listing 8-14. Progress Bar

```
function progressBar():Void{
    delete group.content;
    var t = 0.0;
    var w = 1.0;
    var rect = Rectangle{
        width: 350
        height: 50
        arcHeight: 15
        arcWidth: 15
        fill: bind createLinearGradient(30,[
                Stop{color: createColor(w,w, 1,1), offset: 0.0},
                createStop(Color.WHITE, t),
                createStop(Color.BLUE, t+.5),
                Stop{color: createColor(w,w, 1,1), offset: 1.0},
                ]);
        stroke: Color.LIGHTGRAY
        strokeWidth: 2
    }
    var anim = Timeline{
        repeatCount: Timeline.INDEFINITE;
        keyFrames: [
            KeyFrame{
                time: 1s
                values: [
                    w => 0.0
                ]
            },
            KeyFrame{
                time: 2s
                values: [
                    t => 1.0,
                    w => 1.0
                ]
            }
            ]
    }
    anim.play();
    var hgloss = Rectangle{
        width: 350
        height: 50
        arcHeight: 15
        arcWidth: 15
        fill: LinearGradient{
            startX: 0
            endX: 0
            stops: [
                Stop{
                    color: Color.TRANSPARENT
                    offset: 0.0
```

```
                    },
                    Stop{
                        color: Color{red: 1, green: 1, blue: 1, opacity: .4}
                        offset: 0.3
                    },
                    Stop{
                        color: Color.TRANSPARENT
                        offset: 1.0
                    },
                ]
            }
        }
    var vgloss = Rectangle{
        width: 350
        height: 50
        arcHeight: 15
        arcWidth: 15
        fill: LinearGradient{
            startY: 0
            endY: 0
            stops: [
                Stop{
                    color: Color{red: 1, green: 1, blue: 1, opacity: .3}
                    offset: 0.0
                },
                Stop{
                    color: Color.TRANSPARENT
                    offset: 0.1
                },
                Stop{
                    color: Color.TRANSPARENT
                    offset: 0.8
                },
                Stop{
                    color: Color{red: 1, green: 1, blue: 1, opacity: .3}
                    offset: 1.0
                },
            ]
        }
    }
    var holder = Group{
        translateX: 640/2-350/2;
        translateY: 480/2-50
    }
    insert rect into holder.content;
    insert hgloss into holder.content;
    insert vgloss into holder.content;
    insert holder into group.content;
}
```

In this case, the fill of rect is set using a new version createLinearGradient that can be found in Listing 8-15. This new version will be discussed shortly, but first let's look at the Stops used. There are four Stops. The first and last Stops are fixed at the offset 0.0 and 1.0, but their color is animated. Let's call the first and last Stops the end Stops, since they are at either end of the gradient. The two middle Stops have fixed colors—one is fixed to white and the other fixed to black—so let's call these the middle Stops.

The Timeline named anim moves the middle stops to the right by increasing the value of t. The Timeline also animates the value of w. The variable w controls how much red and green are applied to the color of the end stops. I named the variable w because it affects how white the end stops are. So the idea here is that the white and blue bands created by the middle stops move to the right and then wrap around and start back at the beginning. And while the middle bands move, the end stops change color to create a seamless gradient from the middle stops to the end of the gradient.

In Figure 8-8 it looks as if there are more than just four Stops. Listing 8-15 explains the new version of createLinearGradient and how it creates the impression that there are many more Stops.

Listing 8-15. createLinearGradient(new)

```
public function createLinearGradient(length:Number,stops:Stop[]):LinearGradient{
    return LinearGradient{
        startX: 0
        endX: length
        startY: 0
        endY: 0
        cycleMethod: CycleMethod.REPEAT
        proportional: false
        stops: sortStops(stops);
    }
}
```

Listing 8-15 shows a function very similar to the one found in Listing 8-7. However, this version takes a new parameter called length, which is used to set the parameters startX and endX. It says, Draw this complete gradient from the x value 0 to the x value length. The parameters startY and endX are set to zero, which means there is no vertical component to the gradient and it goes from left to right. The property cycleMethod is being set to CycleMethod.REPEAT, which causes the gradient to be copied over the entire shape to which it is applied. By setting these additional properties on the LinearGradient it makes it appear that there are many more Stops on the rectangle from Figure 8-8.

Summary

This chapter showed you the basics of creating colors and both linear and radial gradients. This included understanding the two modes in which gradients operate—proportional and non-proportional. Several functions were defined to animate the colors and gradients. Examples of using these functions showed you how to dynamically change the color and offset of the Stops found in the gradients, to produce a number of interesting results with very little code.

CHAPTER 9

∎ ∎ ∎

Effect: Audio Visualizer

I have always been amazed how the human mind is capable of connecting sounds we hear with something that we see. When my cat meows, I hear the sound and see the motion of the cat, and somehow these two different sensory experiences are combined into a single event. Computers have been used for years to visualize audio data, and being able to see the data update as you hear the sound being analyzed provides insight into sounds that would not be possible by just listening alone. JavaFX is an excellent tool for graphics, and Java has passable media support; this chapter will show how to combine these tools to create our own live graphical representations of audio.

We will explore how to create an audio visualization in JavaFX. We will discuss a little bit about what digital audio is in the first place and what it means to visualize sound. We will take a quick look at media support in JavaFX and see that it won't give us access to the live raw data we need. We will then explore the Java Sound API to learn how to create our own audio processing thread, which will enable us to perform calculations on the raw audio data as it is being played.

Since we will be working with both Java and JavaFX, we will look at how these two environments can work together to create a JavaFX-friendly audio API. The end of the chapter will then use our new JavaFX audio API to make a simple player and three different examples of audio visualizations.

What Is an Audio Visualizer?

In the simplest terms, an *audio visualizer* is any graphic that is derived from audio data. To understand what that means, it is worth starting from the beginning and describing a little bit about what sound is and how digital audio works. In the most basic terms, sound is a change of air pressure on our eardrums. When we speak, our throat and mouths rapidly change the air pressure around us, and this change in pressure is propagated through the air and is eventually detected by our listener's ears.

Understanding that a particular sound correlated to a pattern in air pressure allowed early inventors to create ways of recording sounds and playing it back. If we consider the phonograph, we can see that the cylinder that holds the recording has captured a particular pattern of changing air pressure in its grooves. When the needle of a phonograph is vibrated by those grooves, it re-creates the original sound by moving a speaker, which in turn re-creates the changes in air pressure, which comprised the original sound.

Digital audio works by measuring the change in pressure several thousand times a second and saving those measurements in a digital file. So when digital audio is played back, a computer reads each of those values in the file and creates a voltage in a speaker wire proportional to that value. The voltage in the wire then moves the membrane of a speaker by a proportional amount. The movement of the speaker moves the air around it, which eventually moves the air in our ears. So, in essence, each value stored in an audio file is proportional to the change in pressure on our eardrums when we are hearing the same sound as was recorded.

Therefore, an audio visualization is simply any graphic that is in some way proportional to those values in the digital file. When the visualization is created at the same time as the sound is played back, it creates an opportunity for the eyes to see something that is synchronized with what we are hearing. In general, this is a pretty compelling experience.

There are numerous examples of audio visualizations in the world. Some visualizations are useful to audio engineers, allowing them get another perspective on the data on which they are working. Other visualizations are more decorative and simply exist as another way of enjoying music. Many home-stereo components include a display, which shows the sound levels of whatever is playing; this usually takes the form a column of small LED lights. The more lights that are illuminated, the louder the sound. Sometimes there are two columns of lights, one representing the left channel and the other representing the right channel. Other times there are numerous columns, which break down the song into different pitches; these are more complex since some computational work must be done to separate the different parts of the music.

Most applications for playing music on computers these days come with a view that shows the music as a psychedelic composite of colors. This is the type of visualization we are going to focus on in this chapter.

In Figure 9-1 we can see the end result of this chapter. We have a scene with a control panel for starting and stopping the audio. There are a number of buttons on the right to control which of our three example visualizations are visible.

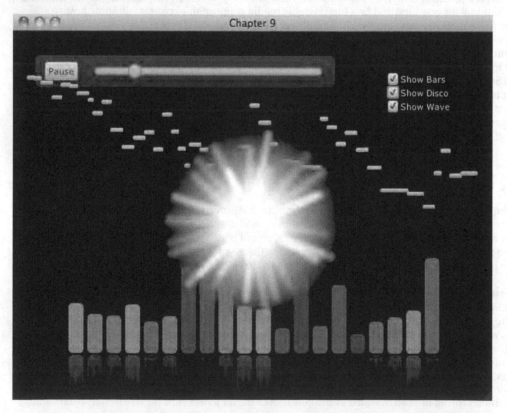

Figure 9-1. *Audio visualizer in JavaFX*

Audio and the JVM

As mentioned earlier, the JavaFX media API will not work for our purposes because it does not provide access to the raw audio data as it is being played. The JavaFX API focuses on simple playback, which I am sure provides all of the functionality most people require. It is worth taking a look at the JavaFX media API anyway, because it becomes useful in other cases and will provide context for what we will be implementing later in the chapter.

There are other ways to work with media and audio, in particular with Java. We will take a look at the Java Sound API, which we will use to implement our audio visualizations.

Audio and JavaFX

JavaFX comes with classes that allow the playing of several media types including audio files. The following are the core classes:

```
javafx.scene.media.AudioTrack
javafx.scene.media.Media
javafx.scene.media.MediaError
javafx.scene.media.Media.Metadata
javafx.scene.media.MediaPlayer
javafx.scene.media.MediaTimer
javafx.scene.media.MediaView
javafx.scene.media.SubtitleTrack
javafx.scene.media.Track
javafx.scene.media.TrackType
javafx.scene.media.VideoTrack
```

As we can see, JavaFX provides us with a simple set of classes for playing back video and audio. Using these classes, loading and playing media in a JavaFX application is straightforward. Listing 9-1 shows a simple example of doing this.

Listing 9-1. *JavaFXMediaExample.fx*

```
function run():Void{
    var media = Media{
        source: "file:///Users/lucasjordan/astroidE_32_0001_0031.avi"
    }
    var mediaPlayer = MediaPlayer{
        media: media;
    }
    var mediaView = MediaView{
        mediaPlayer: mediaPlayer;
    }

    Stage {
        title: "Chapter 9 - JavaFX Media Support"
        width: 640
        height: 480
        scene: Scene{
```

```
        content: [mediaView]
    }

  }

  mediaPlayer.play();
}
```

As we can see in Listing 9-1, a `Media` object is created with a URI pointing to the media file. The `Media` object is then used to create a `MediaPlayer` object. `MediaPlayer` is a class that provides functions for playing media, such as play, pause, reset, and so on. If the media is a video, then a `MediaView` object must be created to display the video in our scene. `MediaView` is a `Node`, so it can be used just like any other node in the scene, meaning it can be translated, can be animated, or can even have an effect applied to it. Keep in mind that for both audio and video JavaFX does not provide a widget for starting and stopping media. It is up to the developer to create actual start and stop nodes, which the user can click.

The `javafx.scene.media` package includes a few other classes not used in this simple example. These other classes allow the developer to get some additional details about a particular piece of media, specifically, details about tracks.

You might have noticed in this simple example that the movie file was not read from the JAR file like images often are. This is because of a bug in JavaFX; let's hope this issue will be addressed in the next release of JavaFX. If you are looking at the accompanying source code, you will notice that I included the movie file in the source code. This is so you can run this example if you want; simply copy the movie file to somewhere on you local hard drive, and change the URI accordingly.

So, the good news is that JavaFX has pretty good media support and the API is very easy to use. Unfortunately, the JavaFX media API provides no way to get access to the content of the media programmatically. The next section explores how we can use the Java Sound API to get the data we need out of an audio file.

Java Sound

One of the strengths of the JavaFX platform is that it runs on top of the Java platform. This means that all the functionality that comes with the JVM is available to your JavaFX application. This also means that all the thousands of libraries written in Java are also available. Since we can't use JavaFX's media package to create an audio visualization, we have to find another library to do our work. When it comes to media support, Java is as capable as many other platforms and includes several ways of playing a sound file. In fact, if you are developing a JavaFX application for the desktop, you have available at least four APIs from which to choose:

- JavaFX media classes

- Java Media Framework (JMF) API

- AudioClip API

- Java Sound

I found it very interesting that these APIs seem to support different formats of music files. I do not have a good explanation for this, but be warned that Java's codec support is a wonderland of confusion. For the examples in this chapter, we will be using an MP3 file. (I had some trouble getting all MP3 files to work with Java Sound, but this one works.)

There are other differences between these libraries as well. JMF, for example, is a powerful and complex tool designed to process any sort of media. I am sure audio visualizations have been created with the JMF library, but Java Sound has a more modern and simpler API, so it makes for better example code. The `AudioClip` class is part of the Applet API; it provides only the most basic functionality, so it is not suitable for our uses.

To use the Java Sound API, we have to do a couple of things in our code: we must prepare the audio file for playback, buffer the song, create a thread that reads and writes the audio data, and write some code that analyzes the audio data as it is being played.

Figure 9-2 is a graphical representation of all the classes and threads required to sample the audio as it is playing as well as expose the audio stream to JavaFX. As we can see, there are three threads involved in making this all work, but only the Audio thread and the Accumulate thread are defined by our code. The JavaFX rendering thread is responsible for drawing the scene and is implicitly defined when any JavaFX application is created.

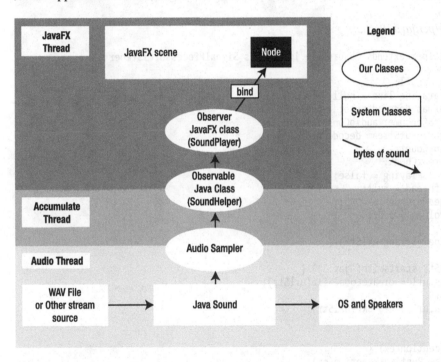

Figure 9-2. *Interaction between classes*

The Audio Thread reads from the source of the audio and uses Java Sound to play it through the speakers. The Accumulate Thread samples the sound data as it is being played and simplifies the data so it is more useful to our application. It must be simplified because it is hard to create an interesting visualization from what is effectively a stream of random bytes. The Accumulate Thread informs the JavaFX thread that there are changes to the data through the Observable/Observer pattern. Lastly, changes are made to the scene based on the simplified audio data. The following sections explain how this is implemented in code.

Preparing the Audio File

In the source code you will find that a WAV file is provided for use in this example. Before we get into details of how the code works, I would like to thank J-San & The Analogue Sons for letting me use the title track of their album *One Sound* in this example. If you like modern reggae, go check them out at http://www.jsanmusic.net.

You can find the MP3 file used in the example in the folder org/lj/jfxe/chapter9/media of the accompanying source code. Since it is in the source code, it will be put into the JAR that makes up this NetBeans project. Since it is in the JAR file, it can be accessed by the running process. However, Java Sound, like JavaFX, has an issue where sound files cannot be played directly from the JAR. To get around this, we must read the file out of the JAR and write it to disk someplace. Once the file is written to disk, we can get Java to play the sound file. Listing 9-2 shows some of the source code from the class SoundHelper, which is a Java class that is responsible for preparing and playing the sound file.

Listing 9-2. SoundHelper.java (Partial)

```java
public class SoundHelper extends Observable implements SignalProcessorListener {

    private URL url = null;
    private SourceDataLine line = null;
    private AudioFormat decodedFormat = null;
    private AudioDataConsumer audioConsumer = null;
    private ByteArrayInputStream decodedAudio;
    private int chunkCount;
    private int currentChunk;
    private boolean isPlaying = false;
    private Thread thread = null;
    private int bytesPerChunk = 4096;
    private float volume = 1.0f;

    public SoundHelper(String urlStr) {
        try {
            if (urlStr.startsWith("jar:")) {
                this.url = createLocalFile(urlStr);
            } else {
                this.url = new URL(urlStr);
            }

        } catch (Exception ex) {
            throw new RuntimeException(ex);
        }
        init();
    }

    private File getMusicDir() {
        File userHomeDir = new File(System.getProperties().getProperty("user.home"));

        File synethcDir = new File(userHomeDir, ".chapter9_music_cache");
        File musicDir = new File(synethcDir, "music");
```

```java
        if (!musicDir.exists()) {
            musicDir.mkdirs();
        }
        return musicDir;
    }

    private URL createLocalFile(String urlStr) throws Exception {
        File musicDir = getMusicDir();

        String fileName = urlStr.substring(urlStr.lastIndexOf('/')).replace("%20", " ");

        File musicFile = new File(musicDir, fileName);

        if (!musicFile.exists()) {
            InputStream is = new URL(urlStr).openStream();
            FileOutputStream fos = new FileOutputStream(musicFile);

            byte[] buffer = new byte[512];
            int nBytesRead = 0;

            while ((nBytesRead = is.read(buffer, 0, buffer.length)) != -1) {
                fos.write(buffer, 0, nBytesRead);
            }

            fos.close();
        }
        return musicFile.toURL();
    }

    private void init() {

        fft = new FFT(saFFTSampleSize);
        old_FFT = new float[saFFTSampleSize];
        saMultiplier = (saFFTSampleSize / 2) / saBands;

        AudioInputStream in = null;
        try {

            in = AudioSystem.getAudioInputStream(url.openStream());
            AudioFormat baseFormat = in.getFormat();

            decodedFormat = new AudioFormat(AudioFormat.Encoding.PCM_SIGNED,
                    baseFormat.getSampleRate(), 16, baseFormat.getChannels(),
                    baseFormat.getChannels() * 2,
                    baseFormat.getSampleRate(), false);

            AudioInputStream decodedInputStream =
AudioSystem.getAudioInputStream(decodedFormat, in);
            ByteArrayOutputStream baos = new ByteArrayOutputStream();
```

```
            chunkCount = 0;
            byte[] data = new byte[bytesPerChunk];
            int bytesRead = 0;
            while ((bytesRead = decodedInputStream.read(data, 0, data.length)) != -1) {
                chunkCount++;
                baos.write(data, 0, bytesRead);
            }
            decodedInputStream.close();
            decodedAudio = new ByteArrayInputStream(baos.toByteArray());

            DataLine.Info info = new DataLine.Info(SourceDataLine.class, decodedFormat);
            line = (SourceDataLine) AudioSystem.getLine(info);

            line.open(decodedFormat);
            line.start();

            audioConsumer = new AudioDataConsumer(bytesPerChunk, 10);
            audioConsumer.start(line);
            audioConsumer.add(this);

            isPlaying = false;

            thread = new Thread(new SoundRunnable());
            thread.start();

        } catch (Exception ex) {
            throw new RuntimeException(ex);
        }
    }
```

In Listing 9-2 we can see that a SoundHelper class is created by calling a constructor and providing a URL. If the provided URL starts with the word *jar*, we know we must copy the sound file out of the JAR and into the local file system; the method createLocalFile is used to do this. Looking at the implementation of createLocalFile, we can see that a suitable location is identified in a subdirectory created in the user's home directory. If this file exists, then the code assumes that this file was copied over during a previous run, and the URL to this file is returned. If the file did not exist, then the createLocalFile method opens an input stream from the copy in the JAR and also opens an output stream to the new file. The contents of the input stream are then written to the output stream, creating a copy of the sound file on the local disk.

Once the class SoundHelper has a URL pointing to valid sound file, it is then time to decode the sound file so we can play it. The method init uses the static method getAudioInputStream from the Java Sound class AudioSystem. The AudioInputStream returned by getAudioInputStream may or may not be in a format we want to work with. Since we are going to do some digital signal processing (DSP) on the contents of this stream, we want to normalize the format so we only have to write one class for doing the DSP.

Using the original format of the AudioInputStream as stored in the variable baseFormat, a new AudioFormat is created called decodedFormat. The variable decodedFormat is set to be PCM_SIGNED, which is how our DSP code expects it to be formatted.

So, now that we know what format we want our audio data in, it is time to actually get the audio data. The audio data will ultimately be stored as a byte array inside the variable decodedAudio. The variable decodedAudio is a ByteArrayInputStream and provides a convenient API for working with a byte array as a stream.

An AudioInputStream is an InputStream and works just like other InputStream objects, so we can just read the content to an AudioInputStream like we would any other InputStream. In this case, we read the content from decodedInputStream and write the data to the ByteArrayOutputStream object's baos. The variable baos is a temporary variable whose content is dumped into the variable decodedAudio. This is our end goal—to have the entire song decoded and stored in memory. This not only allows us to play the music but also give us the ability to stop and start playing the song form any point.

Working with the Audio Data

The last thing that the method init does is use the AudioSubsystem class again to create a DataLine. A DataLine object allows us to actually make sound come out of the speakers; the class SoundRunnable, as shown in Listing 9-3, does this in a separate thread.

Listing 9-3. SoundRunnable

```
private class SoundRunnable implements Runnable {

public void run() {
        try {
            byte[] data = new byte[bytesPerChunk];
            byte[] dataToAudio = new byte[bytesPerChunk];

            int nBytesRead;
            while (true) {
                if (isPlaying) {
                    while (isPlaying && (nBytesRead = decodedAudio.read(data, 0,
data.length)) != -1) {

                        for (int i = 0; i < nBytesRead; i++) {
                            dataToAudio[i] = (byte) (data[i] * volume);
                        }

                        line.write(dataToAudio, 0, nBytesRead);
                        audioConsumer.writeAudioData(data);
                        currentChunk++;
                    }
                }
                Thread.sleep(10);
            }

        } catch (Exception e) {
            throw new RuntimeException(e);
        }
    }
}
```

In Listing 9-3 we can see that the class SoundRunnable implements Runnable, which requires the method run to be implemented. In the run method there are two while loops. The outer loop is used to toggle whether sound should be playing or not. The inner loop does the real work; it reads a chunk of

185

data from decodedAudio, which contains our decoded audio data and writes it to both line and audioConsumer. The variable line is the Java Sound object that actually makes the sound. The write method on line is interesting because it blocks until it is ready for more data, which in effect keeps this loop in sync with what you are hearing. audioConsumer is responsible for actually doing the digital signal processing.

I am going to leave out the details of how the audio data is actually processed, because it is a rather complex topic and I didn't write the class that does the work. The class comes from a subproject of the JDesktop Integration Components (JDIC) project called the Music Player Control API. You can find the JDIC project at https://jdic.dev.java.net.

In general, though, the DSP classes take the audio data as it is being written and break the signal up into 20 values. Each value represents how much of the sound is coming from a particular frequency in the audio, which is known as a *spectral analysis*. The values are stored in the variable levels of the class SoundHelper. The variable levels is simply an array of 20 doubles, each having a value between 0.0 and 1.0. A value of 0.0 indicates that that particular frequency is not contributing at all to what you are hearing, and a value 1.0 indicates that it is contributing as much as possible.

JavaFX and Java

The class SoundHelper now provides us with the ability to play an audio file and get information about which levels are high or low as the music is being played. The next step is to expose this functionality to a JavaFX application. When creating applications that bridge the two environments of JavaFX and Java, it is recommended that the Observer/Observable pattern be used.

The Observer/Observable pattern is pretty simple; it just states that an observable object should be able to inform observers when some value has changed. Let's look at the classes and interfaces provided by Java to implement this pattern. First the class java.lang.Observable implements a number of methods, but the three we are interested in are addObserver, setChanged, and notifyObservers. The method addObserver takes an Observer that should be informed whenever the Observable's data changes. To inform the Observer that changes have taken place, the Observable should first call setChanged and then notifyObservers. Calling these two methods causes the update method from the interface Observer to be called. This pattern is very much like the listener pattern common in Swing programming.

Looking at Listing 9-2 we can see that the class SoundHelper extends Observable. This means it can inform any observers that a change has happened. If we look at the JavaFX class SoundPlayer in Listing 9-4, we can see the other half of this relationship.

Listing 9-4. SoundPlayer.fx

```
public class SoundPlayer extends Observer{

    public var volume:Number = 1.0 on replace {
        soundHelper.setVolume(volume);
    }

    public var currentTime:Duration;

    public var songDuration:Duration;

    public var url:String;
    public var file:File;
```

```
    var soundHelper:SoundHelper;
    override function update(observable: Observable, arg: Object) {
        FX.deferAction(
        function(): Void {
            for (i in [0..(soundHelper.levels.length-1)]){
                levels[i] = soundHelper.getLevel(i);
            }
            currentTime =
(soundHelper.getCurrentChunk()*1.0/soundHelper.getChunkCount()*1.0)*soundHelper.getSongLengt
hInSeconds()*1s;
        }
        );
    }

    //20 channels
    public var levels: Number[] = for (i in [1..20]) 0.0;

    public var hiChannels:Number = bind levels[19] + levels[18] + levels[17] + levels[16] +
levels[15] + levels[14] + levels[13];

    public var midChannels:Number = bind levels[7] + levels[8] + levels[9] + levels[10] +
levels[11] + levels[12];

    public var lowChannels:Number = bind levels[0] + levels[1] + levels[2] + levels[3] +
levels[4] + levels[5] + levels[6];

    init{
        soundHelper = new SoundHelper(url);
        soundHelper.addObserver(this);
        songDuration = soundHelper.getSongLengthInSeconds() * 1s;
        soundHelper.setVolume(volume);
        reset();
    }

    public function reset():Void{
        soundHelper.pause();
        soundHelper.setTimeInMills(0);
    }

    public function stop():Void{
        soundHelper.pause();
    }
    public function pause():Void{
        soundHelper.pause();
    }
    public function play():Void{
        soundHelper.play();
    }
    public function setTime(time:Duration){
        soundHelper.setTimeInMills(time.toMillis());
    }
```

```
    public function isPlaying():Boolean{
        return soundHelper.isPlaying();
    }
}
```

In Listing 9-4 we can see the class SoundPlayer. The class SoundPlayer is intended to wrap a SoundHelper and provide a JavaFX-style interface to any application that requires the feature of SoundHelper. We can see SoundPlayer implements the interface Observer and thus has an update function. It is very simple for JavaFX classes to extend Java interfaces; the only real difference is in the syntax of declaring the function. In the init function, we can see that SoundPlayer creates a new SoundHelper and then registers itself as an observer. Now any time the levels change in the SoundHelper, the update function of SoundPlayer will be called.

Looking at the update function of SoundPlayer, we can see that the levels in SoundHelper are copied into the sequence levels of class SoundPlayer. But notice that the for loop that does the copying is actually performed in a function that is passed the static function FX.deferAction. The function FX.deferAction is a utility function that causes any function passed into it to be called by the JavaFX event thread. This is important because this allows other JavaFX objects to bind to the sequence levels in a reliable way.

In fact, SoundPlayer has a number of other variables, which are bound to levels such as hiChannels, midChannels, and lowChannels. These variables are simply aggregates of the values in levels and will be used later to allow audio visualization to bind to just the high, middle, or low parts of the song.

SoundPlayer also has a number of functions that simply wrap methods on the soundHelper; this is done to make SoundPlayer a complete package and prevents developers who use SoundPlayer from needing to know anything about SoundHelper and the whole Java side of things.

One last thing to note is how simple it is for JavaFX classes to make calls to Java objects. On the JavaFX side, the Java object is created as normal, and method calls are made just like they were native JavaFX objects. Calling JavaFX functions from Java is a bit trickier; there are particulars with the differences in JavaFX primitive types and Java's primitive types that can confound any developer. The trick here was to have the JavaFX class implement a Java interface that ensures that the types used in the function calls are going to be familiar from the Java perspective.

Audio Visualizations

Now that we have a nice JavaFX interface for our sound processing code, we can start using SoundPlayer in an example application that will illustrate how easy it is to create compelling audio visualizations in JavaFX. Figure 9-1 shows the sample application we will be talking about.

In Figure 9-1 we can see scene composed of a control for starting and pausing the music, as well as a control bar where we can change which part of the song is playing. There are also three check boxes that control which three of our example effects are displayed. In this screenshot, all three are displayed. Let's start by looking at Main.fx and how this example was set up (Listing 9-5).

Listing 9-5. Main.fx

```
var soundPlayer = SoundPlayer{
    url: "{__DIR__}media/01 One Sound.mp3";
}
var bars = Bars{
    translateX: 50
```

```
        translateY: 400
        soundPlayer:soundPlayer
        visible: bind barsButton.selected
}
var barsButton = CheckBox{
        graphic: Label{text: "Show Bars", textFill: Color.WHITESMOKE}
}
var disco = DiscoStar{
        translateX: 320
        translateY: 240
        soundPlayer:soundPlayer
        visible: bind discoButton.selected
}
var discoButton = CheckBox{
        graphic: Label{text: "Show Disco", textFill: Color.WHITESMOKE}
}
var wave = Wave{
        translateX: 620
        translateY: 380
        soundPlayer:soundPlayer
        visible: bind waveButton.selected
}
var waveButton = CheckBox{
        graphic: Label{text: "Show Wave", textFill: Color.WHITESMOKE}
}
var scene = Scene {
        fill: Color.BLACK
        content: [
            SoundControl{
                translateX: 30
                translateY: 30
                soundPlayer:soundPlayer
            }, wave, disco, bars
        ]
}
function run():Void{
        var vbox = VBox{
            translateX: 500
            translateY: 50
            content: [barsButton, discoButton, waveButton]
        }
        insert vbox into scene.content;
        Stage {
            title: "Chapter 9"
            width: 640
            height: 480
            scene: scene
        }   barsButton.selected = true;
}
```

In Listing 9-5 the first thing we do is create a SoundPlayer pointing at our sample song. The SoundPlayer will then be passed to the other objects that require access to it. For example, in the Scene, a SoundControl is created that uses the SoundPlayer. A SoundControl is a class that contains the Play/Pause button as well as the seek track.

One instance of each of our three example effects is created as well as a CheckBox. For each effect the visible attribute is bound to the selected attribute of each CheckBox. I noticed while creating this example that CheckBox does not have an action function attribute in the same way Button does; I think this is an oversight. It would be very handy. I will have to talk to somebody about that!

Controlling the Audio

Before we get into how each effect was created, let's take a look at SoundControl and see how it provides a graphical interface into our SoundPlayer class. Listing 9-6 shows the source code.

Listing 9-6. SoundControl.fx

```
public class SoundControl extends AudioVisualization{
    var playButton:Button;

    init{
        var background = Rectangle{
            width: 400
            height: 40
            arcHeight: 10
            arcWidth: 10
            fill: grayGradient
            opacity: .3
        }
        insert background into content;

        playButton = Button{
            translateX: 13
            translateY: 8
            action: buttonClicked;
            text: "Play";
        }
        insert playButton into content;

        var group = Group{
            translateX: 80
            translateY: 15
            onMouseReleased:mouseReleased;
            onMouseDragged:mouseDragged;
        }
        insert group into content;

        var track = Rectangle{
            width: 300
            height: 8
```

```
                arcWidth: 8
                arcHeight: 8
                fill: grayGradient
                strokeWidth: 2
                stroke: Color.web("#339afc");
        }

        insert track into group.content;

        var playhead = Circle{
                translateY: 4
                translateX: bind calculateLocation(soundPlayer.currentTime,dragLocation);
                radius: 8
                fill: grayGradient
                strokeWidth: 2
                stroke: Color.web("#339afc");
        }
        insert playhead into group.content;

}

    var mouseIsDragging:Boolean = false;
    var dragLocation:Number;

    function calculateLocation(currentTime:Duration,dragX:Number):Number{
        var rawLocation:Number;
        if (mouseIsDragging){
            rawLocation = dragX;
        } else{
            rawLocation = currentTime/soundPlayer.songDuration*300;
        }
        if (rawLocation < 0){
            return 0
        } else if (rawLocation > 300){
            return 300
        } else {
            return rawLocation
        }
    }
    function buttonClicked():Void{
        if (soundPlayer.isPlaying()){
            soundPlayer.pause();
            playButton.text = "Play";
        } else {
            soundPlayer.play();
            playButton.text = "Pause";
        }
    }
function mouseReleased(event:MouseEvent):Void{
        mouseIsDragging = false;
        soundPlayer.setTime(event.x/300.0*soundPlayer.songDuration);
```

```
    }
    function mouseDragged(event:MouseEvent):Void{
        mouseIsDragging = true;
        dragLocation = event.x;
    }
}
```

In Listing 9-6 we can see that SoundControl extends AudioVisualization, which is a simple base class used by this example. We will take a look at it in a moment in Listing 9-7. In the init function of SoundControl, we see that the background rectangle is added as well as the Pause/Play button. When the button is clicked, the function buttonClicked is called, which updates the text of the button and tells the soundPlayer to either play or pause.

The seek bar is bit more interesting; it is composed of two shapes: a Rectangle for the long horizontal part and a Circle that has its translateX bound to the function calculateLocation. This function takes the current time and the location of any drag event. Even though both of these values are in scope within the function calculateLocation, by passing them in to the function, we cause the bound value to be updated whenever they change. Remember, binding to a function with no parameters causes the bound value to never update.

By adding event functions to the group's onMouseDragged and onMouseRelease attributes, we can respond when the user clicks and drags the seek bar. The function onMouseDragged sets mouseIsDragging to true and updates the value of dragLocation, which in turn causes the bound translateX attribute of the circle to be updated. When the mouse is released, the circle goes back to the current time of the song.

Let's take a quick look the class AudioVisualization, since it gets used by four of our classes in this example. Listing 9-7 shows the source code.

Listing 9-7. *AudioVisualization.fx*

```
public class AudioVisualization extends Group{
    public-init var soundPlayer:SoundPlayer;
}
```

In Listing 9-7 we can see that it is a very simple class; AudioVisualization extends Group and allows a SoundPlayer to be specified when it is created. SoundPlayer and all three example effects extend this class.

Now that we have the basic framework spelled out, we can explore the details of these effects.

Bars

The first visualization we'll look at will show a number of bars, one for each level, which grow and shrink along with the values stored in the sequence levels of the class SoundPlayer. Figure 9-3 shows our first example visualization.

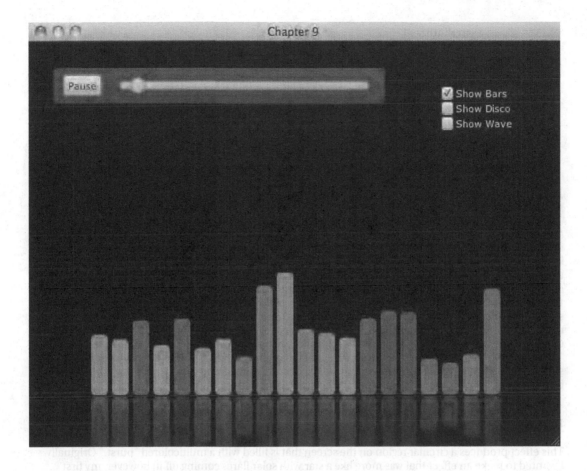

Figure 9-3. *Bars effect*

In Figure 9-3 the bars visualizer is displayed. There are 20 bars; each bar's height is proportional to the sound at one of the 20 frequencies presented by the class SoundPlayer. Let's take a look at the source code in Listing 9-8.

Listing 9-8. *Bars.fx*

```
public class Bars extends AudioVisualization{
    init{
        for (i in [0.. <sizeof(soundPlayer.levels)]){
            var rect = Rectangle{
                translateX: 500-i*25
                translateY: bind -soundPlayer.levels[i]*200
                width: 20;
                height: bind soundPlayer.levels[i]*200
                arcHeight: 10
```

```
                    arcWidth: 10
                    fill: Color.BLUE
                    effect: ColorAdjust {
                            brightness: bind soundPlayer.levels[i] * 1.5 - .75;
                            contrast: bind soundPlayer.levels[i] * 3 + 0.25;
                            hue: bind soundPlayer.levels[i] * 1.5 - .75;
                    };
            }
            insert rect into content;
        }
        effect = Reflection{}
    }
}
```

In Listing 9-8 we can see that this is actually a pretty simple class. The class Bars extends AudioVisualizer from Listing 9-7, so it has a soundPlayer available and is also a Group. The init function in the class Bars creates one Rectangle for each item in the sequence levels of class AudioPlayer. Each Rectangle has its translateX value set so they are laid out right to left; this puts the higher frequency bars to the right and the lower frequency bars to the left, as is common in these types of displays. The height of each Rectangle is bound to a value of levels times 200 to make them tall enough to see. The translateY is also bound to levels, which keeps the bottom of the Rectangles aligned as they change size. Remember, a Rectangle's origin is the upper-left corner. Lastly, a ColorAdjust is applied to each rectangle; the ColorAdjust has attributes bound to levels as well, and this makes the Rectangle change color as it gets taller. Applying a Reflection to the entire class gives it that nice reflection at the bottom.

In my opinion, the Bars class does an excellent job of showing exactly what all that work on the Java side was for, because we can clearly see that we have successfully decomposed the audio. The next effect is much more abstract but is still interesting because it is synced to only part of the music.

Disco

This effect produces a circular region on the screen that is filled with a multicolored "burst." Originally I wanted to make an effect that was more like a star with solar flares coming off it; however, my first attempt didn't look quite right. It reminded me of disco lights, and I thought that was more appropriate anyway, so I ran with it. Figure 9-4 shows the effect by itself.

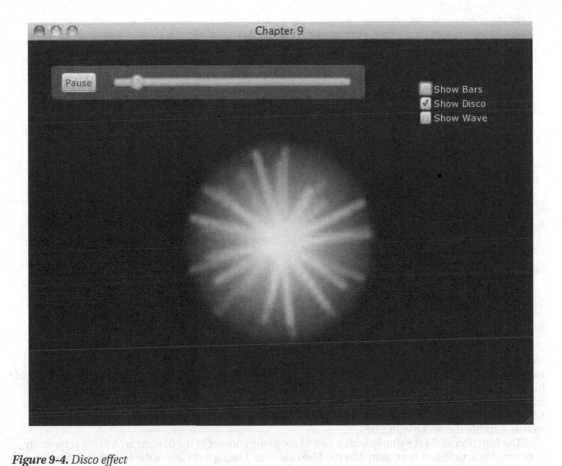

Figure 9-4. Disco effect

In Figure 9-4 we can see a circular region of the screen composed of rays emitting from the center. The rays are multicolored. This effect borrows heavily from the chapter on particles, as the source code in Listing 9-9 shows.

Listing 9-9. DiscoStar.fx

```
public class DiscoStar extends AudioVisualization{
    var lastEmit = DateTime{}

    var showFlare = bind soundPlayer.hiChannels on replace {
        if (soundPlayer.hiChannels > 3){
            var now = DateTime{};
            if (now.instant - lastEmit.instant > 100){
                lastEmit = now;
                addFlare();
            }
        }
    }
```

```
    var anim = Timeline{
        repeatCount: Timeline.INDEFINITE
        keyFrames: KeyFrame{
            time: 1/30*1s
            action: function(){
                for (node in content){
                    (node as Flare).update();
                }
            }
        }
    }

    init{
        anim.play();
        blendMode = BlendMode.ADD;
    }

    function addFlare():Void{
        var flare = Flare{}
        insert flare into content;
    }
}
```

In Listing 9-9 we can see again that the class DiscoStar extends AudioVisualization. The variable showFlare is bound to the variable hiChannel of the soundPlayer. The variable hiChannel is simply the sum of the higher-frequency values found in soundPlayer.levels. The idea here is that when the value of hiChannel changes, we check to see whether it is greater than 3. If it is, we check to make we have not added one within the last tenth of a second, and if we have not, then we call addFlare. The time check is just to make sure we don't add too many too fast, because that would cause performance problems as well as saturate the scene with flares.

The function addFlare simply adds a new Flare to the content of the DiscoStar. A Flare is basically a very simple particle that is animated by the Timeline anim. Listing 9-10 shows the source code for Flare.

Listing 9-10. *Flare.fx*

```
def flareImage = Image{
    url: "{__DIR__}media/flare.png"
}
def random = new Random();

public class Flare extends ImageView{
    public var totalSteps:Number = 1000;
    public var delteRotation:Number;
    var currentStep = totalSteps;

    init{
        image = flareImage;
        translateX = flareImage.width/-2.0;
        translateY = flareImage.height/-2.0;
        effect = ColorAdjust{
            hue: -1 + random.nextFloat()*2
```

```
        }
        delteRotation = random.nextFloat()*.04;
        rotate = random.nextInt(360);
    }

    public function update():Void{
        currentStep--;
        if (currentStep == 0){
            delete this from (parent as Group).content;
        } else{
            rotate += delteRotation;
            opacity = currentStep/totalSteps;
        }
    }
}
```

In Listing 9-10 we can see that Flare extends ImageView and shows the Image flareImage. The init function sets the effect to a ColorAdjust with a random value; the value deltaRotation is also set to a random value as well as the starting rotation. When the Timeline anim from the class DiscoStar calls the function update, this class behaves much like some of the other particles we have looked at. First we check to see whether the particle is done living as tracked by the value of currentStep. If the particle is still alive, it is rotated a little bit, and it becomes more transparent. Figure 9-5 shows what one Flare looks like.

Figure 9-5. *Source image for Flare*

What you can't see in Figure 9-5 is that the source image for the flare particles is all red. By using the ColorAdjust, we can set the color to anything at runtime.

I like this effect; I like the way it shows up with the horns in the music.

Wave

This last example uses the bass and the midrange from the song to generate a wave of dots. This again uses the pattern of particles to generate its effect. Figure 9-6 shows this effect.

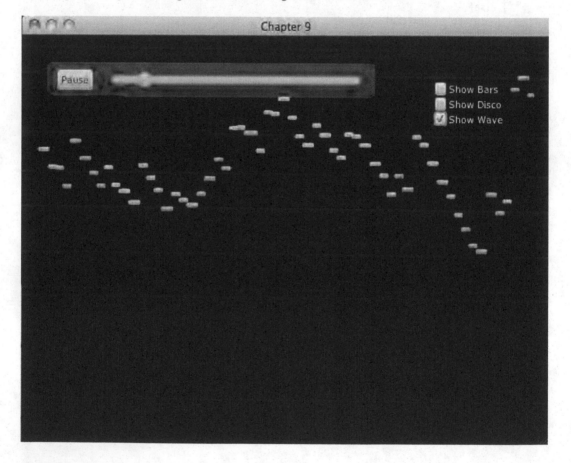

Figure 9-6. Wave effect

In Figure 9-6 we can see a number of dots scattered about the screen; when you run the example, you can see they are being created on the right of the screen and in a straight line go to the left. Each dot's height on the screen is dictated by the amount of bass in the song when it is created. The color of the dot is derived from the midrange. Listing 9-11 shows how we did this.

Listing 9-11. Wave.fx

```
public class Wave extends AudioVisualization{

    var count = 0;
    var anim = Timeline{
        repeatCount: Timeline.INDEFINITE
        keyFrames: KeyFrame{
            time: 1/30*1s
            action: function(){
                count++;
                for (node in content){
                    (node as WaveDot).update();
                }
                if (count mod 30 == 0){
                    emit();
                }
            }
        }
    }

    init{
        anim.play();
    }

    function emit():Void{
        if (soundPlayer.isPlaying()){
            insert WaveDot{
                radius: 3
                translateY: -soundPlayer.lowChannels*100;
                fill: Color.CRIMSON
                effect: ColorAdjust{
                        hue: -1 + soundPlayer.midChannels/3.5
                }
            } into content;
        }
    }
}
```

In Listing 9-11 we see that Wave creates a Timeline called anim that does two things; first it calls update on each WaveDot, and second it calls emit every 30th time. The function emit simply creates a new WaveDot and inserts it into the Wave's content. When creating the WaveDot, its height on the screen is determined by sampling the soundPlayer's lowChannel value. A ColorAdjust is also used in conjunction with soundPlayer's midChannel value.

By having the height be a function of the lowChannel and the color be a function of the midChannel, we create a kind history of the song as it plays, since only the most recently created WaveDot is a reflection of the music you are hearing. Let's take a look at the source code for WaveDot to make sure we understand how this works (Listing 9-12).

Listing 9-12. WaveDot

```
public class WaveDot extends Circle{
    var totalSteps = 6000;
    var currentStep = totalSteps;
    var deltaX = -0.1;

    public function update():Void{
        currentStep--;
        if (currentStep == 0){
            delete this from (parent as Group).content;
        } else{
            translateX += deltaX;
        }
    }
}
```

In Listing 9-12 we see a very simple particle class; it is worth looking at this because it shows that just few lines of JavaFX code can create some really interesting animations. As we can see in the function update, we simply check to see whether the WaveDot is ready to be removed; if not, we move it to the left.

Summary

This chapter started with an introduction to the JavaFX media classes and then explored some of the other audio-related libraries that come with Java. We created a class that could play audio using Java Sound as well as perform digital signal processing on the sound as it is being played. We then wrapped this class in a JavaFX API to allow us to create animations in JavaFX driven by the music. By creating a JavaFX-friendly API, it's simple to get to the real work of creating interesting animations in JavaFX based on an audio stream.

CHAPTER 10

■ ■ ■

Effects: Physics and Particles

Particles are capable of creating some eye-catching animations that produce vibrant and fluid effects. Physics engines, on the other hand, create animations that satisfy our sense of motion. Combining these two excellent effects offers the best of both worlds, and this chapter explores two examples of intertwining physics with particles.

Particles as Bodies

In Chapter 6 I used the open source physics engine Phys2D to implement a number of physics-based examples in JavaFX. This chapter will continue to use Phys2D because it provides so much functionality.

As you'll recall from Chapter 6, an object in a physics simulation is called a body. This first example explores how to implement a particle system where each particle is a body. Basically, the particle emitter will create particles that are JavaFX Nodes and have reference to a Body. As the World is updated and the location of the Body changes, the location of the Node is updated to reflect this.

This is different from the original particle examples in Chapter 6 wherein each Node updated its location based on a set of fixed parameters. Figure 10-1 shows a particle system that utilizes physics.

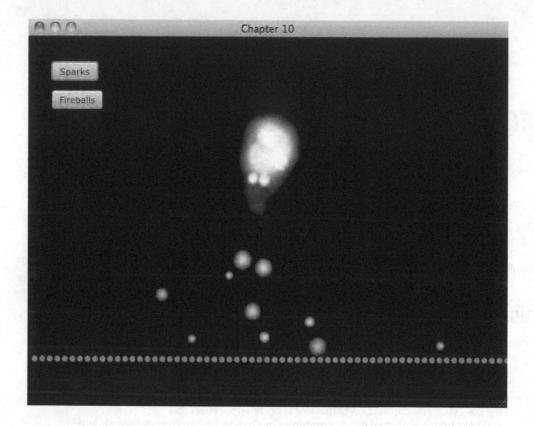

Figure 10-1. *Particles as bodies*

Figure 10-1 shows a bunch of falling particles, and as they fall they bounce off each other and the line of dots at the bottom of the screen. There are two types of particles being emitted—one is big and puffy and the other is smaller.

In Figure 10-2 we see that the two different particles are simulating different aspects of a shower of sparks.

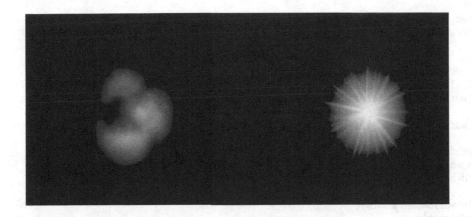

Figure 10-2. Two types of particles

The bigger ones try to capture the sense of smoke and fire at the point where the sparks are being emitted, and the little particles try to capture the sense of sparks falling and bouncing. Listing 10-1 shows the majority of the Main.fx file for this example.

Listing 10-1. Main.fx

```
public var cloud = Image{
    url: "{__DIR__}cloud.png"
}
public var spark = Image{
    url: "{__DIR__}spark.png"
}
public var random = new Random();

var worldNodes:WorldNode[];
var emitters:Emitter[];

var particles = Group{
        blendMode: BlendMode.ADD
        }
var obstacles = Group{}

var world = new World(new Vector2f(0,600), 1);
var worldUpdater = Timeline{
    repeatCount: Timeline.INDEFINITE
    keyFrames: KeyFrame{
        time: 1.0/30.0*1s
        action: update;
    }
}
public function update():Void{
    world.<<step>>();
```

```
        for (worldNode in worldNodes){
            worldNode.update();
        }
    }
    public function addWorldNode(worldNode:WorldNode):Void{
        if (worldNode instanceof Particle){
            insert (worldNode as Node) into particles.content;
        } else {
            insert (worldNode as Node) into obstacles.content;
        }
        insert worldNode into worldNodes;
        for (body in worldNode.bodies){
            world.add(body);
        }
        for (joint in worldNode.joints){
            world.add(joint);
        }
    }
    public function removeWorldNode(worldNode:WorldNode):Void{
        if (worldNode instanceof Particle){
            delete (worldNode as Node) from particles.content;
        } else {
            delete (worldNode as Node) from obstacles.content;
        }
        delete worldNode from worldNodes;
        for (body in worldNode.bodies){
            world.remove(body);
        }
        for (joint in worldNode.joints){
            world.remove(joint);
        }
    }
    public function addEmitter(emitter:Emitter):Void{
        insert emitter into emitters;
        emitter.play();
    }
    public function removeEmitter(emitter:Emitter):Void{
        emitter.stop();
        delete emitter from emitters;
    }

    public function clear(){
        var wn = worldNodes;
        for (node in wn){
            removeWorldNode(node);
        }
        var em = emitters;
        for (emitter in emitters){
            removeEmitter(emitter);
        }
    }
}
```

```
function run():Void{
    worldUpdater.play();

    var sparksButton = Button{
        text: "Sparks"
        action: sparks
    }
    var fireballsButton = Button{
        text: "Fireballs"
        action: fireballs
    }
    var buttons = VBox{
        translateX: 32
        translateY: 32
        spacing: 12
        content: [sparksButton, fireballsButton]
    }
    Stage {
        title: "Chapter 11"
        width: 640
        height: 480
        scene: Scene {
            fill: Color.BLACK;
            content: [buttons, obstacles, particles]
        }
    }
}

function sparks():Void{
    clear();
    for (x in [1..64]){
        addWorldNode(Peg{
            radius: 4
            translateX: x*10
            translateY: 400
        });
    }
    var emitter = SparkEmitter{
        x: 640/2
        y: 130
    }
    addEmitter(emitter);
]
```

The function run sets up the scene and the buttons that present each example. The function sparks is the entry point for this first example—it simply creates a number of Pegs and a SparkEmitter. The Pegs create the line of circles seen in Figure 10-1, while the SparkEmitter specifies from where the sparks should come. The Pegs are added by the function addWorldNode; the Emitter is added by the function addEmitter.

In this example an Emitter is not a JavaFX Node. It is just an object that controls when particles are added, though it does specify where the particles are created. In Chapter 6 on particles, an emitter is a

Group and the particles are children of that Group. But for this example, that arrangement is not ideal. Since all bodies in the simulation have coordinates in the same coordinate space, it makes sense to keep all Nodes in a Group that is located at 0.0. This allows the coordinates of each node to be exactly the same as their corresponding body.

Keeping all of the particles in a single Group has another advantage: It allows particles from different Emitters to be blended together. This is done in the code in Listing 10-1 by setting the blendMode of the Group particles to Add. The Nodes that represent the StaticBodies are stored in the Group obstacles, so they are not included in the blend effect.

Listing 10-1 shows that a World object is created and animated by the Timeline worldUpdater. Bodies are added and removed from the world with the functions addWorldNode and removeWorldNode. The two functions also manage which Groups are used for a particular WorldBody.

The function addEmitter is used to keep track of all running emitters in the scene so that they can be stopped and removed by a call to removeEmitter. The function clear resets the scene for a new example to be displayed.

Looking back at the function sparks we can see that a number of Pegs are added. Listing 10-2 shows the implementation of Peg.

Listing 10-2. *Peg.fx*

```
public class Peg extends WorldNode, Circle{
    init{
        bodies[0] = new StaticBody(new net.phys2d.raw.shapes.Circle(radius));
        bodies[0].setPosition(translateX, translateY);
        bodies[0].setRestitution(1.0);
        fill = Color.GRAY;
    }
    public override function update():Void{
        //static bodies do not move
    }
}
```

In Listing 10-2 we see the class Peg, which simply creates a circular StaticBody at the same location as the Peg. Peg extends Circle, so the graphical representation of the StaticBody is taken care of.

Besides the Pegs, a SparkEmitter is involved in this example, as it is the class that creates the falling sparks from Figure 10-1. Listing 10-3 shows the implementation.

Listing 10-3. *SparkEmitter*

```
public class SparkEmitter extends Emitter{
    public var x:Number;
    public var y:Number;

    var cloudTimeline:Timeline = Timeline{
        repeatCount: Timeline.INDEFINITE;
        keyFrames: KeyFrame{
            time: 1/5.0*1s;
            action: emitCloud;
        }
    }
```

```
var sparkTimeline:Timeline = Timeline{
    repeatCount: Timeline.INDEFINITE;
    keyFrames: KeyFrame{
        time: 1/4.0*1s;
        action: emitSpark;
    }
}
function emitCloud():Void{
    var particle = PhysicsParticle{
        scaleX: .8
        scaleY: .8
        translateX: x;
        translateY: y;
        image: Main.cloud;
        radius: 4;
        weight: 1;
        totalSteps: 10 + Main.random.nextInt(30);
        effect: ColorAdjust{
            hue: .3
        }
        fadeInterpolator: Interpolator.LINEAR;
    }
    Main.addWorldNode(particle);
}

function emitSpark():Void{
    var size:Number = 2.0 + Main.random.nextFloat()*3.0;
    var direction = 225 + Main.random.nextInt(90);
    var speed = Main.random.nextInt(50);
    var particle = PhysicsParticle{
        scaleX: size/11.0
        scaleY: size/11.0
        translateX: x;
        translateY: y;
        image: Main.spark;
        radius: 5;
        weight: 1;
        startingSpeed: speed
        startingDirection: direction
        totalSteps: 1/size*400
        effect: ColorAdjust{
            hue: .3
        }
        fadeInterpolator: Interpolator.SPLINE(0.0, .8, 0.0, .8)

    }
    Main.addWorldNode(particle);
}

public override function play():Void{
    cloudTimeline.play();
```

207

```
        sparkTimeline.play();
    }

    public override function stop():Void{
        cloudTimeline.stop();
        sparkTimeline.stop();
    }
}
```

Listing 10-3 shows the class SparkEmitter. This class creates two Timelines, one for each particle type. The Timeline cloudTimeline calls the function emitCloud, which creates a PhysicsParticle and adds it to the world through the function addWorldNode. Likewise, the Timeline sparkTimeline calls the function emitSpark, which creates a PhysicsParticle and adds it to the world. The difference between the functions emitCloud and emitSpark is just the settings used to create the particle.

The cloud particles are created using the Image cloud set to a yellow color and set to live for 10 to 40 steps. Since a PhysicsParticle has a body, this particle will drop straight down. A linear interpolator controls how the particle fades.

The spark particles are created based on a random size, which dictates the scale, the startingSpeed, and the totalSteps. Large particles are slower than smaller ones, and smaller ones also live longer. The particles start out with a random velocity in a random upward direction and use the Image spark.

Listing 10-4 shows the implementation of PhysicsParticle.

Listing 10-4. *PhysicsParticle*

```
public class PhysicsParticle extends Group, WorldNode, Particle{
    public-init var image:Image;
    public-init var radius:Number;
    public-init var weight:Number;
    public-init var totalSteps:Number = 100;
    public-init var startingDirection:Number;
    public-init var startingSpeed:Number;
    public-init var fadeInterpolator:Interpolator=Interpolator.LINEAR;
    var stepsLeft = totalSteps;

    init{
        insert ImageView{
            translateX: image.width/-2.0;
            translateY: image.height/-2.0;
            image: image;
        } into content;

        var body = new Body(new Circle(radius), weight);
        body.setRestitution(.8);

        body.setPosition(translateX, translateY);
        body.setRotation(Math.toRadians(rotate));
        body.adjustAngularVelocity(5.0);

        var theta = Math.toRadians(startingDirection);
```

```
        body.adjustVelocity(new Vector2f(Math.cos(theta)*startingSpeed,
Math.sin(theta)*startingSpeed));

        insert body into bodies;
    }

    public override function update():Void{
        stepsLeft--;
        if (stepsLeft <= 0){
            Main.removeWorldNode(this)
        }

        var ratio = stepsLeft/totalSteps;
        if (ratio < 0){
            ratio = 0;
        }

        opacity = fadeInterpolator.interpolate(0.0, 1.0, ratio) as Number;


        translateX = bodies[0].getPosition().getX();
        translateY = bodies[0].getPosition().getY();
        rotate = Math.toDegrees(bodies[0].getRotation());
    }
}
```

Listing 10-4 shows the class PhysicsParticle, which extends Group, WorldNode, and Particle. The init function of PhysicsParticle adds an ImageView to the content. A Body is also created with the same location and rotation as the PhysicsParticle, and it's given a velocity based on the startingDirection and startingSpeed.

The update function is called after each step of the world object, and the location and rotation of the PhysicsParticle is adjusted to match the Body. The lifecycle of the PhysicsParticle is also handled by the function update. The value of stepsLeft is reduced by one, and if it reduces to zero, the entity is removed from the scene and the world.

If fadeInterpolator is set, the opacity of the PhysicsParticle is adjusted. The actual opacity is calculated by figuring out what ratio of the PhysicsParticle's steps have expired. This ratio is then fed into the fadeInterpolator to get the final result. The spark particles in this example use a spline interpolator with its value set so that most of the fading is put off until the end of the lifecycle.

Emitters as Bodies

The next example uses only a few bodies, but each body specifies the location of a more traditional particle emitter. As the emitters move about the screen, the particles they create basically stay in place. The advantage of this technique is that the number of bodies in the simulation is greatly reduced, so there are performance gains.

Figure 10-3 shows a number of fireballs bouncing down a field of pegs. As the fireball moves, a particle is created that drifts slightly upward, giving each fireball a trail effect—something required by fireballs.

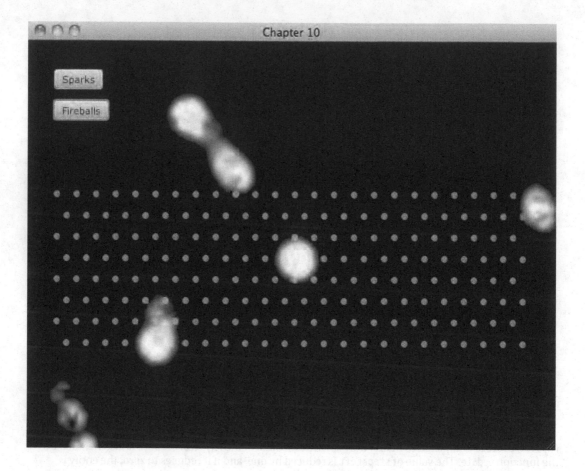

Figure 10-3. *Fireballs*

This example builds on the code from Listing 10-1 with the remainder of the `Main.fx` class shown in Listing 10-5.

Listing 10-5. *Fireballs (part of Main.fx)*

```
function fireballs():Void{
    clear();
    for (y in [1..4],i in [1..2],x in [1..24]){
        addWorldNode(Peg{
            radius: 4
            translateX: x*24+i*12
            translateY: 100+y*48+i*24
        });
    }
```

```
    addEmitter(FireballEmitter{});
}
```

Listing 10-5 shows the function fireballs, which sets up the next example. The function creates a number of Pegs in a sort of Pachinko pattern and adds a FireballEmitter. The class FireballEmitter creates a number of Fireball particles as Listing 10-6 illustrates.

Listing 10-6. FireballEmitter.fx

```
public class FireballEmitter extends Emitter{
    var emitTimeline = Timeline{
        repeatCount: Timeline.INDEFINITE;
        keyFrames: KeyFrame{
            time: 2s
            action: emit;
        }
    }
    function emit():Void{
        var fireball = Fireball{
                translateX: 100 + Main.random.nextInt(440)
                translateY: -30
                effect: ColorAdjust{
                    hue: Main.randomFromNegToPos(1.0);
                }
            }
        Main.addWorldNode(fireball);
        Main.addEmitter(fireball);
    }
    public override function play():Void{
        emitTimeline.play();
    }
    public override function stop():Void{
        emitTimeline.stop();
    }
}
```

Listing 10-6 shows the class FireballEmitter, which extends Emitter. This simple class creates a Timeline that periodically calls emit. The function emit creates a new Fireball with a random color and sets it loose. Listing 10-7 shows the implementation of Fireball.

Listing 10-7. Fireball.fx

```
public class Fireball extends Group, WorldNode, Particle, Emitter{
    var emitTimeline = Timeline{
        repeatCount: Timeline.INDEFINITE
        keyFrames: KeyFrame{
            time: 1/15.0*1s
            action: emit;
        }
    }
```

```
init{
    blendMode = BlendMode.ADD;

    bodies[0] = new Body(new Circle(4), 1);
    bodies[0].setPosition(translateX, translateY);
    bodies[0].setRestitution(.9);
}
function emit():Void{
    var fireParticle = FireParticle{
        image: Main.cloud;
        scaleX: .5;
        scaleY: .5;
        initialSteps: 10;
        direction: 270;
        speed: 2
    }
    insert fireParticle into content;
}
public override function update():Void{

    var dX = translateX - bodies[0].getPosition().getX();
    var dY = translateY - bodies[0].getPosition().getY();

    translateX = bodies[0].getPosition().getX();
    translateY = bodies[0].getPosition().getY();
    //rotate = Math.toDegrees(bodies[0].getRotation());

    for (node in content){
        node.translateX += dX;
        node.translateY += dY;
        (node as FireParticle).doStep();
    }

    if (translateX > 660){
        translateX = -20;
        bodies[0].setPosition(translateX, translateY);
    }
    if (translateX < -20){
        translateX = 660;
        bodies[0].setPosition(translateX, translateY);
    }
    if (dX == 0){
        bodies[0].adjustVelocity(new Vector2f(.2,0));
    }
    if (translateY > 500){
        Main.removeWorldNode(this);
        Main.removeEmitter(this);
    }
}
public override function play():Void{
    emitTimeline.play();
```

```
    }
    public override function stop():Void{
        emitTimeline.stop();
    }
}
```

The interesting thing about the class Fireball as shown in Listing 10-7 is that Fireball extends Group, WorldNode, Particle, and Emitter. It extends Group so it can contain the FireParticles it produces. It extends WorldNode and Particle because it is has to bounce around the screen, and these interface classes provide that functionality. Lastly, Fireball extends Emitter, and it does this so its Timeline—emitTimeline—will be started and stopped.

For the most part, Fireball is just like the other Emitters in this book: It creates a particle that animates in some way. Fireball is also much like the other nodes used with the physics engine. It creates a Body that it uses in the method update to synchronize its location on the screen with its location in the physics model.

Fireball adds some other features to the update method. For example, if the Fireball is off the screen to the left, it is moved to the right side. And if it is off to the right, it will be moved to the left so it will fly back onto the screen. This is why the fireballs wrap around the screen. If the Fireball is below a certain level, it removes itself.

The update function also adjusts the location of the FireParticles the Emitter has created. This is done to keep the location of the particles steady while the Emitter moves about the screen.

The particles created by Fireball are defined by the class FireParticle. Listing 10-8 shows the implementation of FireParticle.

***Listing 10-8.** FireParticle.fx*

```
public class FireParticle extends ImageView, Particle{

    public-init var initialSteps:Integer;//number of steps until removed
    public-init var startingOpacity = 1.0;
    public-init var speed:Number;//pixels per step
    public-init var fadeout = true;
    public-init var direction = -90.0;
    public-init var directionVariation = 10.0;

    var deltaX;//change in x location per step
    var deltaY;//change in y location per step
    var stepsRemaining = initialSteps;

    init{

        smooth = true;
        translateX -= image.width/2.0;
        translateY -= image.height/2.0;

        rotate = Math.toDegrees(Main.random.nextFloat()*2.0*Math.PI);

        opacity = startingOpacity;
        //random direction in radians
        var startingDirection = direction + Main.randomFromNegToPos(directionVariation);
```

```
        var theta = Math.toRadians(startingDirection);
        deltaX = Math.cos(theta)*speed;
        deltaY = Math.sin(theta)*speed;
    }

    package function doStep(){
        //remove particle if particle has expired
        if (--stepsRemaining == 0){
            delete this from (parent as Group).content;
        }
        //advance particle's location
        translateX += deltaX;
        translateY += deltaY;

        if (fadeout){
            opacity = startingOpacity*(stepsRemaining as Number)/(initialSteps as Number);
        }
        rotate += 4;
    }
}
```

In Listing 10-8 we see the class FireParticle, which extends ImageView and Particle. This class borrows many ideas from the particles in Chapter 2. We can see that the variable initialSteps determines how long each FireParticle will be present in the scene, just like before. The other parameters work as expected Note, however, that direction is preset to -90. This causes the FireParticle to move upward like fire does. In the init function we can see that the variable startingDirection is set to the value of direction plus a random value. This gives each FireParticle a little variation in its motion.

The doStep method also works much as expected— when stepsRemaining reaches zero the FireParticle is removed from the scene. The position of the FireParticle is updated by adding deltaX to translateX and adding deltaY to translateY. Lastly, the opacity of the FireParticle is set based on how far along the FireParticle is in its life cycle.

Summary

This chapter presented two examples of using particle effects with a physics engine. The first example used a body for each particle. This created a complex effect, but at the expense of performance. The second example used one body per emitter, and each emitter created its own small particle effect. Both techniques are excellent ways to add advanced graphics elements to any application, but especially to games.

CHAPTER 11

■■■

Pulling It All Together:
Clown Cannon

Throughout this book I have presented techniques and examples in isolation so that you can examine details of the implementation. They represent the experience that I have gained from trial and error when working with JavaFX. But an application is more than just the sum of its features and effects, which is why, in this chapter, we will explore an entire application from start to finish. We will look at the design process, the workflow, and the implementation of an example application.

Design Phase

I wanted to find a way to bring the examples in this book together, and I thought an example application would do the job. While some of the techniques in this book could be used in many different types of applications, a game is the only application where it makes sense to use all of them. It seemed each chapter could add something to a game that contributed to specific design goals: Physics, for example, quickly creates compelling game play. Animated lighting gives a unique and interesting look to a game. What about animated gradients? There must be some use for them in a game.

Game Design

So I followed my own advice from Chapter 1 and opened up Adobe Illustrator and started designing a game from scratch. My goal was to use as many examples from the book as I could without it seeming contrived, but upon reflection I gave up worrying about that. Let me present to you Clown Cannon, a game where the goal is to fire a clown out of a cannon and into a bucket of water. Figures 11-1 and 11-2 show the initial design concept.

In Figure 11-1 a very simple start screen is described with a thematic background, a title, and two buttons. The four notes are self-explanatory. But I want to point out that the use of transitions is nearly identical to the case presented in Chapter 3—using transitions to move from one screen to another.

Clown Cannon – Start Screen

1. Title for clown cannon, 'circus' like font, animated gradient.

2. Play Game button, wipe transitions screen to Game Screen, starts a new game.

3. About Button, transitions screen to about screen. Random transition.

4. Circus tent background, with circus floor.

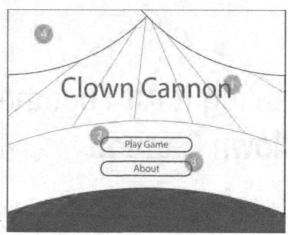

Figure 11-1. *Clown Cannon start screen*

Figure 11-2 explains the idea of the game.

Clown Cannon – Game Screen

1. The cannon fires the clown out of the cannon; the angle can be adjusted with the mouse scroll wheel or the up and down arrow keys.

2. If the clown lands in the water bucket then points are scored.

3. Power bar; this cycles up and down to indicate the starting velocity of the clown when the user clicks the fire button (left mouse or space bar)

4. If the clown passes through a Bonus Balloon the score received if they land in the bucket is doubled.

5. Random pegs appear before each clown is fired, the clown will bounce off of these in the air, these add difficulty.

6. The ladder has clowns climbing up it: the number of clowns indicates the number of shots the player has left.

7. A net to catch the clown, the clown cannot pass below this level. When the clown lands on the net the shot is over.

8. Firework launchers shoot fireworks when the clown lands in the water bucket.

9. The current score of the player is posted here.

Figure 11-2. *Clown Cannon game screen*

A user can aim the cannon and shoot a clown into the water bucket on the right, and the power meter on the upper left determines the speed at which the clown leaves the cannon. The power meter cycles up and down—it is up to the user to time her clicks in order to achieve the desired power. The animation of the power meter will be an animated gradient, like those presented in Chapter 8. A number of pegs appear to block the path of the clown. These pegs are randomly positioned to provide a unique experience every time the game is played. The flight of the clown and how it bounces off the pegs will use the concepts from Chapter 6 on physics to provide realistic motion. If the clown passes through the balloon, the score is doubled for that shot. An interpolator, as seen in Chapter 5, drives the motion of the balloon. Lastly, landing in the water bucket should reward the player with some fancy graphics, and this is where the firework launchers come in. When the clown lands in the bucket, a short fireworks display is presented to the user, which, of course, is a great use of the particle effects from Chapter 2.

Graphic Design

Now that we have the basic design in place, it is time to give the game graphics an overhaul. Since the initial design was done in Adobe Illustrator, it makes sense to use that same tool to create the graphics for the game. We simply export the content to a JavaFX-friendly format. Figure 11-3 shows the contents of the final Illustrator file.

Figure 11-3. *Final game assets*

In Figure 11-3, all of the game assets are presented. It is sort of a garbled mess— every graphic used in the game is laid over each other. This is intentional, because for this chapter I decided to use a single Illustrator file to store all of the assets in the game. There are advantages and disadvantages to using a single file instead of multiple files, but before we discuss that, let me explain how the Illustrator file is organized. (By the way, the Illustrator file used to create the assets in this game is included with the source code, so you can inspect it. The file is saved as a CS3 file.)

On the right of Figure 11-3 we see the Layer tool from Illustrator, which displays each component in the file. Each of those items will become a JavaFX Node when exported. For example, the item named jfx:score is the graphic that says "Score: 00000." This will become a Text node named score in the JavaFX code and will enable the code to change the displayed text dynamically at runtime. In fact, each component updated at runtime is given a name with the prefix jfx:, which allows the export tool, in conjunction with NetBeans, to create a JavaFX class that represents this content. This class will be called GameAssetsUI. Chapter 1 describes working with the JavaFX Production Suite in more detail.

The game is composed of three screens—the start screen, the welcome screen, and the game screen. Each of these screens will be an instance of GameAssetsUI. Since each screen does not require all of the content found in each GameAssetsUI, the game code must prune nodes to create exactly the right content. For example, neither the start screen nor the game screen require the about panel, just as the welcome screen and the about screen don't require the text "Game Over," as this is only used by the game screen. When each screen is initialized, all unneeded nodes will be removed.

It might make sense to simply create an Illustrator file for each screen, removing the need to delete unwanted nodes. You could also create one master Illustrator file or a number of smaller Illustrator files this is a question of workflow. For this game, however, I decided to create a single file because all of the screens shared a background; I did not want to update three different illustrator files every time I changed the color of the background. I could have also chosen to create a background Illustrator file and then three other Illustrator files for each screen. This, of course, would work. But once we get to the code we will see that initializing each GameAssetsUI for use as three different screens is not all that complicated. Let me say this: The Illustrator to JavaFX workflow is not perfect. In most cases there will be JavaFX code that does some sort of initialization on each illustrator file, and I leave it up to you to figure out what is best for your application and workflow.

There are a few graphics at the bottom of Figure 11-3—five pegs, a flying clown, and a balloon. These graphics will be placed dynamically on the game screen, so there is no reason to lay them out with the rest of the graphics. The initialization code of the game screen will handle these graphics specifically, as they will be at many different locations in the course of a game.

While most of the design was done with Illustrator, some had to happen with JavaFX code. For the background I wanted searchlights moving back and forth to add to the sense that the action is happening in a circus tent. Figure 11-4 and Figure 11-5 show the difference between the Illustrator file and the game in JavaFX.

Figure 11-4. Back of tent revealed in asset file

Figure 11-5. *Back of tent after lights are applied in JavaFX*

In Figure 11-4 we can see the back of the tent. It is composed of a number of brightly colored shapes. The arced horizontal band is supposed to be the back wall, and the vertically aligned triangular areas are supposed to be the ceiling of the tent. Without any shading the scene is pretty flat. In Figure 11-5 we can see the same scene with a JavaFX SpotLight applied to the background. The light moves in a figure eight pattern and distorts as it gets farther from the center. This creates a convincing sense of depth.

In Figure 11-6 we can see the game screen with the clown in mid-air. The five pegs have been randomly placed to impede the flight of the clown, and the bonus balloon is floating out of reach of the clown.

Figure 11-6. The game screen

The power level on the upper left shows that the user clicked the mouse when the meter was at about 80%. Note that the power level is a gradient. We will use the animated gradient technique from Chapter 8 to implement this.

If the clown makes it to the water bucket on the right, points are awarded and there is a small fireworks display. Figure 11-7 shows the firework display.

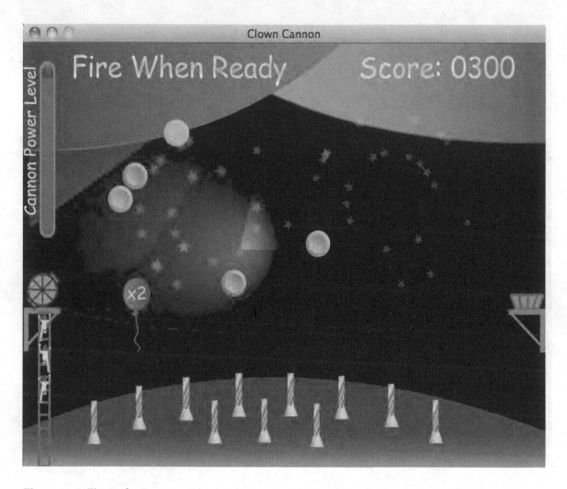

Figure 11-7. Fireworks

In Figure 11-7 there are two dots that came out of the launchers below them. The dots represent a firework shell, and when they reach the top of their animation a bunch of star particles are created. Each star particle moves outward in a random direction to create a firework effect.

Implementation

You learned how to implement the effects used in this game in previous chapters; the following code examples will focus on how these effects are used in an application. We will also look at the code that glues these effects together to create a complete game and some tricks you can use when working with content created in Illustrator.

Game Life Cycle

All applications, including games, require some sort of life cycle that moves the user from a starting screen to each feature in the application. In Figure 11-8 we can see the life cycle of Clown Cannon. When the game is first launched, the start screen is displayed. From the start screen the user can either view the about screen or play the game. The game screen, in turn, allows the user to play again, which means staying on the game screen, or go back the start screen. This is a very rudimentary application life cycle, but it is complicated enough to require some set-up code. Listing 11-1 shows how the game sets itself up.

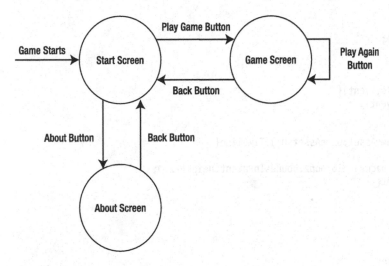

Figure 11-8. *Game life cycle*

Listing 11-1. *Main.fx*

```
public def random = new Random();

public var startScreen = GameAssetsUI{}
var aboutScreen = GameAssetsUI{}
var gameModel:GameModel;

var rootGroup = Group{
    content: startScreen
    onKeyReleased: keyReleased;
}

var scene = Scene {
        width: 640
        height: 480
        content: [rootGroup]
        fill: Color.BLACK
    }
```

```
public var blockInput = false;
public var lightAnim:Timeline;

function run():Void{
    initStartScreen();
    initAboutScreen();
    Stage {
        title: "Clown Cannon"
        resizable: false;
        scene: scene
    }
    rootGroup.requestFocus();
    lightAnim.play();
}

function keyReleased(event:KeyEvent){
    gameModel.keyReleased(event);
}

public function addLights(gameAsset:GameAssetsUI):Timeline{

    var yCenter = gameAsset.backPanelGroup2.boundsInParent.height/2.0;
    var spotLight = SpotLight{
            x: 320
            y: yCenter
            z: 50;
            pointsAtZ: 0
            pointsAtX: 320
            pointsAtY: yCenter
            color: Color.WHITE;
            specularExponent: 2
        }

    gameAsset.backPanelGroup1.effect = Lighting{
        light: spotLight
        diffuseConstant: 2
    }

    var anim = Timeline{
        repeatCount: Timeline.INDEFINITE;
        keyFrames: [
KeyFrame{
                time: 0s
                values: [spotLight.pointsAtX => 320 tween Interpolator.EASEBOTH,
                        spotLight.pointsAtY => yCenter tween Interpolator.EASEBOTH]
            },
            KeyFrame{
                time: 1s
                values: spotLight.pointsAtY => yCenter+100 tween Interpolator.EASEBOTH
            },
            KeyFrame{
                time: 2s
```

```
                    values: spotLight.pointsAtX => 30 tween Interpolator.EASEBOTH
                },
                KeyFrame{
                    time: 3s
                    values: spotLight.pointsAtY => yCenter-100 tween Interpolator.EASEBOTH
                },
                KeyFrame{
                    time: 4s
                    values: spotLight.pointsAtX => 320 tween Interpolator.EASEBOTH
                },
                KeyFrame{
                    time: 5s
                    values: spotLight.pointsAtY => yCenter+100 tween Interpolator.EASEBOTH
                },
                KeyFrame{
                    time: 6s
                    values: spotLight.pointsAtX => 610 tween Interpolator.EASEBOTH
                },
                KeyFrame{
                    time: 7s
                    values: spotLight.pointsAtY => yCenter-100 tween Interpolator.EASEBOTH
                },
                KeyFrame{
                    time: 8s
                    values: [spotLight.pointsAtX => 320 tween Interpolator.EASEBOTH,
                             spotLight.pointsAtY => yCenter tween Interpolator.EASEBOTH]
                }
                ]
        }
    return anim;
}

function initStartScreen():Void{
    simplifyGradients(startScreen);
    lightAnim = addLights(startScreen);
    removeFromParent(startScreen.aboutPanel);
    removeFromParent(startScreen.waitingClownGroup);
    removeFromParent(startScreen.startGameInstructions);
    removeFromParent(startScreen.endButtons);
    removeFromParent(startScreen.gameOverText);
    makeButton(startScreen.startButton, startGame);
    makeButton(startScreen.aboutButton, showAbout);
}

function initAboutScreen():Void{
    simplifyGradients(aboutScreen);
    removeFromParent(aboutScreen.startButton);
    removeFromParent(aboutScreen.aboutButton);
    removeFromParent(aboutScreen.startGameInstructions);
    removeFromParent(aboutScreen.waitingClownGroup);
    removeFromParent(aboutScreen.endButtons);
```

```
        removeFromParent(aboutScreen.gameOverText);
        makeButton(aboutScreen.backButton, backToStart);
        aboutScreen.effect = ColorAdjust{
            hue: .2
        }
    }

    public function removeFromParent(node:Node):Void{
        var parent:Object = node.parent;
        if (parent instanceof Group){
            delete node from (parent as Group).content;
        } else if (parent instanceof Scene){
            delete node from (parent as Scene).content
        }
    }
    public function makeButton(node:Node,action:function()){
        node.blocksMouse = true;
        node.onMouseClicked = function(event:MouseEvent):Void{
            if (not blockInput){
                action();
            }
        }
        node.onMouseEntered = function(event:MouseEvent):Void{
            node.effect = Glow{}
        }
        node.onMouseExited = function(event:MouseEvent):Void{
            node.effect = null;
        }
    }
    public function allowInput():Void{
        blockInput = false;
    }
    function startGame():Void{
        lightAnim.stop();
        gameModel = GameModel{}
        FlipReplace.doReplace(startScreen, gameModel.screen, gameModel.startingAnimationOver);
    }
    function showAbout():Void{
        lightAnim.stop();
        blockInput = true;
        WipeReplace.doReplace(startScreen, aboutScreen, allowInput);
    }
    function backToStart():Void{
        lightAnim.play();
        blockInput = true;
        WipeReplace.doReplace(aboutScreen, startScreen, allowInput);
    }
    public function offsetFromZero(node:Node):Group{
        var xOffset = node.boundsInParent.minX + node.boundsInParent.width/2.0;
        var yOffset = node.boundsInParent.minY + node.boundsInParent.height/2.0;
```

```
        var parent = node.parent as Group;
        var index = Sequences.indexOf(parent.content, node);

        delete node from (parent as Group).content;

        node.translateX = -xOffset;
        node.translateY = -yOffset;

        var group = Group{
            translateX: xOffset;
            translateY: yOffset;
            content: node;
        }
        insert group before parent.content[index];

        return group;
}

public function createLinearGradient(stops:Stop[]):LinearGradient{
    return LinearGradient{
        startX: 1
        endX: 1
        startY: 0
        endY: 1
        proportional: true
        stops: sortStops(stops);
    }
}
public function sortStops(stops:Stop[]):Stop[]{
    var result:Stop[] = Sequences.sort(stops, Comparator{
        public override function compare(obj1:Object, obj2: Object):Integer{

            var stop1 = (obj1 as Stop);
            var stop2 = (obj2 as Stop);

            if (stop1.offset > stop2.offset){
                return 1;
            } else if (stop1.offset < stop2.offset){
                return -1;
            } else {
                return 0;
            }
        }
    }) as Stop[];

    return result
}

public function randomFromNegToPos(max:Number):Number{
        if (max == 0.0){
            return 0.0;
        }
```

```
            var result = max - random.nextFloat()*max*2;
            return result;
    }

public function simplifyGradients(node:Node):Void{
        if (node instanceof Shape){
            var shape  = node as Shape;
            if (shape.fill instanceof LinearGradient){
                var linearGradient = (shape.fill as LinearGradient);
                if (sizeof(linearGradient.stops) > 2){
                    var newStops:Stop[];

                    insert linearGradient.stops[0] into newStops;
                    insert linearGradient.stops[sizeof(linearGradient.stops)-1] into newStops;

                    var newGradient = LinearGradient{
                        endX: linearGradient.endX
                        endY: linearGradient.endY
                        proportional: linearGradient.proportional;
                        startX: linearGradient.startX
                        startY: linearGradient.startY
                        stops: newStops;
                    }
                    shape.fill = newGradient;
                }
            }
        }
        if (node instanceof Group){
            for(n in (node as Group).content){
                simplifyGradients(n);
            }
        }
    }
}
```

In Listing 11-1 the variables startScreen and aboutScreen are instances of GameAssetsUI. Each GameAssetsUI is a complete set of Nodes from the original Illustrator file. The functions initStartScreen and initAboutScreen prepare startScreen and aboutScreen for use in the game. The function initStartScreen simplifies the gradients, creates an animation for the spotlight, removes a number of unwanted Nodes and turns the Nodes startScreen.startButton and startScreen.aboutButton into buttons. Let's take a look at each of these steps.

The gradients generated when exporting from Illustrator are oddly complex. Listing 11-2 shows one of these gradients.

Listing 11-2. *GameAssets.fxz (partial)*

```
SVGPath {
        id: "floor"
        fill: LinearGradient{proportional: false startX: 320.31 startY:385.22 endX: 320.31
endY: 480.00 stops: [
        Stop {offset: 0.005 color: Color.rgb(0x5e,0x43,0x19)},
```

```
        Stop {offset: 0.5751 color: Color.rgb(0x66,0x47,0x19)},
        Stop {offset: 0.6603 color: Color.rgb(0x6e,0x4c,0x1a)},
        Stop {offset: 0.7159 color: Color.rgb(0x76,0x51,0x1b)},
        Stop {offset: 0.7582 color: Color.rgb(0x7e,0x56,0x1c)},
        Stop {offset: 0.7927 color: Color.rgb(0x86,0x5b,0x1d)},
        Stop {offset: 0.8220 color: Color.rgb(0x8e,0x60,0x1e)},
        Stop {offset: 0.8478 color: Color.rgb(0x96,0x65,0x1f)},
        Stop {offset: 0.8707 color: Color.rgb(0x9e,0x6a,0x20)},
        Stop {offset: 0.8914 color: Color.rgb(0xa6,0x6e,0x20)},
        Stop {offset: 0.9104 color: Color.rgb(0xae,0x73,0x21)},
        Stop {offset: 0.9279 color: Color.rgb(0xb6,0x78,0x22)},
        Stop {offset: 0.9441 color: Color.rgb(0xbe,0x7d,0x23)},
        Stop {offset: 0.9593 color: Color.rgb(0xc6,0x82,0x24)},
        Stop {offset: 0.9736 color: Color.rgb(0xce,0x87,0x25)},
        Stop {offset: 0.9872 color: Color.rgb(0xd6,0x8c,0x26)},
        Stop {offset: 1.000 color: Color.rgb(0xde,0x91,0x27)},
    ]}
    stroke: null
    content: "M0.31,480.00 L0.31,439.00 Q299.31,318.00 640.31,439.00 L640.31,480.00 Z "
}
```

In Listing 11-2, a LinearGradient is defined with 17 Stops, but in Illustrator this gradient is defined with just 2 colors. I am not exactly sure why all of the extra Stops are included. Perhaps the algorithm Illustrator used for tweening colors is different than that of JavaFX. Since gradients are a performance pain point in JavaFX, it makes sense to simplify these gradients to use just 2 Stops. There might be a fidelity issue with doing this, but I couldn't tell the difference between the LinearGradient with 17 Stops and the simplified LinearGradient with only 2 Stops. In Listing 11-1, the functions that initialize the two GameAssetUIs use the function simplifyGradient to recursively traverse the Node tree and simplify all LinearGradients. Be warned that if your Illustrator file uses gradients, which should have more than 2 Stops, the simplifyGradients function will not correctly preserve the intended look.

The function initStartScreen creates a Timeline for animating the SpotLight by calling the function addLights. The function addLights creates a Lighting effect with a SpotLight and applies it to the Group backPanelGroup2. The Group backPanelGroup2 contains the ceiling and wall of the circus tent. The SpotLight that is created is positioned in the center of the Group backPanelGroup2, and the Timeline anim is then created to change the location where the SpotLight is pointing. The Timeline anim is returned from the function addLights to allow the animation to be started and stopped. This is important because applying lighting effects is computationally expensive and should be turned off when not in use.

The functions initStartScreen and initAboutScreen use the function removeFromParent to get rid of unwanted content. This is a simple utility function found in Listing 11-1 that I find handy, because Node.parent returns a Node of type Parent, which is not very useful. Both of the classes Scene and Group extend Parent, since these are the two types that might contain a Node. Unfortunately the class Parent does not require an attribute named content. Rather it requires the function removeFromParent to cast node.parent to the correct class before deleting it from the content that contains it.

The last thing the functions initStartScreen and initAboutScreen do is create buttons out of some of the Nodes in the fxz content. The function makeButton does not create an instance of javafx.scene.control.Button, but instead just adds button-like functionality to the Node passed to the function. Adding some event listeners to the Node does this. The onMouseClicked attribute is used to call the function action when the user clicks on the Node, and setting blocksMouse to true prevents the click from being processed by some other listening node. The two properties onMouseEntered and onMouseExited make the button Node change color as the mouse passes over it, which tells the user that the Node is interactive in some way.

The Node startScreen now has two buttons wired up to actions. When the user clicks on the Node aboutScreen.startButton, a new game is started by calling the function startGame. When the user clicks on startScreen.aboutButton, the startScreen Node is replaced with the Node aboutScreen using a WipeReplace. Conversely, when the user clicks on the Node aboutScreen.backButton, a WipeReplace replaces the Node aboutScreen with the Node startScreen. This allows the user to navigate from the start screen to the about screen and back. When the user clicks on the Node startScreen.startButton, the Node startScreen is replaced with the Node gameModel.screen. This starts the game proper.

Round Life Cycle

Once the user is ready to actually play the game, the class GameModel initializes and starts accepting user input. Playing the game constitutes firing a clown five times at the bucket of water. Let's call that a round. Each time a clown is fired the application will go from waiting for the user, to animating the scene, to back to waiting for the user. We will start by looking at how GameModel initializes and then how the state of the game is managed. Let's take a look at the class GameModel and get into the meat of the game.

Listing 11-3. GameModel.fx (partial)

```
public class GameModel {
    //local variables omitted for brevity, please see the source code.

    init{
        initScreen();
    }

    function initScreen():Void{
        Main.simplifyGradients(screen);
        Main.removeFromParent(screen.aboutPanel);
        Main.removeFromParent(screen.aboutButton);
        Main.removeFromParent(screen.startButton);
        Main.removeFromParent(screen.title);

        screen.powerLevel.visible = true;
        screen.backFromPlayButton.visible = false;
        screen.playAgainButton.visible = false;
        screen.gameOverText.visible = false;
        Main.makeButton(screen.backFromPlayButton, goBack);
        Main.makeButton(screen.playAgainButton, playAgain);

        screen.onMouseWheelMoved = mouseWheelMoved;
        screen.onMouseClicked = mouseButtonClicked;

        clownNode = Main.offsetFromZero(screen.flyingClown);
        cannonNode = Main.offsetFromZero(screen.cannon);
        bucketNode = Main.offsetFromZero(screen.waterBucket);
        balloonNode = Main.offsetFromZero(screen.bonusBalloon);
        net = Main.offsetFromZero(screen.net);
```

```
        insert Main.offsetFromZero(screen.peg0) into pegs;
        insert Main.offsetFromZero(screen.peg1) into pegs;
        insert Main.offsetFromZero(screen.peg2) into pegs;
        insert Main.offsetFromZero(screen.peg3) into pegs;
        insert Main.offsetFromZero(screen.peg4) into pegs;

        for (firework in (screen.fireworkGroup as Group).content){
            insert Main.offsetFromZero(firework) into fireworks;
        }

        lightsAnim = Main.addLights(screen);
        lightsAnim.play();
    }

    public function startingAnimationOver():Void{
        Main.allowInput();
        var startingAnimation = Timeline{
            keyFrames: [
                    KeyFrame{
                        time: 10s
                        values: screen.startGameInstructions.opacity => 0.0 tween
Interpolator.SPLINE(1.00,0.00,1.00,0.00)
                        action: startRound;
                    }
                    ]
        }
        startingAnimation.play();
    }

    function startRound():Void{
        cannonAngle = -45;
        world.clear();
        clownsAvailable = 5;
        for (peg in pegs){
            peg.translateX = 100 + Main.random.nextInt(400);
            peg.translateY = 100 + Main.random.nextInt(200);
            var circleBody = StaticCircleBody{
                node: peg;
            }
            world.add(circleBody.body);
        }
        //adding wall on right edge of screen
        for (i in [0,,40]){
            var wall = new StaticBody(new net.phys2d.raw.shapes.Circle(12));
            wall.setPosition(640+6, i*12);
            world.add(wall);
        }

        readyLaunch();
    }
```

```
function mouseButtonClicked(event:MouseEvent):Void{
    fireClown();
}
function mouseWheelMoved(event:MouseEvent):Void{
    adjustCannon(event.wheelRotation);
}
public function keyReleased(event:KeyEvent):Void{
    if (event.code == KeyCode.VK_SPACE){
        fireClown();
    } else if (event.code == KeyCode.VK_UP){
        adjustCannon(-2);
    } else if (event.code == KeyCode.VK_DOWN){
        adjustCannon(2);
    }
}

function adjustCannon(amount:Number):Void{
    cannonAngle += amount;
    if (cannonAngle < -85){
        cannonAngle = -85
    }
    if (cannonAngle > -15){
        cannonAngle = -15;
    }
}

function readyLaunch():Void{
    (screen.status as Text).content = "Fire When Ready";
    if (clownBody != null){
        world.remove(clownBody.body);
    }

    balloonAnim.stop();
    balloonAnim = Timeline{
    repeatCount: Timeline.INDEFINITE;
        autoReverse: true;
        keyFrames: [
                KeyFrame{
                    time: 0s
                    values: balloonNode.translateY => 100.0 tween Interpolator.EASEOUT;
                },
                KeyFrame{
                    time: 4s
                    values: balloonNode.translateY => 400.0 tween Interpolator.EASEIN;
                }
        ]
    }

    clownNode.translateX = cannonNode.translateX;
    clownNode.translateY = cannonNode.translateY;
    clownNode.rotate = cannonAngle;
```

```
        balloonNode.translateX = 100 + Main.random.nextInt(400);
        balloonNode.visible = true;
        balloonAnim.playFromStart();
        balloonMulti = 1;

        canFire = true;
        powerAnim.playFromStart();
}

function fireClown():Void{
    if (canFire){
        powerAnim.stop();

        canFire = false;
        clownsAvailable--;

        clownNode.translateX = cannonNode.translateX;
        clownNode.translateY = cannonNode.translateY;
        clownNode.rotate = cannonAngle;

        clownBody = ClownBody{
            startingPower: cannonPower;
            clown: clownNode
        }
        world.add(clownBody.body);
        worldUpdater.play();
    }
}

function update():Void{
    world.<<step>>();
    clownBody.update();

    checkBalloon();

    if (collision(clownNode, bucketNode)){
        worldUpdater.stop();
        score+=100*balloonMulti;
        celebrate();
    } else if (clownNode.translateY > net.boundsInParent.minY){
        worldUpdater.stop();
        nextClown();
    }
}

function checkBalloon():Void{
    if (collision(clownNode, balloonNode)){
        balloonNode.visible = false;
        balloonMulti = 2;
    }

}
```

```
function celebrate():Void{
    (screen.status as Text).content = "Well Done!";
    var timeline = Timeline{}

    var count = (Main.random.nextInt(sizeof(fireworks))+1)*balloonMulti;

    for (i in [0..count]){
        var firework = fireworks[Main.random.nextInt(sizeof(fireworks)-1)];
        insert KeyFrame{
            time: i*.5s;
            action: function(){
                    doFirework(firework);
                    };
        } into timeline.keyFrames;
    }

    insert KeyFrame{
            time: count*.5s + 1s;
            action: function(){
                    nextClown();
                    }
        } into timeline.keyFrames;

    timeline.play();
}

// fireworks related functions found in Listing 11-6

function nextClown():Void{
    if (clownsAvailable > 0){
        readyLaunch();
    } else {
        endRound();
    }
}

// section omitted for brevity
}
```

In Listing 11-3 we can see class GameModel, whose job it is to coordinate the state of the GameAssetsUI call screen. In the init function we can see that a call to initScreen is made. The function initScreen simplifies the gradients, removes some unwanted Nodes, and creates two buttons for managing game state—just like the functions initStartScreen and initAboutScreen from Listing 11-1.

The function initScreen also does some other bookkeeping. There are a number of local variables such as clownNode, cannonNode, bucketNode, and net that are assigned by a call to Main.offsetFromZero. The function Main.offsetFromZero can be seen in Listing 11-1. This function is used to wrap a Node within screen with a new Group. This is necessary because the Nodes defined within an fxz file do not have their translateX and translateY values set. Looking at Nodes with an fxz file will help explain this. Listing 11-4 shows the Node bonusBalloon from the fxz file.

Listing 11-4. GameAssets.fxz (bonusBalloon)

```
Group {
    id: "bonusBalloon"
    content: [
            SVGPath {
                    fill: null
                    stroke: Color.rgb(0x9b,0x85,0x78)
                    strokeWidth: 1.0
                    content: "M426.43,585.43 Q428.83,581.53 428.83,580.02 C428.83,578.52
422.67,574.92 422.67,572.36 C422.67,569.81 427.03,564.40 427.03,562.00 C427.03,559.59
422.82,540.37 424.92,538.26 "
            },
            Polygon {
                    points: [422.84,537.66,420.09,543.59,427.92,543.59,425.81,537.03]
                    fill: LinearGradient{proportional: false startX: 420.09 startY:540.31
endX: 427.92 endY: 540.31 stops: [
Stop {offset: 0.000 color: Color.rgb(0xd4,0x47,0x99)},
Stop {offset: 1.000 color: Color.rgb(0x72,0x38,0x95)},
]}
                    stroke: null
            },
            SVGPath {
                    fill: LinearGradient{proportional: false startX: 409.17 startY:519.59
endX: 441.62 endY: 519.59 stops: [
Stop {offset: 0.000 color: Color.rgb(0xd4,0x47,0x99)},
Stop {offset: 1.000 color: Color.rgb(0x72,0x38,0x95)},
]}
                    stroke: null
                    content: "M441.62,519.59 C441.62,529.77 434.36,538.02 425.40,538.02
C416.44,538.02 409.17,529.77 409.17,519.59 C409.17,509.41 416.44,501.16 425.40,501.16
C434.36,501.16 441.62,509.41 441.62,519.59 Z "
            },
            Text {
                    transforms:
[Transform.affine(1.000000,0.000000,0.000000,1.000000,413.540470,525.303710)]
                    fill: Color.rgb(0xf9,0xed,0x33)
                    stroke: null
                    x: 0.0
                    y: 0.0
                    textOrigin: TextOrigin.BASELINE
                    font: Font.font( "ComicSansMS", FontWeight.REGULAR, FontPosture.REGULAR,
19.80)
                    content: "x2"
            },                      ]
}
```

In Listing 11-4 we can see that the Node with id equal to bonusBalloon is defined by a number of SVGPath Nodes. The coordinates that comprise each SVGPath are defined in terms of the upper left of the entire GameAssetUI. This means that when you set bonusBalloon's translateX and translateY to zero, it is placed at the original location form the Illustrator file. If we look at Figure 11-3 we can see that the original location is somewhere below the bottom of the screen. Since we will be moving bonusBalloon around the screen and we want to know if the Node flyingNode intercepts it, it makes sense to normalize both the coordinates of the bonusBalloon and the flyingClown Nodes.

Main.offsetFromZero from Listing 11-1 performs this function by wrapping each Node in a new Group and adjusting the translateX and translateY values of the Group and the Node so that the Node stays in the same visual location on the screen. But the returned Group's translateX and translateY values reflect its position relative to the upper left of the screen.

The function initScreen is called by the init function of the class GameModel. If we look at the function startGame from Listing 11-1, we see that the GameModel is constructed before the transition FlipReplace is called. Recall from Chapter 3 that each transition allows the caller to specify a function that should be called when the transition is complete. When the FlipReplace is done it calls the function GameModel.startingAnimationOver, which actually gets the GameModel ready to start playing the game. Figure 11-8 shows how the game state is managed by the class GameModel.

In Figure 11-9 we see that the function startingAnimationOver gets the ball rolling by calling startRound after the instructions fade out. The function startRound readies the game by resetting the angle of the cannon, setting the number of clowns to five, and randomly distributing the pegs.

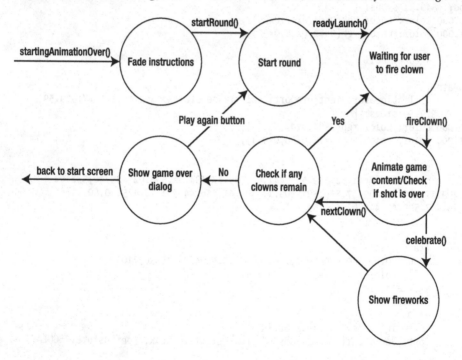

Figure 11-9. *Game state*

In Listing 11-3 we can see that the function startRound adds a Body to a World object. Both Body and World are classes from Phys2d and are used to do our physics simulation. Chapter 6 describes how this works. But be reminded that by adding Bodies to a World you can then use the World object to calculate the location of the clown and the pegs as the game plays out. We can see that the function startRound calls readyLaunch, which resets the location of the Node balloonNode, resets the location of the Node clownNode, and restarts the Timeline powerAnim. The Timeline powerAnim causes the value of cannonPower to change from 0 to 1000 over 1 second. When the value of cannonPower changes, a new LinearGradient is applied to the Node powerFill. This is what animates the power bar on the upper left of the scene.

Once readyLaunch is called, the game is ready for the user to fire the clown. When the user clicks the mouse button or presses the spacebar, the function fireClown is called. The function fireClown stops the Timeline powerAnim and uses the current value of cannonPower and the current value of cannonAngle to create a new ClownBody. The class ClownBody is used to synchronize the position and rotation of the Node clownNode with the Body that represents the clown in flight. Listing 11-5 shows the class ClownBody.

Listing 11-5. ClownBody.fx

```
public class ClownBody {
    public-init var startingPower:Number;
    public-init var clown:Node;
    public var body:Body;

    init{
        body = new Body(new net.phys2d.raw.shapes.Circle(4), 1);
        body.setPosition(clown.translateX, clown.translateY);

        var rotationInRadians = Math.toRadians(clown.rotate);

        var x = Math.cos(rotationInRadians) * startingPower;
        var y = Math.sin(rotationInRadians) * startingPower;

        body.adjustVelocity(new Vector2f(x,y));
    }

    public function update():Void{
        clown.translateX = body.getPosition().getX();
        clown.translateY = body.getPosition().getY();
        var velocity = body.getVelocity();
        var vX = velocity.getX();
        var vY = velocity.getY();
        var tanTheta = vY/vX;
        var arcTan = Math.atan(tanTheta);
        clown.rotate = Math.toDegrees(arcTan);
    }
}
```

In Listing 11-5 we see that the class ClownBody does a few things. When the init function is called, a new Body is created, and its position and rotation are set the same as the Node clown. The Body is also given an initial velocity based on the angle of the cannon and the startingPower. The update function is called by GameMode to synchronize the position and rotation of the Node clown based on the position and velocity of the body. By setting the rotation of the Node clown based on the velocity of body keeps clown pointed in the direction it is traveling.

Once the clown is prepared to fly through the scene by the function fireClown, the Timeline worldUpdater is started, which calls the function update every 30th of a second. The function update advances world by one step and updates the location of flyingClown. The function update also checks to see if the clown has intercepted the balloon, if the clown has landed in the bucket, and lastly, if the clown has fallen below the top of the net. If the clown is in the bucket or has fallen into the net, the current shot is over.

If the clown is in the bucket, then the function celebrate is called, which creates a number of firework effects. In Listing 11-3 we can see that the function celebrate creates a Timeline called timeline, which kicks off a firework every .5 seconds by calling doFirework. The Timeline also calls nextClown when the fireworks display is over. Looking at the function doFirework, we see it creates yet another Timeline that animates a Circle called shell up into the scene. This Timeline also calls doExplosion when shell reaches its apex. Listing 11-6 shows the functions related to displaying the fireworks. The function doExplosion adds a new Explosion to the scene and then creates a Timeline that will remove the Explosion after 4 seconds. Listing 11-7 shows the implementation of the class Explosion.

Listing 11-6. *GameModel.fx (firework-related functions)*

```
function doFirework(firework:Group):Void{
        var shell = Circle{
            radius: 4
            fill: Color.DARKBLUE
        }

        insert shell into firework.content;

        var timeline = Timeline{
            keyFrames: [
                KeyFrame{
                    time: .5s
                    values: shell.translateY => -250 tween Interpolator.SPLINE(.43, .79,
.84, 1.0)
                    action: function(){
                        doExplosion(firework, shell.translateX, shell.translateY);
                        delete shell from firework.content;
                    }
                }
            ]
        }
        timeline.play();
    }

    function doExplosion(firework:Group, x:Number, y:Number):Void{
        var explosion = Explosion{
                translateX: x;
                translateY: y;
            }
        insert explosion into firework.content;

        var timeline = Timeline{
            keyFrames: KeyFrame{
                time: 4s
```

```
                action:function(){
                    explosion.stop();
                    delete explosion from firework.content;
                }
            }
        }

        timeline.play();
}
```

Listing 11-7. *Explosion.fx*

```
public class Explosion extends Group{
    var moveSparks = Timeline{
        repeatCount: Timeline.INDEFINITE
        keyFrames: KeyFrame{
            time: 1/30*1s
            action: function(){
                for (node in content){
                    (node as Particle).doStep();
                }
            }
        }
    }
    init{
        var hue1 = ColorAdjust{
            hue: -1 + Main.random.nextDouble()*2.0;
        }
        for (i in [0..10]){
            insert Particle{
                fadeout: true
                speed: .7
                initialSteps: 200;
                direction: 0
                directionVariation: 360;
                gravity: .002
                effect: hue1;
                scaleX: .4
                scaleY: .4
            } into content;
        }
        var hue2 = ColorAdjust{
            hue: -1 + Main.random.nextDouble()*2.0;
        }
        for (i in [0..10]){
            insert Particle{
                fadeout: true
                speed: .4
                initialSteps: 200;
                direction: 0
                directionVariation: 360;
```

239

```
                    gravity: .002
                    effect: hue2;
                    scaleX: .4
                    scaleY: .4
                } into content;
        }
        moveSparks.play();
    }

    public function stop():Void{
        moveSparks.stop();
    }
}
```

In Listing 11-7 we see that the class Explosion is very much like the class Emitter from Chapter 2. The init function of Explosion adds two sets of Particles to its content, and these two sets create the firework effect. The class Particle is a direct copy of the class from Chapter 2. As the Timeline moveSparks runs, it calls the doStep function on each Particle, causing each Particle to animate in the scene. In this case, each Particle travels away from the location of the Explosion in a random direction, fading as it goes.

Once all of the Explosions are done animating, the code path is then identical to the code path when the clown hit the net instead of the bucket. The function nextClown is called and checks to see if the user has fired all of his clowns or not. If clowns remain, the function readyLaunch is called and the process repeats. If there are no more clowns the user is presented with a dialog, allowing him to either play again or go back to the start screen.

Summary

This chapter started with a design for a game that incorporated many of the effects described in this book. That initial design was used to create game assets in Adobe Illustrator. The details and workflow decisions of working with the JavaFX Production Suite provided a real-world context for using this tool. The implementation of Clown Cannon showed how to glue all of the effects together to create a complete game. This glue included understanding the life cycle of the entire game as well as each round.

Index

■A

aboutButton function, 228, 230
aboutScreen function, 228, 230
Abstract Windowing Toolkit (AWT), 2–3
Accumulate Thread, 181
action function, 190, 229
ADD setting, blend effect, 38
Add value, blendMode effect, 206
addBodies function, 134–135
addEmitter function, 205–206
addFlare function, 196
addLights function, 229
addObserver method, 186
addWorldNode function, 117, 124, 205–206, 208
Adobe After Effects, 141
Adobe Illustrator, 14–15, 21, 215, 217–218
Adobe Photoshop, 20
After Effects, 141
angle variable, 63
anim Timeline, 160, 171, 175, 196–197, 199
animation
    in applications
        controls and layout, 1–5
        overview, 1
    gradients, 153–175
        animated stops, 171
        multi-colored linear gradient, 165–166
        opacity, 169–171
        progress bar, 172–175
        proportional property, 155–158

simple color example, 159–160
simple linear gradient, 160–163
simple radial gradient, 163–165
image sequences, 137–152
    creating images, 137–143
    design considerations, 151–152
    implementing, 143–151
lighting, 71–86
    basics of, 71–73
    design considerations, 86
    examples of, 75–86
    implementation of, 73–86
looping, 142–143
particle system visual effect, 25
animator class, 28
animis Timeline, 229
appearance, of particles, 25
Apple iPhone, 8
Arcs class, 119
Audacity tool, 21
audio files, 182–186
Audio Thread, 181
audio visualizer, 177–200
    bars effect, 192–194
    controlling audio, 190–192
    disco effect, 194–198
    JVM and, 179–188
        Java, 186–188
        Java Sound, 180–186
        JavaFX, 179–188
    overview, 177–178
    wave effect, 198–200
AudioClip class, Applet API, 181

AudioSubsystem class, 185
AudioVisualization class, 192
AWT (Abstract Windowing Toolkit), 2–3
azimuth property, 72

B

backButton function, 230
background parameter, 147
backgroundLoading variable, 149
Ball class, 119
balloonNode function, 236
baos variable, 185
Bars class, 194
bars effect, 192–194
baseFormat variable, 184
bind keyword, 33
bitmaps, 40
blend mode, 38–40
Blender application, 21, 137–138, 140, 149
BlendMode class, 40
blendMode variable, 38, 40
bodies
    emitters as, 209–214
    overview, 113
    particles as, 201–209
Bodies class, 117, 122, 128
Body class, 114, 236
bonusBalloon variable, 234–235
bucketNode variable, 234
built-in interpolators, 91–94
    EASEBOTH, 92
    EASEIN, 92
    EASEOUT, 92
    linear, 91
    overview, 91
    spline, 93–94
burn replace, 66–68
buttonClicked function, 192

C

calculateLocation function, 192
callback function, 56
cannonNode variable, 234

celebrate function, 238
centerX argument, 155, 165
centerY argument, 155, 165
checkCleanup function, 134
checkProgress method, 146, 150
Circle class, 28, 65, 119, 206
Circle shape, 86, 192
classpath variable, 115, 149
clear function, 206
cloud image, 42
Clown Cannon example application, 215–240
    design phase, 215–222
        game design, 215–217
        graphic design, 217–222
        overview, 215
    implementation, 222–240
        game life cycle, 223–230
        overview, 222
        round life cycle, 230–240
    overview, 215
clown node, 237
ClownBody class, 237
clownNode variable, 234, 237
coefficients function, 100
Collections class, 163
Color class, 153–154, 162
color property, 153
Color value, 95
ColorAdjust class, 44, 66, 68
Control node, 134
ControlHandler class, 134
ControlHelper class, 135
Controls class, 128, 131
createColor function, 160, 162, 165
createLinearGradient function, 162, 169, 175
createLocalFile method, 184
createRadialGradient function, 165
createStop function, 162, 165
cross-platform dialog box, 7
cubic function, 99
cubic interpolator, 97–99
CubicInterpolator class, 99
currentImage variable, 151

currentStep value, 197
currentValue value, 91
curve function, 95–96, 98, 101
custom interpolators, 94–108
    cubic, 97–98
    extending, 95
    overview, 94
    polynomial, 99–101
    quadratic, 96
    step, 103–108
    windup-overshoot, 101–103
CustomLookAndFeelUI class, 17
cycleMethod property, 155, 175
cycling images, 143
Cylon eye effect, 168

■D

DataLine object, 185
decodedAudio variable, 184–185
deferAction function, 188
deltaRotation value, 197
deltaX attribute, 28, 34, 46, 214
deltaY attribute, 28, 34, 46–47, 214
deployment, 18
design considerations, 1–21
    animated image sequences, 151–152
    animated lighting, 86
    deployment, 18
    graphics and animations in
        applications, 1–8
        animations, 8
        controls and layout, 1–5
        graphics, 5–8
        overview, 1
    NetBeans, 18–20
    open source tools, 20–21
    overview, 1
    physics engine, 135
    scene graph, 13–14
    visual transitions, 69
designers and developers, 9–12
    overview, 9
    setting realistic expectations, 12
    showing off platform, 12

    tools for, 14–17
    workflow, 9–12
digital signal processing (DSP), 184
direction, 44–46
direction attribute, 46
directionVariation variable, 46
disco effect, 194–198
DiscoStar class, 195–196
displayed variable, 51
distant light, 75–77
DistantLight class, 72, 77, 84
doAfter function, 55, 134
doExplosion function, 238
doFirework function, 238
doReplace function, 55, 134
doStep function, 28, 37, 43, 47, 214, 240
draw function, 91
drawCircle function, 13
drawImage function, 13
DropShadow class, 84
DSP (digital signal processing), 184
duration attribute, 28, 34

■E

ease interpolator, 110–111
EASEBOTH interpolator, 92, 95
EASEIN interpolator, 92
EASEOUT interpolator, 92
Eclipse, 17
effect attribute, 44
Effect class, 66
effect property, 71
effects, audio. See audio visualizer
elevation property, 72
emit function, 27, 31, 44, 199, 211
emitCloud function, 208
emitSpark function, 208
Emitter attributes, 29–35
Emitter class, 25, 27–29, 31, 33, 44, 48, 240
emitter node, 24
Emitter object, 27, 205
emitters, 24, 209–214
emitTimeline attribute, 27, 31
end argument, 95

endX property, 155, 175
endY property, 155
ExampleNodeA class, 51
ExampleNodeB class, 51
Explosion class, 238, 240
extending interpolators, 95

F

Fade Out checkbox, 36
fade replace, 53–56, 110, 131
fadeout attribute, 37
falling ball example, 115–121
false value, proportional property, 155, 163
fill property, 153, 158–160, 162
fill value, 165
Fireball class, 211, 213
FireballEmitter class, 211
fireballs function, 211
fireClown function, 237
Firefox login dialog box, 3
FireParticle class, 213–214
Fixed Radial gradient, 156
Fixed Width Linear gradient, 156
Flare particle, 196
flip replace, 58–63, 111, 236
flyingNode variable, 236
for loop, 188
fraction argument, 95
frequency attribute, 31
frequency slider, 30
FXDNode, 17
fxz file, 15–16, 234

G

GameAssetsUI class, 218
GameModel class, 230, 234, 236
GaussianBlur class, 66, 68
getAudioInputStream method, 184
getImage function, 147–148
getImageSequence function, 147–148
GIMP tool, 20
gradients, 153–175
    animated stops, 171

examples of, 155–156
    multi-colored linear, 165–166
    opacity, 169–171
    overview, 221
    progress bar, 172–175
    proportional property, 155–158
    simple color example, 159–160
    simple linear, 160–163
    simple radial, 163–165
graphical user interfaces (GUIs), 1, 5
graphics, design considerations, 1–8
gravity, 114, 129
Group class, 27, 119, 229
group node, 58
GTK dialog box, 6–7
GUIs (graphical user interfaces), 1, 5

H

heterogeneous particles feature, 47
hiChannel variable, 188, 196
holder variable, 65
hsb function, 154

I

IDE (Integrated Development
        Environment), 17–18
Illustrator, 14–15, 21, 215, 217–218
image function, 147
imageCount variable, 149
ImageMagick tool, 21
images
    animated sequences of, 137–152
        creating images, 137–143
        design considerations, 151–152
        implementing, 143–151
    cycling, 143
    loading, 143
imageSequence function, 146–147
ImageSequenceView class, 146, 150
ImageView class, 42
implementation classes, 25
INDEFINITE value, repeatCount function,
        27

initAboutScreen function, 228–229, 234
initialSteps variable, 214
initScreen function, 234, 236
initStartScreen function, 228–229, 234
Inkscape tool, 21
inner while loop, 185
Integer value, 163
Integrated Development Environment
    (IDE), 17–18
interpolate function, 95
Interpolator class, 47, 95
interpolator property, 91
interpolators, 87–112
    built-in, 91–94
        EASEBOTH, 92
        EASEIN, 92
        EASEOUT, 92
        linear, 91
        overview, 91
        spline, 93–94
    custom, 94–108
        cubic, 97–98
        extending, 95
        overview, 94
        polynomial, 99–101
        quadratic, 96
        step, 103–108
        windup-overshoot, 101–103
    overview, 87–88
    transition example, 108–111
        fade replace, 110
        flip transition, 111
        further considerations, 111
        overview, 108–110
        slide transition, 110–111
    visualizing, 88–91
InterpolatorView class, 91, 112
InterpolatorViewer class, 88
iPhone, 8

■ J

Java, 5, 186–188
Java Archive (JAR), 18, 182–184
Java Media Framework (JMF) API, 181

Java Network Launching Protocol (JNLP),
    18
Java Sound, 180–186
    audio data, 185–186
    preparing audio files, 182–185
Java Swing, 2–3, 5
Java Virtual Machine (JVM), 152, 179–188
JavaFX
    Java and, 186–188
    JVM and, 179–180
    rendering thread, 181
JavaFX Production Suite, 14, 21
javafx.animation.transition class, 49
javafx.scene.media package, 180
java.lang.Observable class, 186
JDesktop Integration Components (JDIC)
    project, 186
JDesktopPane component, 3
JMF (Java Media Framework) API, 181
JNLP (Java Network Launching Protocol),
    18
Joint class, 122, 125
JVM (Java Virtual Machine), 152, 179–188

■ K

KeyFrames class, 25, 55, 63

■ L

Layer tool, Adobe Illustrator, 218
length parameter, 175
levels sequence
    AudioPlayer class, 194
    SoundPlayer class, 192
levels variable, 186
lighting, animated, 71–86
    basics of, 71–73
    design considerations, 86
    examples of, 75–86
    implementation of, 73–86
Lighting class, 71
line variable, 186
linear gradients
    multi-colored, 165–166

overview, 160–163
linear interpolator, 91–92, 104, 110–111
LinearGradient class, 153–155, 162, 168, 229
loading images, 143
login dialog box
    Firefox, 3
    OS X VPN, 4
look and feel dialog boxes, 6
LookAndFeel class, 5
lowChannels variable, 188
lx variable, 63
ly variable, 63

M

Main class, 25
main function, 145
Main.fx file, 25, 31, 143, 203, 210
makeButton function, 229
Media object, 180
MediaLoader class, 146–148, 152
MediaPlayer class, 180
MediaView object, 180
midChannels variable, 188
mixing effect, rudimentary, 35
Motif look and feel dialog box, 6–7
moveSparks Timeline, 240
moving emitter feature, 47
multi-colored linear gradients, 165–166
MULTIPLY setting, blend effect, 38
Music Player Control API, 186

N

net variable, 234
NetBeans application, 16–18, 20, 147–148, 218
nextClown function, 240
no blend effect setting, 38
Node class, 36, 229
nodes, 38, 49–53
nodeToReplace function, 55, 58, 62, 68, 134–135
nonlinear changes feature, 47

nonlinear paths, 46–47
nonuniform nodes, 40–44
normalizeHue function, 44
notDisplayed variable, 51
notifyObservers method, 186
Number value, 95
numberToString function, 149

O

Observer interface, 188
Observer/Observable pattern, 186
offsetFromZero function, 234
offsetX property, 86
offsetY property, 86
okButton variable, 16–17
on replace function, 31
onMouseClicked attribute, 229
onMouseDragged function, 192
onMouseEntered property, 229
onMouseExited property, 230
onMouseRelease attribute, 192
opacity, 169–171
opacity attribute, 36
open source tools, 20–21
    Audacity, 21
    Blender, 21, 137–138, 140, 149
    GIMP, 20
    ImageMagick, 21
    Inkscape, 21
    overview, 20
org.lj.jfxe.chapter6.transition package, 128
OS X
    native look and feel dialog box, 7
    VPN login dialog box, 4
outer while loop, 185

P

Paint object, 153, 159
Parent class, 229
Particle class, 25, 27–28, 31, 33, 37–38, 40, 42–43, 46, 240
Particle Opacity slider, 36
particle size slider, 30

particle system visual effect, 23–48
  basic principles of, 23–25
    animation, 25
    particle appearance, 25
    visual density, 25
  examples of
    blend mode, 38–40
    core classes, 25–29
    direction, 44–46
    Emitter attributes, 29–35
    nonlinear paths, 46–47
    nonuniform nodes, 40–44
    transparency, 35–37
  other features of, 47–48
particleDuration attribute, 31
particleHue attribute, 44
particleHueVariation attribute, 44
particleRadius attribute, 31
particles
  appearance of, 25
  as bodies, 201–209
particleSpeed attribute, 31
pause function, 180
PCM_SIGNED value, decodedFormat
    variable, 184
Peg class, 206
Peg.fx file, 206
Pendulum class, 124–125
pendulum example, 122–125
PerspectiveTransform class, 58, 62
Photoshop, 20
Phys2D physics engine, 201
physics engine, 113–135
  design considerations, 135
  examples of
    falling ball, 115–121
    pendulum, 122–125
    Teeter Totter, 126–128
    transition, 128–135
  implementing third-party, 114–128
  simulation, 113–114
PhysicsParticle class, 208–209
pixels, setting values of, 13
play function, MediaPlayer class, 180

PNG (Portable Network Graphics) file, 20,
    140
point light, 77–80
PointLight class, 72, 80
polynomial interpolator, 99–101, 104, 110–
    111
polynomial transition, 108
PolynomialInterpolator class, 102
Portable Network Graphics (PNG) file, 20,
    140
powerAnim Timeline, 237
powerFill node, 237
Production Suite, JavaFX, 14, 21
progress bar, animated, 172–175
progress function, 150
Proportional Linear gradient, 156
proportional property, 155, 158
Proportional Radial gradient, 156

■ Q

quadratic function, 97, 99
quadratic interpolator, 96–97, 99
QuadraticInterpolator class, 98–99

■ R

radial gradients, 163, 165
RadialGradient class, 153, 155
radius attribute, Particle class, 31
radius property, RadialGradient class, 155
randomFromNegToPos function, 44
raster graphics library, 13–14
rect shape, 86
Rectangle class, 120, 192
red variable, 160
removeEmitter function, 206
removeFromParent function, 229
removeWorldNode function, 206
REPEAT value, cycleMethod property, 175
replacementNode node, 55, 58
reset function, MediaPlayer class, 180
rigid body dynamics, 113
rudimentary mixing effect, 35
run function, 185, 205

■ S

scaleX attribute, 44
scaleY attribute, 44
Scene class, 27, 29, 229
scene graph, 13–14
score Text node, 218
SCREEN setting, blend effect, 38
seek bar, 192
selected attribute, 190
seq1 variable, 146
seq2 variable, 146
seq3 variable, 146
Sequence handlers function, 134
Sequence inactives function, 134
Sequences class, 163
sequenceView method, 145
setChanged method, 186
shadows, 83–86
showFlare variable, 196
simpleBalls function, 117
SimpleInterpolator class, 95
simplifyGradients function, 229
simulation, 113–114
slide replace, 56–58, 110–111
Slider class, 29
smooth attribute, 42
solve function, 100
solveFor variable, 100
sort function, 163
sortStops function, 163
SoundControl class, 190, 192
SoundHelper class, 182, 184, 186
SoundPlayer class, 186, 188, 190, 192–193
SoundRunnable class, 185
SparkEmitter class, 206, 208
sparks function, 205–206
spectral analysis, 186
speed attribute, 34
spline interpolator, 93–94, 96, 101, 110–111
spline transition, 108
spot light, 80–83
SpotLight class, 72–73, 80
Stage class, 25, 29
start argument, 95
startButton function, 228, 230

startGame function, 230, 236
startingAnimationOver function, 236
startingDirection variable, 214
startingOpacity attribute, 37
startRound function, 236
startScreen function, 228, 230
startX property, 155, 175
startY property, 155, 175
StaticBody class, 120, 135
staticBody function, 134
step function, 104
step interpolator, 103–108
stepsRemaining attribute, 37
Stop class, 155, 162
stops argument, 155, 165
stroke property, 153
stub class, 16–17
Sun Abstract Windowing Toolkit (AWT), 2–3
Sun NetBeans, 16–18, 20, 147–148, 218
Sun Web Start, 18
SVGPath Nodes, 235
Swing, 2–3, 5

■ T

Teeter Totter example, 126–128
Text node, 171
theta angle, 34
third-party physics engine, 114–128
threads, 181
3D content, software for creating, 21
Timeline class, 25, 31, 55, 77, 134–135, 238
TransitionExampleMain file, 128
transitions, 49–69, 108–111
    design considerations, 69
    examples of
        burn replace, 66–68
        fade replace, 53–56, 110, 131
        flip replace, 58–63, 111, 236
        slide replace, 56–58, 110–111
        wipe replace, 63–65
    overview, 49–53, 108–110
    physics engine, 128–135
translateX value, 192, 194, 214, 234–236

translateY value, 194, 214, 234–236
transparency, 35–38
triangle shape, 86
TrivialInterpolator class, 95
TrivialSimpleInterpolator class, 95
true value, 42, 155, 163

U

ulx variable, 63
uly variable, 63
update function, 118, 134, 188, 197, 200,
        209, 213, 237
updateImage function, 151

V

vector graphics library, 13–14
velocity, 114
Virtual Machine, Java, 152, 179–188
visible attribute, 190
visual density, 25
visual effects
    animated lighting, 71–86
        basics of, 71–73
        design considerations, 86
        examples of, 75–86
        implementation of, 73–86
    particle systems, 23–48
        basic principles of, 23–25
        examples of, 25–47
        other features of, 47–48
    physics engine, 113–135
        design considerations, 135
        examples of, 115–135
        implementing third-party, 114–128
        simulation, 113–114
    transitions, 49–69
        design considerations, 69
        examples, 53–68
        overview, 49–53

W

w variable, 175
Wall class, 128
Wave class, 199
wave effect, 198–200
WaveDot class, 200
web function, 154
Web Start application, 18
while loops, 185
windup interpolator, 110–111
windup-overshoot interpolator, 101–103
wipe replace, 63–65
Wood, Tim, 141
World class, 114, 118, 134, 206, 209, 236
WorldNode class, 117, 119, 135
worldUpdater function, 118, 134–135, 237
write method, 186

X

X per step, deltaX attribute, 34
-Xms option, 152
-Xmx option, 152

Y

Y per step, deltaY attribute, 34

Z

zeroToOne function, 160, 162

You Need the Companion eBook